PRIMARY EDUCATION IN THE VILLAGE OF LUSK

Bun Oideachas Lusca

The History of Lusk National School

Stair Bhunscoil Lusca

1823 – 1992

DERMOT RUSSELL

SUPPORTED BY

Comhairle Contae Fhine Gall
Fingal County Council

First Published 2015

Copyright © Dermot Russell, 2015

Copyright of this publication is with the author
Dermot Russell

ISBN 978-0-9934163-1-6 (PB)
978-0-9934163-0-9 (HB)

No part of this publication may be reproduced in any form or by any means without
the prior permission of the copyright holder.

Design and layout by Artwerk Limited, Dublin

Published by Dermot Russell

Printed by: Colourworld Limited, Kilkenny

Edited by: Dr. Séamus O'Maitiú

www.facebook.com/luskprimaryschoolhistory

"Education is not the filling of a pail but the lighting of a fire".

W.B. Yates

DEDICATION

This publication is dedicated to my parents Jemmy and Bridie Russell who both attended Lusk primary school in the 1920's. My brothers and sisters all of whom attended Lusk school through the 1940's, 50's, 60's and 70's.

My wife Jane, children Karen, Shane, Colm and Brendan, and my grandchildren some of whom are currently experiencing primary education and the remainder who have yet to embark on that journey.

Dermot

CONTENTS

INTRODUCTION		x
CHAPTER 1	Background to the Formation of a National School System in Ireland.	1
CHAPTER 2	The Beginning of National Education in the Village of Lusk.	8
CHAPTER 3	Through the 1800's	15
CHAPTER 4	A New School Building	24
CHAPTER 5	Into The 1900's	33
CHAPTER 6	When One-Hundred years is Aft' and Gone.	54
CHAPTER 7	The 1955 School Building	88
CHAPTER 8	Where Pupils lived:	95
CHAPTER 9	Into the 1960's	97
CHAPTER 10	Pupil Numbers	102
CHAPTER 11	Parents of School Pupils and their Occupations	104
CHAPTER 12	Surnames and First Names	105
CONCLUSION		112
APPENDIX 1	Pupil Attendance	114
APPENDIX 2	Attendance at Examination during the 'Pay by Results' period	117
APPENDIX 3	Teacher Salaries	121
APPENDIX 4	Chronology of Teachers	124
APPENDIX 5	List of pupils registered in Lusk School from c.1862-1992 for Girls, and from 1892-1992 for Boys.	127
	List of Boys 1892 to 1899	128
	List of Boys 1900 to 1970	131
	List of Boys 1971 to 1992	157
	List of Girls c.1862 to 1891	178
	List of Girls 1892 to 1899	191
	List of Girls 1900 to 1970	195
	List of Girls 1971 to 1992	220
BIBLIOGRAPHY		240
INDEX		244

PHOTOS AND ILLUSTRATIONS:

Chapter 1
Fig. 1.1 Hedge School
'The Soldiers are Coming'.

Chapter 2
Fig. 2.1 Rocques Map 1700,s
Fig. 2.2 1823 Penny
Fig. 2.3 Duncans Map 1821
Fig. 2.4 Ordnance Map 1836
Fig. 2.5 Dublin Parish Map 1870/Lusk
Fig. 2.6 and 2.7 Artists Impression of Original Lusk Schoolhouse
Fig. 2.8 to 2.15 Selection of images from school books of early 1800's

Chapter 3
Fig. 3.1 Rev. PJ Tyrrell
Fig. 3.2 Original Fireplace 1874 Lusk School
Fig. 3.3 Original Internal Door 1874 Lusk School
Fig. 3.4 Inspectors report 1857

Chapter 4
Fig. 4.1 1874 Lusk School Building
Fig. 4.2 1874 School Nameplate
Fig. 4.3 Ordnance Survey Map 1906
Fig. 4.4 Plate on Document Case, Presented to John Donnelly
Fig. 4.5 Coat-Rack from the 1874 School Building
Fig. 4.6 Irish Times article 1894
Fig. 4.7 Childrens Bible History

Chapter 5
Fig. 5.1 Original Invoice, George Carton
Fig. 5.2 Mrs O'Sullivan
Fig. 5.3 Envelope, Mrs Rooney

Chapter 6
Fig. 6.1 Mary Doran-Seaver
Fig. 6.2 Mrs Mansfield
Fig. 6.3 Girls Class 1920
Fig. 6.4 Junior Boys Class 1920
Fig. 6.5 Senior Boys Class 1920
Fig. 6.6 Boys early 1920's
Fig. 6.7 Girls Class 1925
Fig. 6.8 Boys Class 1925
Fig. 6.9 Jack Browne, Jemmy Russell, Joe Dennis
Fig. 6.10 Larry Dunne
Fig. 6.11 Mrs Mary Dunne
Fig. 6.12 Boys Class c.1929-30
Fig. 6.13 Boys Class c.1934
Fig. 6.14 How Butter is Made (Jackie Brogan)
Fig. 6.15 Local Fields (Maureen Devine)
Fig. 6.16 Forges (Maura McCann)
Fig. 6.17 Weather (May McGuigan)
Fig. 6.18, 6.19 School Copybook Cover
Fig. 6.20 Primary Cert 1948
Fig. 6.21 Primary Cert 1962
Fig. 6.22 Aisti Gearra, Irish Essays School Book
Fig. 6.23 Oifig and Phoist – Essay
Fig. 6.24 Mo Cat – Essay
Fig. 6.25 Miss Kathleen Moloney
Fig. 6.26 Mrs Kathleen Moloney
Fig. 6.27 Mrs Annie Dunne
Fig. 6.28 Annie Durkin
Fig. 6.29 Girls Class 1945
Fig. 6.30 Girls Class c. 1947
Fig. 6.31 Maureen McCann
Fig. 6.32 Rose Kelly-Knight
Fig. 6.33 John Kelly
Fig. 6.34 Girls Senior Class c.1952

Chapter 7
Fig. 7.1 Invitation to Tender for Construction of Lusk Primary School, 1954
Fig. 7.2 1955 School
Fig. 7.3 1955 School Name Plate
Fig. 7.4 Irish Independent 1956, Opening of New School
Fig. 7.5 Irish Press 1956, Opening of New School
Fig. 7.6 Girls Class 1955
Fig. 7.7 Confirmation 1955

Chapter 9
Fig. 9.1 Michael Browne, Kenneth Knott, Fintan Sherry, c.1965
Fig. 9.2 Boys Class 1965-66
Fig. 9.3 Mr and Mrs Daniel Doherty
Fig. 9.4 Confirmation 1967
Fig. 9.5 Confirmation 1970
Fig. 9.6 Class 1971
Fig. 9.7 Class 1973
Fig. 9.8 School Reunion Ticket 1988
Fig. 9.9 Mr. Des O'Leary and Ladies Committee
Fig. 9.10 Mr Des O'Leary, Principal 1925 - 2007
Fig. 9.11 Lusk Primary School Pupils, Athletics Winners, 1992

FOREWORD

Mr. Paul Comiskey

Parish of St. Maccullin

It is a great honour for me as the current Principal of Lusk National school to contribute a small piece on our school as it is today. Dermot has carried out a fascinating study on the history of our school which will be a wonderful resource for our community in telling the story of the generations of children who have passed through our doors.

It is hard to imagine what the founders of the first school in Lusk would make of our current school, a large school with 834 children on the roll at present, 44 teachers and 15 SNA and ancillary staff. Our children come from 29 different countries and 12 religious faiths. However among them we still have many of the family names that dominate the roll books of the 19th century, names such as Kelly, Skelly, Browne, Cruise and Donnelly. These children now sit beside children with family names such as Akpufore, Borisevic, Mockapetris and Okuson, changed times indeed.

The curriculum taught to the children has also changed significantly over the years. In years gone by schools focused on 'the three r's', reading, writing and arithmetic. We now have eleven subjects including Art, Drama, P.E., Science, SPHE, and SESE, subjects never even heard of in the 1830's.

It is interesting too for us to look at the make up of the teaching staff in the school. For years the school had two teachers each for girls and boys. Boys and girls are now educated together by teachers who come from all parts of the country. We are proud also that amongst our teaching staff are four past pupils of our school. We are also a co-educational school with boys and girls mixed in every class.

This history of our school gives us a fantastic picture of life in days gone by, of the changes that have taken place, but also of the similarities between school in the 1800's and school in the 21st century. It shows that Lusk has been a centre of learning for generations. We hope to continue to be a centre of learning for generations to come and that our school serves the community of Lusk just as well as the school has in days gone by.

Principal: Paul Comiskey, B.Ed., Dip. Ed. Man., M.St.

2015

Fr. Paul Hampson

Lusk National School is a vibrant and dynamic school, because of its history and the many great people who worked and attended over many years. Saying thanks can appear to fall short of what we want to portray in our appreciation of past students and staff, so I welcome Dermot Russell's book entitled 'The History of Lusk Primary School 1823-1992' as it affords us the opportunity to review our past and look forward in hope which is a great testament of thanksgiving.

In the Village of Lusk we are blessed with a sense of our history right back to the 5th Century and the figure of St. MacCullin our patron. The Legends and tales of Cuchulainn and Eimear are prominent in our memories so much so, that we have named an area of our town in Eimear's honour.

I believe this background has contributed enormously to who we are now because we like to recall ancient and personal history. This book by Dermot taps into our local school and its contribution to the lives of the people of the area. It reminds us of the many great people with vision who founded pipe bands, G.A.A. and Soccer clubs, most of whom attended our Local Lusk National School.

I want to both congratulate and thank Dermot for all his work affording us the opportunity to look back and be grateful for the blessing it grants us to move forward in hope.

Paul Hampson P.P.
2015

Chapel Road, Lusk, Co. Dublin
Phone/Fax: 8437738
Email: luskns.ias@eircom.net

Bóthar an tSéipeil, Lusca, BÁC
Guthan/Facs: 8437738
Email: luskns.ias@eircom.net

ACKNOWLEDGEMENTS

I wish to acknowledge the help, assistance and encouragement of the many people, organisations and institutions that I called upon for information, records, photos and memories in the process of researching the contents of this publication.

People:
Mary McNally, Seamus McNally, David Dunne, Pat Kelly, John Kelly, Joan Donnelly, Martin Ryan, Dr. Séamas Ó'Maitiú, Moya Doherty, John Aungier, Dr. Susan Parkes, Colman Dunne, Mattie Devine, Ann Cullen, Aidan Carroll, Yvonne Duignam-Lusk parish office, Fr. Paul Hampson PP Lusk, Paul Comiskey principal Lusk school, Frances Murtagh vice-principal Lusk school, Liz Murphy, secretary Lusk school, Paul Gilmartin caretaker Lusk school, Tom Seaver, Pat Seaver, Deirdre Steale (Dunne), Emer Johnston (Taylor), Dickie Clare, Eamon Clare, Maureen Wright, Susan Morgan, Kathleen Sandford, Christy Russell, Christina Conroy (Gaffney), Barbara Gibbons (Mansfield), Des O'Leary, Pearl Finnegan, Yvonne Cheevers, Billy Sherry, Nellie Moore, Jackie Kelly and all the people of Lusk and surrounding area who showed an interest. Thanks also to Fingal County Council, 'Arts and Culture', for supporting this project.

Organisations/Institutions:
National Archives of Ireland; National Library of Ireland; Dublin City Library and Archives; Valuations Office; Ordnance Survey Ireland; Dublin Diocesan Archive Clonliffe; Fingal Co. Co. Archives; St. Patricks Teacher Training College Drumcondra; Mount St. Joseph College Roscrea; Church of Ireland College of Education; Archives of the Society of the Sacred Heart-Irish/Scottish Provincial, General Registrations Office-Dublin, Irish Architectural Archive, UCD National Folklore Dept., Royal Irish Academy.

Dermot Russell
2015

INTRODUCTION

For the benefit of local history and for current and future local communities, this publication sets out to explore, record, document and trace the evolution and development of primary education in the village of Lusk, North Co. Dublin, covering a period of 170 years.

The formation of national primary education in the village is explored, along with school attendance, attendance patterns, the teachers, personalities and participants in the education process along with particular events and occurrences that will be of interest not only to the community past and present but to future generations from a local, social, general historical and genealogical perspective.

CHAPTER 1

Background to the Formation of a National School System in Ireland

Early Schools
Evidently some attempt at formal education for children existed in the seventeenth century. Cromwellian records refer to 'The Popish Schoole Matsr who taught the Irish youth, trayning them up in Supersticion, Idolatry, and the Evil Customs of the Nation'. [1]

16th Century
Tudor legislation established a system of parish elementary schools (1537) and diocesan grammar schools (1570's).

The aim was that the native Irish would be Anglicised. This proved to be generally ineffective due to dependency on local clerical initiatives which evidently was not present.

17th Century Royal Schools
These were planned as part of plantation of Ulster. Seven schools were established, e.g. Portora Royal School, Cavan Royal School.

18th Century Charter Schools
These schools were established by a Royal Charter. Called after a Charter given by George II in 1734 to the Incorporated Society in Dublin for promoting English Protestant schools in Ireland and to bring up the children of the Irish poor (mainly Catholic) as Protestants. These schools were in some respects a response to the rise in popularity of 'hedge schools' as the penal laws began to take effect. Once again these attempts were not very successful, with evidence of schools being poorly run.

---

[1] *Memories of Dromleigh, (Co. Cork) a Country School 1840-1990*, n.d.

Charity Schools
Increasingly evident from the 1700's
Proselytising (attempt to convert) resulting from an increasing awareness that Catholicism is not disappearing but in fact showing resurgence.

The charity schools were supported by: Landlords, Philanthropists, Clergy and Municipal Boards.

At this time there was still no 'formal national education system' in place in Ireland.

Pay Schools (Hedge Schools)
The penal laws of the eighteenth-century where Catholics were prohibited from teaching in either private or public, or being provided with any education other than in schools teaching the doctrines of the 'established Church' (Church of Ireland), and forbade any Catholic from going abroad to be educated. The penal laws were introduced following the Williamite victory over the Catholic King James II and were mainly concerned with ensuring that the wealth and power remained in the hands of members of the Church of Ireland by restricting access to education. The penal laws were to a great extent counter-productive ironically leading to the growth and development of 'hedge schools', which were essentially illegal schools. Parents paid the teachers, with considerable variation in the amount paid, most earning no more than a basic wage. Teachers' pay was often supplemented by donations of food or fuel. For some teachers pay was occasional, as schools were ill-attended particularly in areas where parents were very poor and needed to keep their children at home to plant potatoes and spread manure in the spring and later in the year to pick potatoes, leaving only four months of the year to attend school.

Never the less in the 1800's between 300,000 and 400,000 children attended 9,000 hedge schools. Classes were conducted in cabins, barns and houses and outdoors in the summer.

The schools however were unregulated, deficient in teacher training, standards and curriculum. The quality of education depended on the capacity of the teacher and few of them had formal training, indeed there were stories of brilliant teachers being abducted by communities who were desperate to have their own hedge school.[2]

Following the repeal of the penal laws in 1782 the number of schools increased rapidly and began to move indoors.[3] By the nineteenth-century, cabins built by local people were used as school-houses.

---

[2] Garrett Fitzgerald, 'Irish Primary Education in the Early Nineteenth Century' (Dublin 2013), p. 2-6. Ed. James Kelly.

[3] How religion made its way into primary school system (http://dialogueireland.wordpress.com/2010/02/16/how-religion-made-its-way-into-primary-school-system/) (28th Oct. 2014).

Debate on a national education system had gone on since the mid eighteenth-century, during which time many private and church agencies took on the job of education.

Early 1800's

The Society for Promoting the Education of the Poor in Ireland (better known as The Kildare Place Society, due to the location of its offices and Model Schools in Dublin city) was one of the most prominent bodies making provision for primary education at this time. It was established in 1811 by a group of philanthropists in Dublin, including Arthur Guinness, Samuel Bewley of the Quaker merchant family, and members of the La Touche banking family.

The Society was non-denominational, its aim being to provide support for schools, and to publish textbooks, primarily to educate poorer Irish children. The society gave grants to help build schools across Ireland, to pay teachers and provide school requisites such as, slates, pens, maps and textbooks. Schools that joined the Kildare Place Society had to follow the society's rules, including not to teach a particular religion. Schoolteachers were permitted however to read the Bible to children but 'without note or comment', i.e. teachers were not permitted to give an interpretation of the Bible nor such instruction to the children. Initially the society had the support of all the churches including the Catholic hierarchy, but such support waned on suspicion about its use of funds to support Protestant missionary agencies and of alleged failure to honour the agreement with regard to reading of scripture without remark.

By 1820 the Kildare Place Society had a total of 381 schools throughout Ireland providing instruction to some 26,474 pupils.[4] By 1825 there were almost 1500 schools catering for about 100,000 pupils.[5] The society had also established teacher training schools.

From 1815 the British government of the time provided funding to the Kildare Place Society to continue its voluntary work. This funding continued up to 1831 whereupon it ceased following 'The Commission of Irish Education Enquiry' and the ensuing national education system. Following the transfer of education funding from the Kildare Place Society to the soon to be established 'national education board' the Society continued as a Protestant education body (Church Education Society) eventually to become the Church of Ireland Training College. The original location of the Kildare Place Society training college is now the site of the Department of Agriculture.

---

[4] Historical commentary for 1818 (http://www.csorp.nationalarchives.ie/context/1818.html) (28th Oct 2014).

[5] The Kildare Place Society and Schooling in the Nineteenth Century National Museum of Ireland: Exhibition 2012/13 held at Decorative Arts & History Collins Barracks, Dublin, http://dublin.anglican.org/news/2012/09/New-Exhibition-Kildare-Place-Society-and-Schooling-in-the-Nineteenth-Century.php (10/01/2015).

The model on which the society functioned became a vehicle for the national education system in Ireland eventually established in 1831.

The Commission of Irish Education Inquiry

In 1824 'The Commission of Irish Education Inquiry' was established and during the summer of that year the commissioners undertook a fact-finding survey of all schools in Ireland. The aim of the survey was to determine the current situation regarding the number of schools in the country, the number of pupils in each school, their sex and religion, the type and cost of the school-house, the names of the teachers, the qualifications and salaries being paid to the teachers, the fees (if any) paid by the pupils, the aid (if any) received by the school, the books used, and whether or not scripture was read.
The results of the survey indicated there was in excess of 10,000 schools in Ireland catering for almost 500,000 pupils.

Almost all of the schools at this time were private fee-paying schools. Access to education for Catholic children was limited. The many hedge schools (pay schools) that existed were unregulated. The quality of education was entirely dependent on the capacity of the teacher, most of whom were untrained, while pupil attendance was intermittent. Parents paid on average eight to ten shillings per year per child.

The report originating from the Commission of Education Inquiry, published in 1825, recommended the establishment of a national school system. In October 1831 (shortly after Catholic Emancipation) chief secretary for Ireland Edward Stanley (Lord Stanley) wrote to the Duke of Leinster setting out the proposed structure and aims for 'a system of National Education in Ireland' and inviting him (Duke of Leinster) to chair a new board of 'commissioners of education'. This was the beginning of our national schools.

The new national school system would be under the auspices of a 'board to superintend the new education system'. A seven-man board was assembled for (Dingfelder, 1982) the first time in December 1831. The board comprised of three members from the Established Church, two Catholics, and two Presbyterians.

Religious instruction was to be separate from other school subjects. Teachers could read the Bible but not comment or interpret its message. No religious iconography was allowed and religious instruction had to take place at a fixed time every week outside of traditional school hours. Eventually the non-religious philosophy waned and schools gradually began to lean towards particular religions.

Schools were under the general direction of the national board and day-to-day direction of local school management. All schooling was to be through the medium of English and the board was responsible for setting the school texts for all schools under the system. Official textbooks for the new school system were not initially available and so the schools made use of books approved by the Kildare Place schools and the Catholic Book Society. The schools also continued to use a collection of texts they had already gathered over time.[6]

With the national school system came the establishment of model schools, a training institution, book publication and an inspectorate. The main offices and central teacher training college were located at Marlborough St. Dublin, where the current Department of Education is still located.

The new national board received an initial grant of £30,000, the money to be spent on school buildings, textbooks, teacher-training and school inspectors. Parishes wishing to establish a school in their locality under the new national school system were required to apply to the board for a grant. To qualify for a grant, potential schools had to identify a site, raise one-third of the sum required to build the school and to pay the teachers. If these requirements were satisfied the commissioners would consider funding the remainder, and also supply furniture and books. Most of the grants allocated by the board were to schools that already existed in some form pre-1831 and who at this stage were seeking incorporation into the new national school system; consequently, few new buildings were constructed with most opting to use existing school-houses.[7]

The new national primary school system was to be interdenominational. The new board of commissioners would accept applications for the establishment of interdenominational schools by different religious schools in each area. The Catholic hierarchy accepted the new interdenominational system but it was strongly opposed by the Protestant religious authorities, which, in some instances refused to make applications in conjunction with the Catholic Church. In 1839 the Church of Ireland created its own organisation to run its schools, referred to as the Church Education Society.

Following on from this the board then felt obliged to accept applications from the Catholic Church for the establishment of schools with a Catholic ethos, and so in effect began a Catholic national school system. In principle however all schools remained open to children of all denominations and no child could be required to attend denominational religious instruction. Schools became interdenominational in principle but not in practice.

---

[6] Garrett Fitzgerald, 'Irish Primary Education in the Early Nineteenth (Commissions of Irish Education Inquiry 1824-25) Century' (Dublin 2013), p. 2-6. Ed. James Kelly.
[7] Ibid.

In an attempt to ensure that all teachers met a set standard, a code of conduct for teachers was introduced, referred to as 'twelve practical rules' and included:

> avoid markets and meetings, but above all political meetings of every kind…., to impress upon their pupils a time and a place for everything and everything in its proper place and time…., to promote cleanliness, neatness and decency…., to discountenance quarreling, cruelty to animals, and every approach to vice.[8]

It was as late as 1965 when the Department of Education under the national school rules entitled, 'schools under the management of different religious denominations', declared that the state 'gives explicit recognition to the denominational character of primary schools'.[9] So the full circle had occurred to some extent, i.e. from non-denominational schools pre 1831, to interdenominational 1831 to 1965, and denominational from 1965 onwards.

The Table opposite show extracts from the 2nd report from the 'Commissioners of Irish Education Inquiry' 1826-27.

Fig. 1.1 Hedge School 'The Soldiers are Coming'. Image courtesy of the National Library of Ireland

---

[8] Garrett Fitzgerald, 'Irish Primary Education in the Early Ninrteenth Century' (Dublin 2013), p. 2-6. Ed. James Kelly.
[9] How religion made its way into primary schools (http://dialogueireland.wordpress.com/2010/02/16/how-religion-made-its-way-into-primary-school-system/) (28th Oct. 2014).

Background to the Formation of a National School System in Ireland

List of School Teachers, in the Baronies of Balrothery and Nethercross 1826-27[10] (Lusk parish straddles the Baronies of Balrothery and Nethercross)

Barony of Nethercross

Name of Teacher	Religion	Parish	Location of School
Byrne, Eliza	RC	Lusk	Rush
Carey, James	RC	Lusk	Lusk
Dogherty, Francis	RC	Lusk	Rush
Fitzgerald, John	RC	Lusk	Rurkeens-Cross
Mahon, Simon	RC	Lusk	Rush
Martin, Thomas	RC	Lusk	Ballough
Reilly, James	RC	Lusk	Corduff
Savage, Alice	RC	Lusk	Kingston
Warren, Catherine	RC	Lusk	Rush

Barony of Balrothery

Name	Religion	Parish	Location of School
Bennett, Anne	RC	Balrothery	Balbriggan
Bradford, Anne and John	Protestant	Donabate	Donabate
Buckley N. Prestige	Protestant	Balrothery	Quay St. Balbriggan
Callaghan, Mary Anne	RC	Balrothery	Clonard St. Balbriggan
Clinton, James	RC	Balrothery	Balrothery
Carey, Mary	RC	Holmpatrick	Skerries
Fenton Rev. G	Protestant	Balrothery	Balbriggan
Fitzpatrick, Patrick	RC	Holmpatrick	Skerries
Finn, James	RC	Holmpatrick	Skerries
Huston, William	Protestant	Balrothery	Balrothery St. Balbriggan
Kiernan, Margaret	RC	Balrothery	Balbriggan
Ryan, Margaret	RC	Holmpatrick	Skerries
Magennis, John	RC	Balrothery	Man-O-War
Morgan, John	RC	Balrothery	Skerries St. Balbriggan
O'Brien, John	RC	Hollywood	Balgee
Rooney, Eliza	RC	Balrothery	Balrothery St. Balbriggan
Sheridan, Peter	RC	Balrothery	Clonard St. Balbriggan
Stewart, Mrs A	Protestant	Balrothery	Balbriggan

[10] National archives of Ireland, list of school teachers, Leinster, 1826 – 1827, (arranged by Dorothy Rines Dingfelder, Sept. 1982).

CHAPTER 2

The Beginning of National Education in the Village of Lusk

Lusk Village

Lusk is a small village in North Co. Dublin, traditionally a rural village although a mere thirteen miles from Dublin city centre.

A medieval village, with a distinctive round tower dating from the 10th century holding a prominent position on an elevated site at the village entrance. The original village of the Middle Ages in common with similar medieval villages throughout the country was contained within the immediate vicinity of the round tower.

An examination of Rocques map of 1756 indicates that Lusk village settlements were confined to the immediate vicinity of the round tower. The area that later became known as 'The Green', where the RC Church and the primary school was eventually built had not yet grown as part of the village.

A Monastery was founded in Lusk c.450AD by St. MacCullin.

It is said that MacCullin died in 497, he was described as abbot and bishop of Lusk.

Fig 2.1 Lusk Village, from Rocques Map, Mid 1700's.
'By permission of the Royal Irish Academy © RIA'

National Education in the Village of Lusk

Children's education was being provided in Lusk village before the formal national education system was introduced in 1831. A pay school was in existence from 1823.

Fig. 2.2 An 1823 penny

In the 'Irish Education Survey' of 1824-25 the master of the school in Lusk was James Carey. He was paid thirty shillings per annum, out of contributions made by the children, ranging from 3d to 7d per week. There were thirty-three Roman Catholic children and 1 Protestant child attending at this time, twenty-five being male and nine females. The school was not affiliated to any education society and scriptures were not read.[11] The school building consisted of mud walls and thatched roof.

Application for Recognition of Lusk School

Following the 'Commission of Irish Education Enquiry' of 1825, and the subsequent establishment of the 'Commissioners of Education' in 1831, an application was made on 30th August 1832 to the commissioners to have a school in Lusk recognised under the newly established national school system and for a grant towards the payment of teachers salaries and other requisites, under the scheme entitled 'Application for the Education of the Poor of Ireland'.

A pay school already existed in the parish before this time. It is most likely that the school was built as a result of local efforts by landowners, clergy and parents. In the application for recognition the name of the school was referred to as 'Lusk Parochial School', and it had been established in 1823. The school derived its only source of funds from occasional charity sermons, and, for those who could afford it, voluntary subscriptions from the children from 1d to 3d (1 pence to 3 pence) per week.

The sum requested in the application was '£40 to pay the masters and mistresses for the school at Lusk, together with what the board will think proper for stationary'.

The annual salary by this stage for a male teacher was £12, while a female teacher was paid £6 per annum, although this depended to some extent on whether the teacher was trained or untrained.

The number of 'scholars' in attendance at that time was ninety males and seventy females during the Summer, and seventy males and fifty females in the Wintertime.[12]

The Early School

With mud walls and a thatched roof the schoolhouse dating from 1823 consisted of two rooms, a boys room 31½ft. x 15ft. and a girls room 37ft x 15ft., accommodating 120 boys and 130 girls. In the application for recognition the school was described as being in a good state of repair, had a thatched roof, and with eight windows to the front and rear. Around this period of time it is recorded that 'Lusk village' had 924 inhabitants.[13]

---

[11] Dublin city and county archives/gilbert library, commissioners of Irish education inquiry 1824-25, house of commons parliamentary papers.
[12] National archives of Ireland, ED/2/15/No. 43-178.
[13] Samuel Lewis, *a topographical dictionary of Ireland, 1837*.

There were eight desks and ten seats for boys, and four desks and ten seats for girls.[14] The desks and seats were most likely long desks seating perhaps up to ten children in a row.

Considering the size of the boys room, 31.5 feet x 15 feet (472.5sq. ft.) to accommodate 120 boys, resulting in just under 4sq. ft. per pupil (scholar), that is 2ft x 2ft., not much elbow room there.

In later years, the late 1800's, the area available per pupil was 7sq. ft.

By comparison, current (2014) Dept. of Education recommended space requirements is 80M² (860 sq. ft.) for a classroom, to include teacher and toilet space.

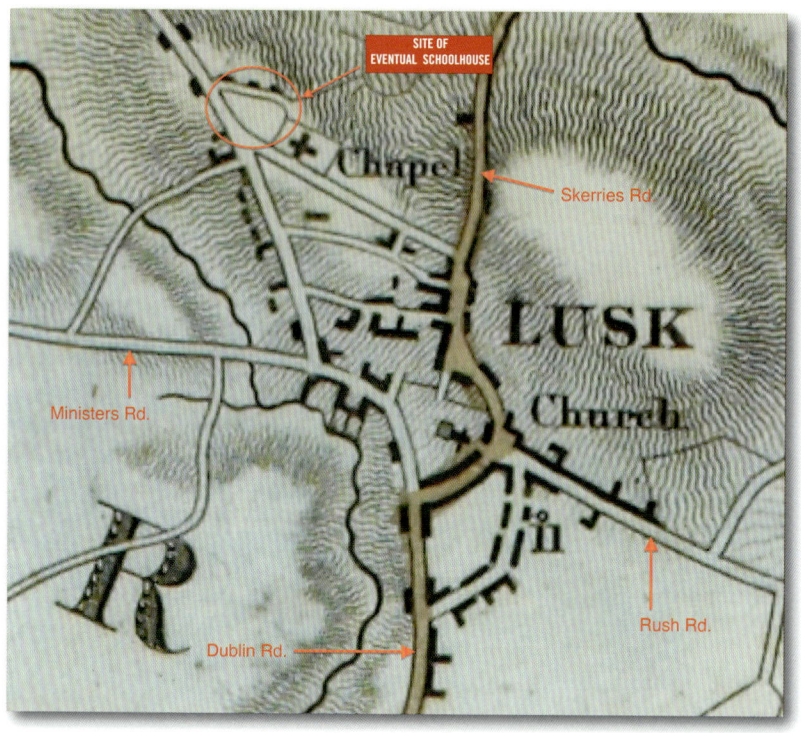

Figure 2.3 – Duncans Map of County Dublin 1821
Image courtesy of the National Library of Ireland

The site on which the original thatched schoolhouse was located comprised an area of ten perches with a valuation in 1847 of £7 and is adjacent to the RC Church.[15]

The schoolhouse was described as built of mud, and was thatched.[16]

Duncans map of 1821 (Fig 2.3) clearly shows the location of the site before any building existed on it, while the 1836 OS Map and the 1870 Parish Map (figures 2.4 and 2.5) shows the position of the first school-house.

The school-house on the 1836 map (Fig. 2.4) indicates a simple rectangular building with an outhouse to the rear, while the 1870 map (Fig. 2.5) clearly indicates an L-shaped building. Whether one or other of the maps is incorrect or whether changes were made to the original thatched school-

---

[14] National archives of Ireland, ED/2/15/No. 43-178.
[15] Primary valuations (www.nli.ie/en/griffiths-valuation.aspx) (Feb 2014).
[16] Dublin city and county archives/Gilbert library, commissioners of Irish education inquiry 1824-25, house of commons parliamentary papers.

house between 1836 and 1870 we can only speculate. It is a distinct possibility that damage occurred to the early school-house resulting from the 'big wind' of January 6th 1839, when thousands of thatched houses throughout the country were destroyed along with additional extensive damage, and it is well documented that the roof of the old church (beside the round tower) was blown off and considerable damage done to the church structure on this occasion. So we know therefore that Lusk did not escape the 'big wind'. It is not beyond the bounds of possibility that the school was damaged on this occasion also, and perhaps the opportunity was used to repair and extend the school-house to the later L-shaped form. This of course is once again pure speculation.

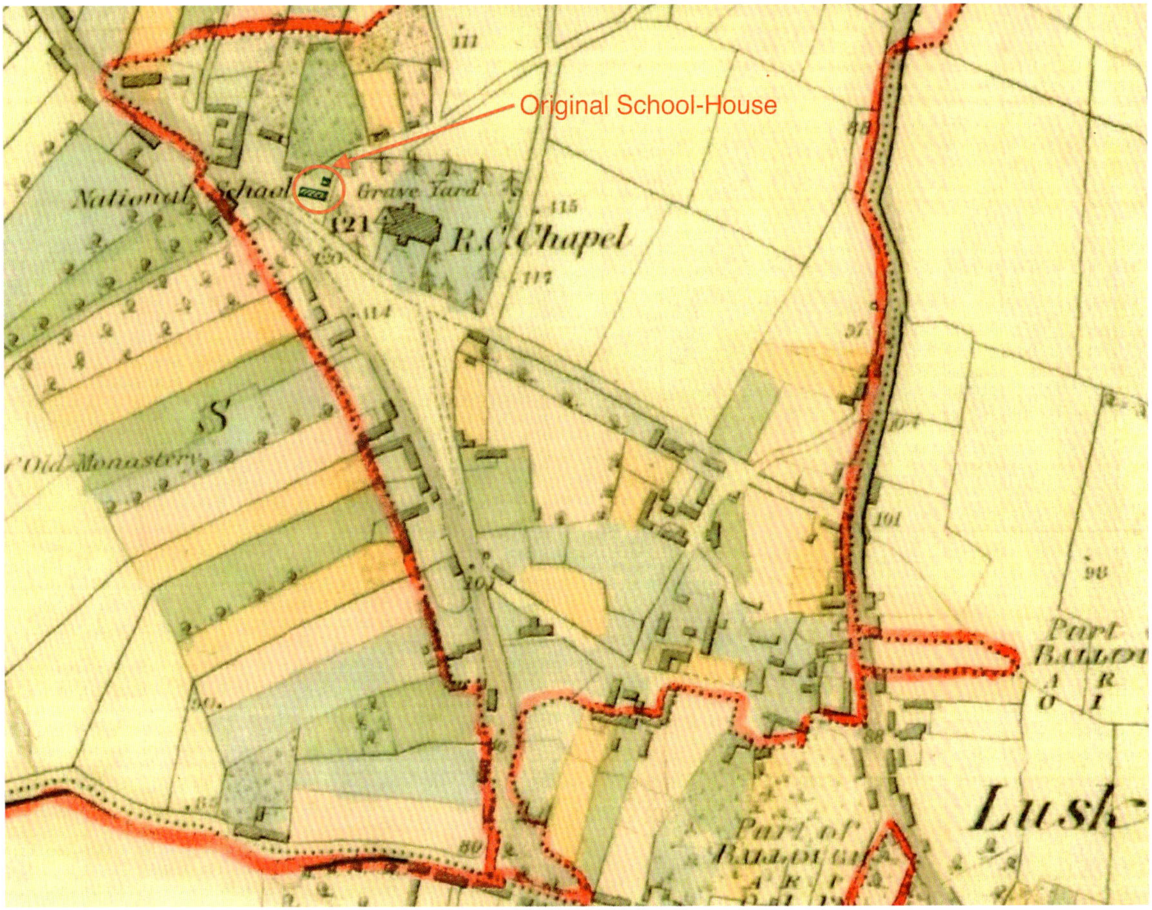

Fig 2.4 1836 OS Map
By permission of Ordnance Survey Ireland

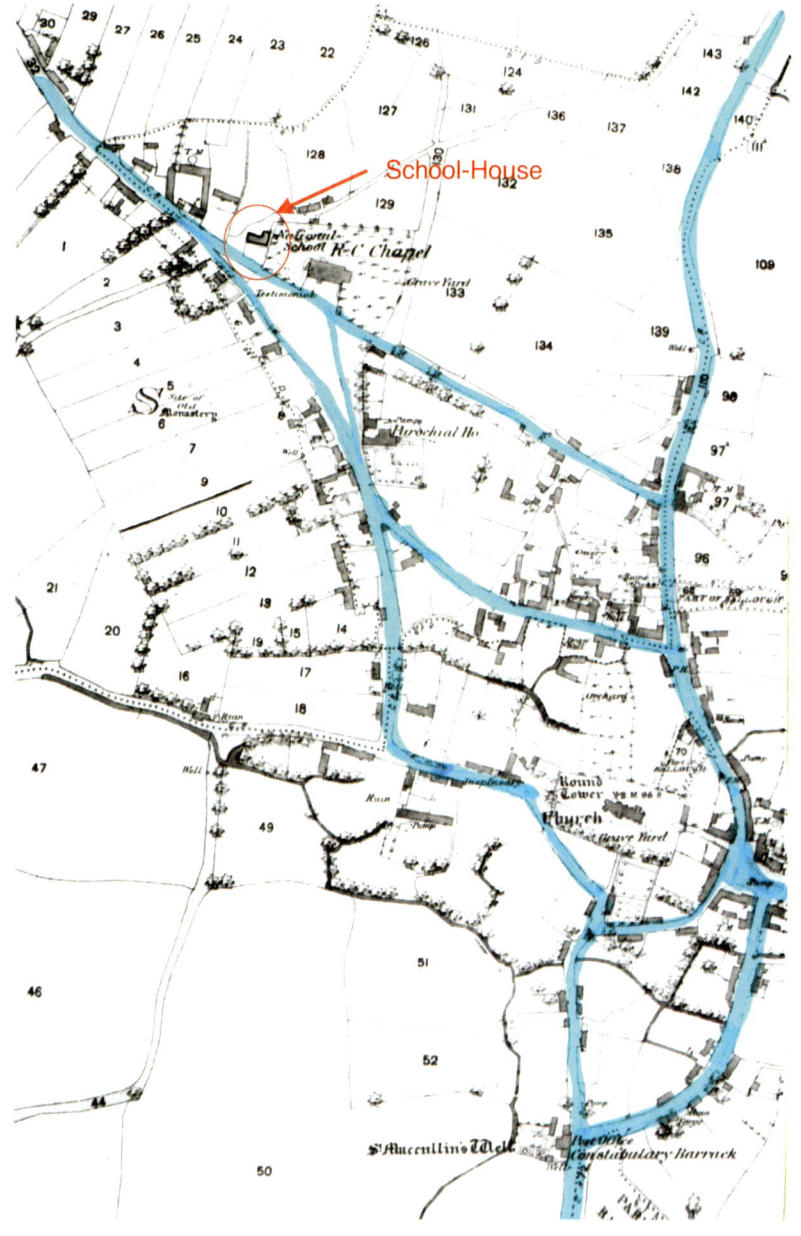

Fig. 2.5
Dublin Parish Maps 1870/Lusk
By permission of the National Library of Ireland

To satisfy the granting of funds it was a requirement for local funds to be raised, the funds to be used for: annual repair of schoolhouse and furniture, towards payment of teachers' salaries and for purchase of books and school requisites. It was further required that a site for the building was to be approved by the commissioners and the schoolhouse to be vested in trustees.[17] As it later transpired the existing thatched school-house in Lusk was approved as the formal school and consequently a new building was not required.

The commissioners also required the school to be kept open for a certain number of hours on four of the five days per week for moral and literary education only, and that the remaining one or two days in the week set apart for giving separately such religious education to the children as may be approved by the clergy of their respective persuasions. The applicants for the grant stated that the school hours were from 9.00am to 3.00pm.

---

[17] National archives of Ireland, ED/1/28 No. 32.

The Beginning of National Education in the Village of Lusk

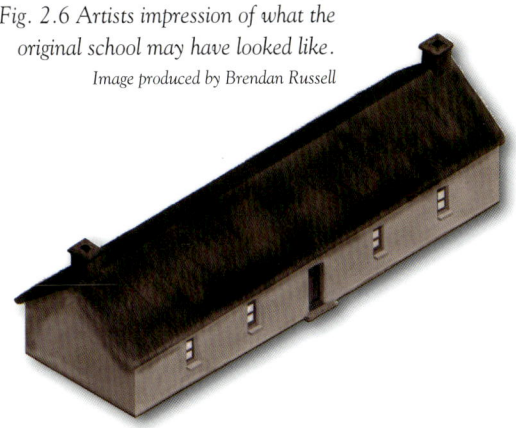

Fig. 2.6 Artists impression of what the original school may have looked like.
Image produced by Brendan Russell

Fig 2.7 Artists impression of the L shaped later school.
Image produced by Brendan Russell

The books in the school at the time were:
- *Discoveries of Columbus.*
- *Histories of useful arts and manufacturers.*
- *Dangerous Voyages of Captain Bligh*
- *Entertaining Medleys, from the Kildare Place Society.*[18]

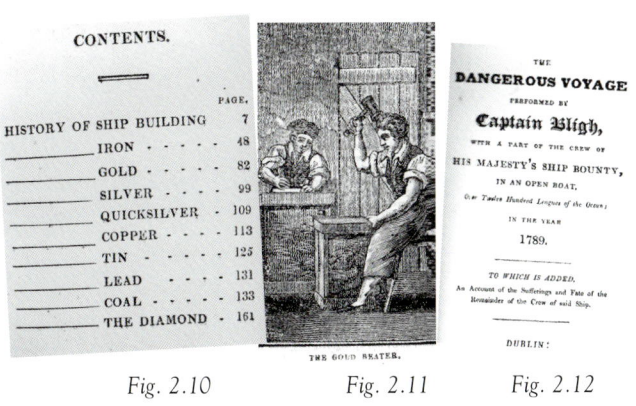

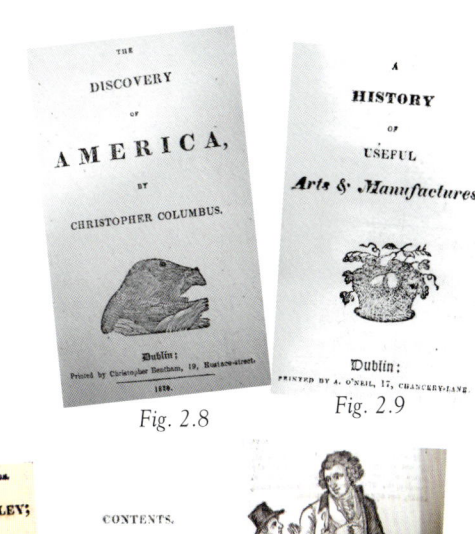

Fig. 2.8

Fig. 2.9

Fig. 2.10   Fig. 2.11   Fig. 2.12

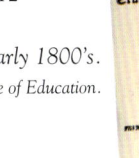

Fig. 2.13   Fig. 2.14   Fig. 2.15

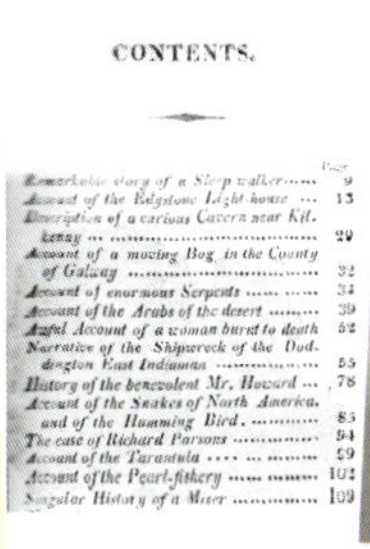

Figs. 2.8 to 2.15, A selection of images from the school books early 1800's.
Reproduced with kind permission of Church of Ireland College of Education.

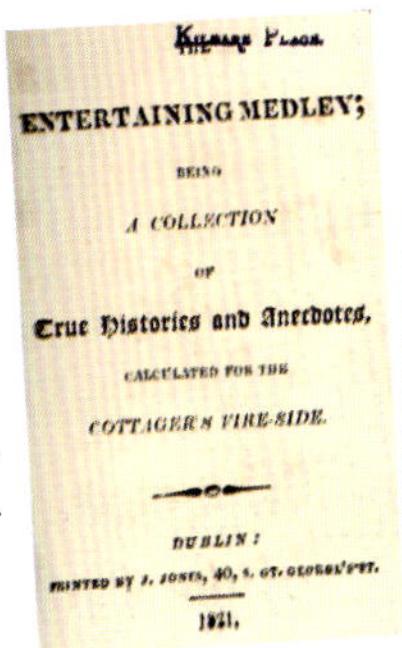

---

18   National archives of Ireland, ED/1/28 No. 32; Church of Ireland education college, Rathmines, Dublin.

At this period in time (1832) the children (or those who could afford it) were required to pay from 1d to 3d per week (slightly less than was indicated in The Irish Education Survey of 1824-25)

Approval is granted

The application was subsequently approved and the school was officially recognised on Dec. 6th 1832. The board of commissioners for national education was first established in December 1831. Lusk school obtained recognition exactly one year later indicating that the school was amongst the first recognised national schools in the country.

The application was signed by three members of the Protestant community: John Rochford, Thomas Knox and Henry Howenden, and seven Roman Catholics; Joseph Smyth, Rev. Patrick Kelly PP, Michael Morgan, Rev. John Fulham CC, Patrick J. Dodd, Richard Smyth and Peter Seaver.[19] Peter Seaver was a farmer living in Rogerstown House at the time.[20]

The official roll number granted for the Lusk school was No. 718 (for the male school) and No. 719 (for the female school) in District No. 30. Male and female schools were considered as separate schools even though contained within the same building, and so each had its own role number and principal teacher.

---

[19] National archives of Ireland, ED/1/28 No. 32.
[20] Interview with Tom Seaver of Co. Limerick (31st March 2015).

CHAPTER 3

Through the 1800's

The First Teachers
As stated above, at the time of the Commissioners of Irish Education Survey, (1825) **James Carey** was the schoolmaster.

At the time of the application for funding (1831) the masters' names were **Christopher Gilmore** and **Patrick McDonagh**.

They were educated at the Roman Catholic School Hanover St. East, (now Westland Row).

The mistress was **Mary Hoey**, educated at a private school paid for by her father.

The school was under the instruction of Rev. P. Kelly, PP Lusk, and Rev. John Fulham CC Lusk.

Teachers in the Earliest Years
In 1834 the teacher in charge of the male school was **Thomas Evlin**, with an average of 66 boys in attendance, while the female pupils were taught by **Anne Evlin.**

In 1836 Thomas Evlin was still the teacher; his salary was £12 and, there were ninety-seven male scholars on the roll. An inspection conducted on 23rd September noted that the teacher was away at the time. This was considered to be 'not favourable' and should be 'looked after'. P.J. Dodd was the acting manager at this time and continued in this role until the appointment of Rev. P.J. Tyrrell PP in 1841 as school manager.

On 15th December it was brought to the attention of the PP that a **Michael McCormick** would be taking up the teaching position as a replacement for Mr. Evlin. Mr. McCormick was a qualified teacher. Shortly afterwards **Anne McCormick** took up the teaching position in the girls school. Mr. McCormick was sixty-nine years old at this time in 1839 and had been in the school for four years.

From 1835 to 1839 the average number of pupils was eighty-five males and seventy-three females.

In 1839 there were ninety-six males and ninety-one females enrolled.

In 1840 and 1841 respectively there were 112 and 104 boys on the school roll, while through 1840 to 1842 the average number of girls was sixty-nine.

In 1839 **Patrick J. O'Brien** was appointed to teach the boys and **Jane Murphy** to teach the girls. Jane Murphy, aged 38, was noted as "not trained", and admonished, presumably based on poor performance, as in the following September is noted as "improved".

These two appointments were to prove somewhat controversial because on March 4th 1841 the school manager and recently appointed PP Rev. P.J. Tyrrell visited and found the school closed. It transpires that the female teacher left the school the previous September "on account of immorality with the teacher of the male school". Miss Murphy was dismissed for immorality.[21] Perhaps it is worth noting that there is no record of Mr. O'Brien being similarly reprimanded.

On December 4th 1843 the school inspector noted the death of Rev. P.J. Tyrrell and the appointment of Rev. Fr. Doran.

On April 15th 1844 Rev. Augustine Costigan was appointed PP for Lusk in succession to Rev. P.J. Tyrrell (Rev. Doran it appears was a temporary appointment).[22]

Fig. 3.1
Rev. P.J. Tyrrell, PP Lusk 1841-43
Image courtesy of the National Library of Ireland

Rev. Peter James Tyrrell was Parish Priest in Lusk from 1841 to 1843 and the first Parish Priest school manager in Lusk. The pyramid shaped monument that still stands in front of the present RC church was erected to commemorate Fr. Tyrrell who, along with Daniel O'Connell and five others campaigned for the repeal of the Act of Union, was arrested and due to be tried for treason, but died in prison before that could happen. The group became known as the 'repeal martyrs'.

James Jordan, teacher in Lusk male school died on 24th May 1844. Mr. Jordan had been teaching in the school for three years. The school was closed for a period of time while awaiting the appointment of a replacement. During this period the boys were taught on a temporary basis by the female teacher.

Anne Jordan was the teacher in the female school also from 1841. Anne Jordan died in 1846 and was replaced by **Maria Thomson**. On July 9th 1847 the school manager and PP, Rev. Costigan records that he removed Maria Thomson from her teaching position, her conduct not having met his approval.[23]

---

[21] National Archives of Ireland, ED/2/15/No.43/178.
[22] National Archives of Ireland, ED/2/15/No.43/178.
[23] National archives of Ireland, ED/2/16/No. 21.

John O'Brien was appointed as the new teacher later that year, following the death of James Jordan. In 1847 John O'Brien was fined ten shillings, to be deducted from his salary, for neglect of school accounts. This was the second report to this effect and having been admonished in the first report, it is noted; "if again reported his salary will be withdrawn".[24]

John O'Brien was later appointed as teacher on Lambay Island school, April 1851 to August 1852. While serving at Lambay school he was fined for being absent from school and inaccuracy in school accounts.[25]

A very notable pattern with regard to the teachers in the male and female schools respectively is evident through some of the preceding years and particularly through the years that follow-for example:

John O'Brien continued as the teacher in the boys school until 1848, during the same period **Anne O'Brien** was the teacher in the female school.

In April 1848 **Thomas Keogh** was appointed teacher in the male school, retaining the position for four years to 1852. During the same period **Anne Keogh** was teaching in the female school. Early in 1852 **Laurence Philips** takes up the teaching position but remains only until August of the same year, while **Susan Philips** was the teacher in the girls school for the same period. **James Wall** was appointed in August of the same year as replacement for Laurence Philips. James Wall held the position for three years, resigning on August 1st 1855, **Sarah Wall** was the female teacher for the same period of time, her salary was withdrawn from April 30th 1855 due to incompetence. It is not certain what personal relationship existed between the male and female teachers of the same surnames but it is most likely they were husband and wife, as this appeared to be a common theme not only in this school but in many schools throughout the country.

In late 1855 the school was closed for a period of time because there was no teacher and an inspector's report of October 10th 1855 asks the school manager, Rev. Costigan, 'if he intends to reopen the school under a qualified teacher?' Rev. Costigan responds to the effect that he will reopen as soon as he can find a competent teacher.[26]

Inspectors Reports Through 1856 to 1859
On June 14th 1856 there was a school inspection: forty-eight pupils were in attendance. There were sixty on the roll for the preceding twelve months, with an average attendance of forty. The average

---
[24] National archives of Ireland, ED/2/15/No. 43-178.
[25] National archives of Ireland, ED/2/16.
[26] National archives of Ireland, ED/2/121/No. 23-24.

age of the pupils was ten years old, with eighteen children under nine, and seventeen aged eleven and above. The inspector requested that, books, blackboard and maps of Europe be obtained and inscriptions renewed.

The inspectors reports were based on three main questions:
1. As to the supply of books and requisites whether adequate or inadequate.
2. As to accounts whether neat and accurate or the opposite.
3. Whether stationery is retrograde or progressing.[27]

On this occasion the inspector noted the following: 'with regard to the character of the school; the supply of books and requisites is inadequate, while accounts are neat and accurate'.

Jeremiah Long was the teacher in the boys school from 24th April 1856 to 6th September 1857, while **Mary Gaynor** was the teacher of the girls.

On October 6th Jeremiah Long was told that 'he cannot be admitted into special class until he shall furnish satisfactory evidence of having properly settled the claims of his former substitute fully, from when he was a teacher in Caher NS'.

Caher NS refers to Cahir national school Co. Tipperary.[28]

On September 4th 1856 there were forty-five pupils present, with an average on the roll for the preceding twelve months of seventy-three and an average attendance of thirty-nine.

On September 19th the following figures apply: thirty-six pupils present on the day, average on the roll for the past twelve months is seventy-two. The average daily attendance is thirty-four, average age is eight, with twenty pupils under nine years of age and four pupils aged eleven or older. Thirty pupils can read books I and II, while six can read books III and IV.

Also in October of 1856 an inspectors report asked for the following requisites: a book press and a teacher's desk or work-table with seat.

A later report indicates seventy-two boys on the roll for the previous twelve months, with an average daily attendance of thirty-four, and an average age of nine, with twenty five under nine years of age, and ten pupils aged eleven and over.

Schoolbooks were classified as; books I and II, books III and IV and book V. The inspection process identifies the number of pupils who can read each grade of book. On this occasion the reports show forty-five pupils can read books I and II, five pupils can read books III and IV, while none are at the

---

[27] National archives of Ireland, ED/2/121/No. 23-24.
[28] Ibid.

standard to read book V. Supply of books and requisites is noted as 'inadequate', accounts 'neat and accurate', and stationery 'progressed'.[29]

	\multicolumn{6}{c}{**NUMBER OF PUPILS IN 1856**}
Year	\multicolumn{2}{c}{Average Number on Roll for preceding 12 Months}	\multicolumn{2}{c}{Average Daily Attendance}	\multicolumn{2}{c}{Average Attendance %}
	Boys	Girls	Boys	Girls	Boys	Girls
1856	68	60	38	26	56%	43%

14th Oct. 1856
(2nd Class)
Writing is pretty fair, the headlines to be treated with more care.
Arithmetic backward
Reading fair
Grammar and geography, tolerably good.
Noted: the house (schoolhouse) at present undergoing repair.

23rd Oct 1857
(3rd Class) A blackboard is indispensably necessary for the effective instruction of the pupils in arithmetic and writing.
The present bookcase is quite unsuitable for the purpose.
(5th Class) The penmanship in general is too angular. This defect should be avoided for the sake of legibility.
The senior pupils should be required to learn needlework and bring materials for that purpose.

On Dec 3rd 1858 repairs were carried out with regard to plaster and whitewash to the walls, and repairs to windows and thatch.[30]

---

[29] National archives of Ireland, ED/2/121/No. 23-24.
[30] Ibid.

24th March 1859

(2nd Class) Cannot yet distinguish the adjective. Only two (pupils) tolerable in outlines of map.

Attendance very irregular.

Walls are reported as in "bad order".

13th Sept. 1859

2nd Class: None able to work correctly a sum of 'three places' in subtraction.

3rd Class: Pretty fair in reading and grammar. Very deficient in tables and in geography.

Regarding the school-room and premises: Roof and windows in bad repair, 6 broken panes, holes in thatch.[31]

The longest serving teacher

Mary Gaynor was first appointed in September 1855, she was twenty years of age. She remained in the position, as principal, until 1894, whereupon she took voluntary retirement,[32] having served a total of thirty-nine years, making her the longest serving teacher in Lusk school in its first one hundred years, if indeed not the longest serving teacher in the history of Lusk school. Mary Gaynor would therefore have spent nineteen years teaching in the original old thatched school and a further twenty years in the later school built in 1874 (currently the parish centre in Lusk). She was awarded a pension of £33-3 shillings from July 1894. Mary Gaynor was originally from Dublin city and unmarried. In her retirement she lived with her brother-in-law Thomas Carroll and his wife Anne, near Merchants Quay in Dublin.[33]

Margaret Coleman was teaching the girls from 1897 and was principal up to 1909, superseding Mary Gaynor. Margaret Coleman spent twelve years teaching in Lusk. For the previous eighteen years she was principal in Balrothery poor law union. She completed her teaching period in Lusk in September 1909,[34] aged 59 years. She was unmarried and lived alone in Lusk during her time in the school and later on lived in Malahide.[35]

Miss Coleman had actually resided in the small upstairs room in the Lusk school for a period of time. Around this period the school manager, Rev. T. Byrne, was making a case for the funding of a teachers residence, near to the school.

---

[31] Lusk primary school, school inspectors reports.
[32] National archives of Ireland, ED/2/121/25, 26.
[33] Census records (www.census/nationalarchives.ie) (April 2014).
[34] National archives of Ireland, ED/9/9001; ED/4/1509.
[35] Census records (www.census/nationalarchives.ie) (April 2014).

Fig. 3.2
The original fire surround in the small upstairs room.
(Authors own photo)

Fig 3.3
The original Victorian door into the small upstairs room.
(Authors own photo)

The schoolroom used by Miss Coleman as a residence resumed as a classroom in October 1909 when it had been used for secular instruction. The room measured 18ft x 10ft., had a fireplace and was said to accommodate eighteen children.

The new teachers residence (opposite the church) was eventually built in 1913.

Joseph McSweeney was the teacher in the boys school from September 1857. He came to Lusk having been teaching in Loughlinstown school. He was dismissed from Lusk by management on 30th January 1858. The school was closed since the dismissal of Mr. McSweeney until the appointment of **Laurence Early** (sometimes written as Eardley) in November 1858. Mr. Earley (Eardley) was a trained teacher and had previously been teaching in Westland Row school. He remained teaching in the school until March 1873.[37]

The inspectors report notes: 'not able to ascertain the cause of McSweeneys dismissal'. Mr. McSweeney at a later stage was teaching in St. Michans, in Dublin city.[38]

---

[36] National archives of Ireland, ED/9/22631.
[37] National archives of Ireland, ED/2.
[38] National archives of Ireland, ED/2/121/25, 26.

An inspectors' report of March 5th 1857 showed a request for 'school tablets to be got'.

On December 1st 1858 there were forty-two pupils present on the day of inspection. There was an average of fifty-eight on the roll over the previous twelve months, with forty-four average daily attendance, thirty six pupils could read book I and II, six pupils could read books III and IV, while there are no pupils deemed capable of reading book V.

The Schoolhouse Deteriorates

Over a period of about six or seven years from 1859 there appears to have been a lax attitude with regard to the running of the school, and perhaps an indication also of deterioration of the old thatched school building. The following series of reports gives rise to this suspicion.

On April 18th 1859 it is recorded that, walls are to be whitewashed, the floor boarded, and black-board, maps of Europe and Ireland, and teachers desks were required.

Later the same year a report notes that repair of the roof, grate, and clock is required, and the need for a blackboard, maps of Europe and Ireland, and the teacher to endeavor to advance his pupils. Needlework is to be taught in the girls school.

A report of October 1861 requires that 'books to be got, and roll book kept correctly'. In 1862 the inspector required children to attend at an earlier hour and for 'Laurence Early [teacher] to exert himself to advance his class and to keep accounts in strict accordance with instructions'. March 11th 1864, floor to be boarded and clock repaired. July 1st 1864, repair grate and clock, and repair floor. October 3rd 1864, repair grate and clock, and repair floor. March 9th 1866, repair windows. An earlier report, in 1863, referred to the "low state of the school", presumably meaning a low state of repair. The report states that the floor needs to be boarded, the clock repaired, and some repairs to the thatch was also required.[39]

Year	Average Number on Roll for preceding 12 Months		Average Daily Attendance		Average Attendance %	
	Boys	Girls	Boys	Girls	Boys	Girls
1860-68	74	58	38	32	51%	55%

NUMBER OF PUPILS 1860'S

---

[39] National archives of Ireland, ED/2/121/25, 26.

The school was closed from 1st April to 6th May 1872 due to an outbreak of smallpox. In early August the school manager, Rev. Nicholas Farrell PP, requested that the usual vacation be reduced to make up for the five weeks lost during the smallpox outbreak.[40]

Francis Flanagan was appointed on June 23rd 1873 replacing Laurence Early who at this stage had been teaching in the school for fifteen years. However Mr. Flanagan's reign was quite short as he left the position in December of the same year.[41] The new school building would have been in the course of construction at this stage.

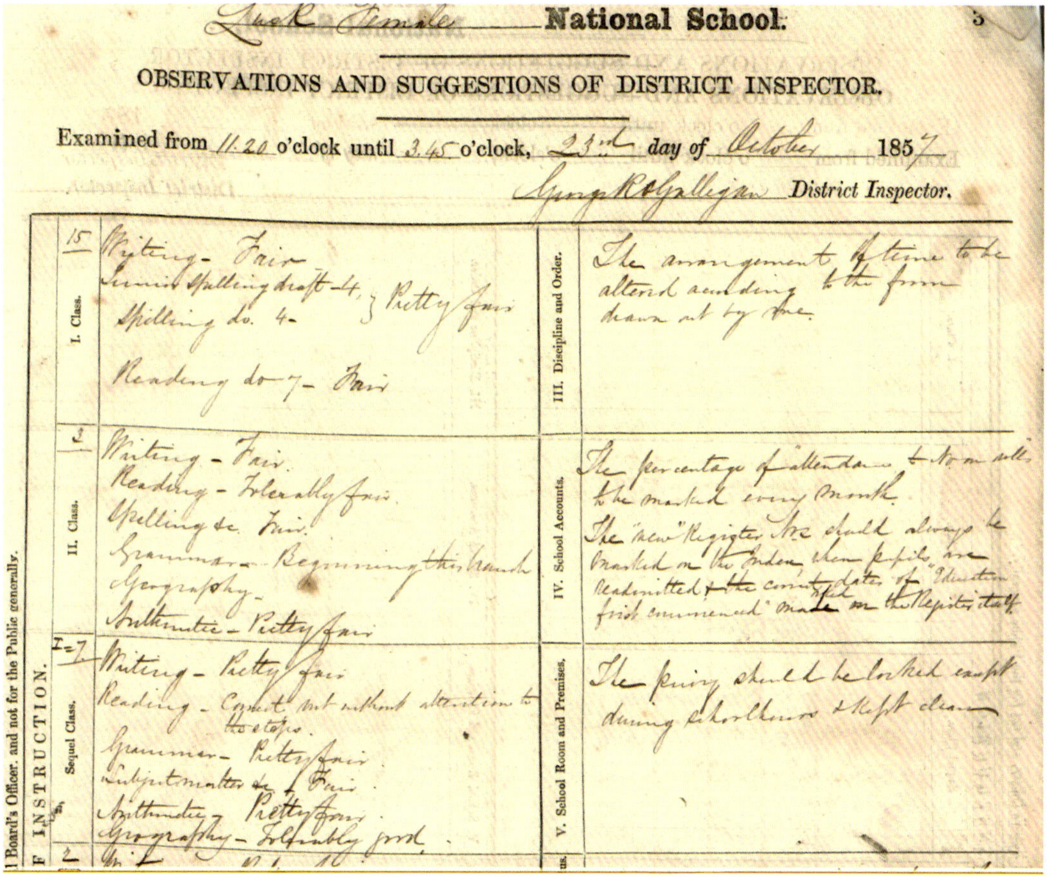
Lusk Female National School.

OBSERVATIONS AND SUGGESTIONS OF DISTRICT INSPECTOR.

Examined from 11.20 o'clock until 3.45 o'clock, 23rd day of October 1857

District Inspector.

I. Class. — Writing – Fair ... Reading do 7 – Fair

II. Class. — Writing – Fair ... Arithmetic – Pretty fair

Sequel Class. — Writing – Pretty fair ... Grammar – Pretty fair ...

III. Discipline and Order.

IV. School Accounts.

V. School Room and Premises.

Fig. 3.4 School Inspectors Report 1857

40 National archives of Ireland, ED/2.
41 National archives of Ireland, ED/4.

CHAPTER 4

A New School Building

On November 11th 1872 a change of house was sanctioned as a temporary arrangement.[42] This presumably refers to the school-house and is most likely the stage when the first school-house was to be vacated and demolished in preparation for the new school building that eventually opened in November 1874. This would indicate that it took two years to construct the 1874 school building. Both buildings were on the same site. The exterior of this building is a 'Protected Structure' under Part IV of the Planning and Development Act 2000, and currently serves as the parish centre.

This 1874 building is a unique structure in many respects. First and foremost there are very few school buildings of this design, certainly in north county Dublin, or for that matter throughout the country. Also, two-storey school buildings from this period are rare. The roof structure consists of four large solid-timber king-post trusses, which in turn support purlin beams and secondary rafters. The walls are pebble-dashed, random-rubble stone, two feet in thickness, with distinctive cut limestone quoins to each of the four main corners. The original windows were all white-painted, timber box-frame vertical sliding-sash, typical of the period. In the early 1980's the windows were replaced with varnished frames and hinged sashes, not quite compatible with good conservation principles, but of course building conservation was not quite so popular at that time and was before the introduction of the 'protected structures' regulations. The original windows internally were fitted with folding timber shutters to splayed reveals. The splayed reveals served to maximise natural light through the windows during daylight hours. Externally the window and door reveals and camber-arch lintels are formed in brick. Brick being more expensive than stone was used sparingly in those days, yet serves to create its own distinctive feature to the building façade. There were four fireplaces in the building, two downstairs and two upstairs, one in each classroom. Open fires being the method of heating in the original school classrooms. The original decorative chimney-pots are still clearly evident externally.

This school building has been standing now for over 140 years. The community of Lusk should value the fine edifice of an historical building that is in its midst. Every effort should be made to ensure

---

[42] National archives of Ireland, ED/2/121/no. 23-24.

that this building and its original design features and character is preserved and protected for future generations to enjoy. Recently the interior of the building has been upgraded to meet current functional uses and demands of modern standards. The year 2024 will be the 150th anniversary of it being first opened as a school, perhaps by then some body will initiate a project and secure funds to replace the windows back to the original sliding sash style of the era along with the internal splayed shutters, and so restore the authentic design features of this building to its full original glory.

The new two-storey building of 1874 replaced the earlier thatched school-house and served as the village school for the next eighty years. A new school building was then constructed on a nearby site in 1955.

Fig 4.1 The 1874 School Building.
Currently a protected structure

Fig. 4.2
The School Name Plate.

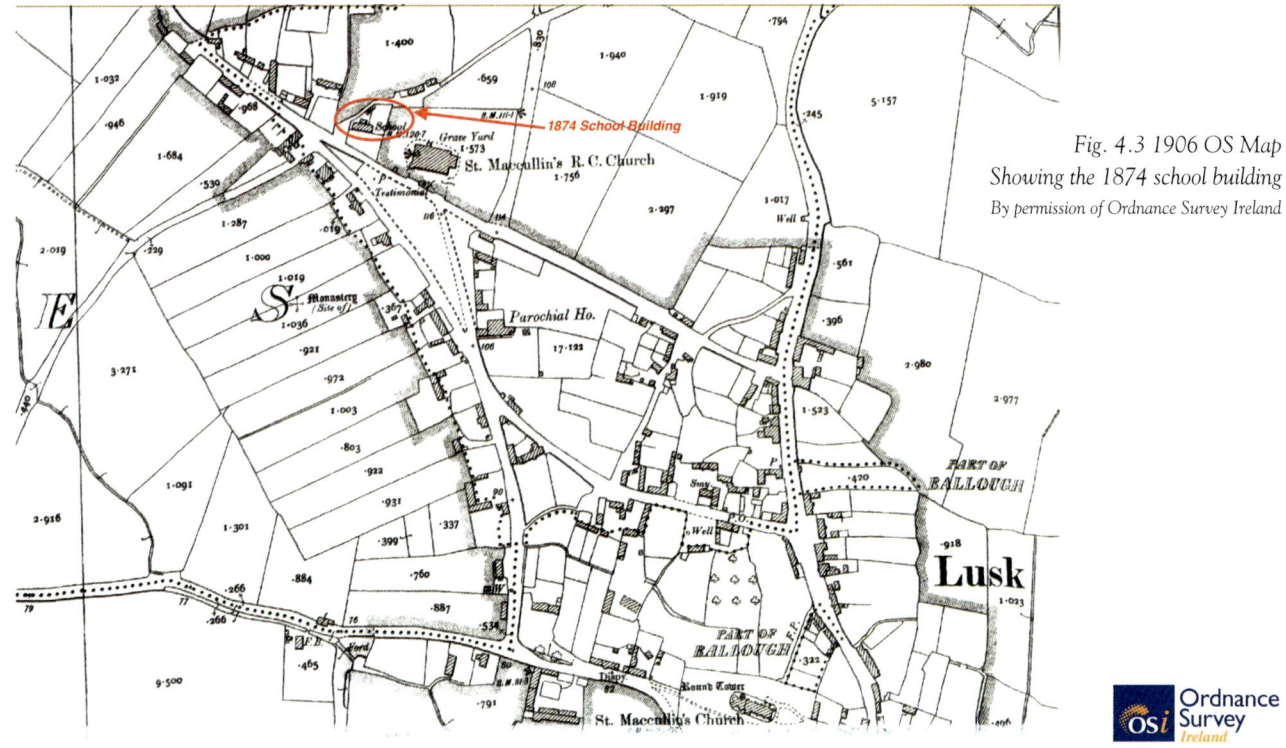

Fig. 4.3 1906 OS Map
Showing the 1874 school building
By permission of Ordnance Survey Ireland

The First teachers in the new 1874 School Building

John Donnelly was a senior monitor[43] in Lusk School from March 1st 1869 (he was 15 years old at this time) through to 1870. He later became a fully fledged teacher in 1871. He was teaching in St. Patrick's, Marlboro St. and from there he transferred to Denmark St. school (Dublin) for a short period. He subsequently returned to Lusk as assistant teacher on January 26th 1874.

John Donnelly was the first male teacher to hold the post in the new 1874 school building. He was appointed principal in 1881, a position he held until 1902.

John Donnelly's position however over this period of time was not without its issues. During these years it was not uncommon for inspectors' reports to be very negative with regard to a teacher's performance, and John Donnelly was on the receiving end of such reports on a few occasions. Part of this may have been due to the fact that from 1872 a teacher's pay was based on pupils performance,

---

[43] Bernadette O'Donovan, B.Ed., M.Ed., Doctor of Education, Thesis, DCU, 2013. A monitor: Often referred to as the Lancastrian Monitorial System, a teaching model used earlier by the Kildare Place Society (also used in many other countries including France, Sweden and Denmark) whereby the better-able older pupils were selected to 'teach' younger pupils.

resulting from tests conducted by a visiting inspector. In November of 1874 10% was deducted from 'results fees' accruing to John Donnelly.[44]

The arrangement of 'payment by results' was introduced in 1872. The setting up of the Powis Commission of 1868 to enquire into the state of the national education system, led to the introduction of teachers pay being partly dependent on the pupils' results at examinations conducted by inspectors. The scheme was quite controversial and considered most unsatisfactory from an educational perspective as teachers began to focus on pupils performance in examinations rather than a more rounded education. Dr. Wm. Starkie (Resident Commissioner for Education) in a speech in the grounds of the education department in 1900 described the system of payment of teachers by 'Results Fees' as an "elaborate mosaic of sixpences and shillings".[45] Payment by results was abandoned in 1900. The 'payment by results' was replaced with a more structured salary scheme whereby teachers were graded in accordance with their qualifications and experience, grade 1, 2 or 3, 1 being the highest with salaries paid accordingly.

The deduction of 10% from John Donnelly's salary from 'results fees' was by no means unique; this happened to many teachers during this period. Due to the introduction of the 'payment by results' scheme every child in attendance had to be accounted for and so a compulsory register/roll book was introduced for the first time.

At a later stage John Donnelly was reprimanded for neglect of 3rd and 4th classes in spelling, arithmetic and geography, and dismissal was threatened. On 18th November he was cautioned against making erasures in school accounts.

On November 22nd 1879 the inspector's report noted the supply of books as fair, house fair, John Donnelly was painstaking in his work, and while records were pretty well kept and proficiency of junior pupils was satisfactory, senior pupils were backward in several subjects.

In October 1880 John Donnelly was reprimanded for 'want of energy and skill, for general low proficiency (of pupils) in writing and of the senior classes in other subjects'. On December 8th 1892 he was admonished for 'extremely low proficiency', with further action threatened. On October 8th 1884 he is once again reprimanded for low proficiency, and yet again on November 21st 1896.[46] John Donnelly continued teaching in the school until his death in 1902 after a long service of 28 years, plus an earlier period as a monitor. There is evidence however that he was held in high esteem by his pupils (See fig. 4.4).

---

[44] National Archives of Ireland, ED2/121/no. 23-24.
[45] Séamus Fenton, *It All Happened, reminiscences of Seamus Fenton*, (1948), Gill and MacMillan.
[46] National archives of Ireland, ED/2/121/No. 23-24.

Following his death some outstanding salary was due to him which was subsequently paid through solicitors P. Tallan 49 Lawrence St. Drogheda, to the executor of his will, his brother Joseph Donnelly.[47]

John Donnelly was 48 years old and a widower at the time of his death. He was a native of Lusk and had one daughter Margaret (Maggie). Maggie was a pupil in the school in the 1890's. The same Maggie Donnelly later married local Lusk man, Johnny Aungier. Their son John Aungier lives in the family home to this day. John Donnelly was John Aungier's grandfather.

John Donnelly's brother Joseph was a local Lusk postman in the late 1800's, early 1900's. Another brother James was a tailor by trade during the same period; they lived where the Credit Union office in Lusk is currently located.

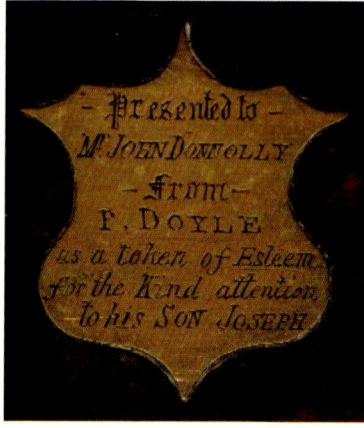

Fig 4.4 An inscribed plate on a small wooden 'document case' presented to John Donnelly by a Mr. P. Doyle on behalf of his son Joseph. This 'document case' is still in existence and is probably at least 120 years old. Courtesy of John Aungier (Authors own photo)

The turn of the century and the abolition of the 'payment by results' saw a new curriculum being introduced to include drawing, elementary science, cookery, laundry work, domestic science, needled work and singing.

In 1920 the Irish language was included in the curriculum for the first time, and all primary school teachers were required to learn Irish. The curriculum was now considered to be too crowded, resulting in some of the other subjects such as elementary science and cookery becoming optional.[49]

Bridget (Bríd) Connor

In November 1874 the school manager and PP Rev. Nicholas Farrell made an application to the commissioners of education for the salary of an assistant teacher to the girls school. In support of the application the size of the room in which the teacher was to work was described as 40ft. x 22ft. This was the new school building (Fig. 4.1) that replaced the original 1823 schoolhouse. This 1874 building although not used as a school since 1955 (apart from for a short period in the 1970's when the newer school became overcrowded) is in fact still in existence and recently, 2012, received a major refurbishment and now used as the parish centre and band hall for the local Black Raven Pipe Band, and, as a structure, is in very good condition.

---

[47] National archives of Ireland, ED/4/802.
[48] 1901 *census records*; birth, marriage and death records; valuations office, valuations records/field books.
[49] *Memories of Dromleigh, (Co. Cork) a Country School, 1840 to 1990*, n.d.; http://www.qub.ac.uk/sites/irishhistorylive/ IrishHistoryResources/ Shortarticlesandencyclopaediaentries/Encyclopaedia/LengthyEntries/Education/, (June 2015).

A New School Building

The application for an assistant teacher on this occasion was on behalf of Bridget (Brid) Connor, aged 18 years. Bridget Connor had been a monitor for the previous six years in Lusk, from February 1st 1869. She was described as 'well qualified and of 'good character'. The number of females on the roll was 78, with an average attendance of 56.8. The inspectors stated; 'as the attendance is high and the candidate competent, I commend the grant to be made'.[50]

Bridget Connor was duly appointed on 1st November 1874 and remained as assistant teacher in Lusk school until 1903, serving a total of thirty-four years, including six years, from March 1869, as a monitor.

Bridget Connors' salary was withdrawn on 30th September 1903 as she was permanently incapacitated; she was aged in her mid forties at the time. Her salary at this time was £60.[51] She was paid an annual pension of £28-5-0 and a disablement pension of £4-14-0.[52]

In 1901 Bridget Connor was living in Lusk village with her bachelor brother Patrick, aged 34, and her younger sister Teresa, aged 30 years.[53]

Bridget Connor was not married, neither, it would appear were any of her siblings, and therefore there are no immediate descendants of this family. However there is strong evidence, from available records, that there is family lineage to a well-known Lusk family, from first-cousins of Bridget Connor, still living in the locality, and this may be of interest from a family history perspective to the family in question.

There were very few teachers in Lusk school down through the years who were in fact natives of Lusk, John Donnelly and Brid Connor were certainly among those few. John Donnellys family lineage can be traced back in Lusk with certainty to the 1700's, while Bridget Connor's family were in Lusk from at least the early 1800's.

Alice Reilly, aged 20, was appointed assistant teacher in October 1903, replacing Bridget Connor and remained in Lusk school until February 1909. She lived in Drumcondra with her parents Thomas, an accountant, and her mother Anne.[54]

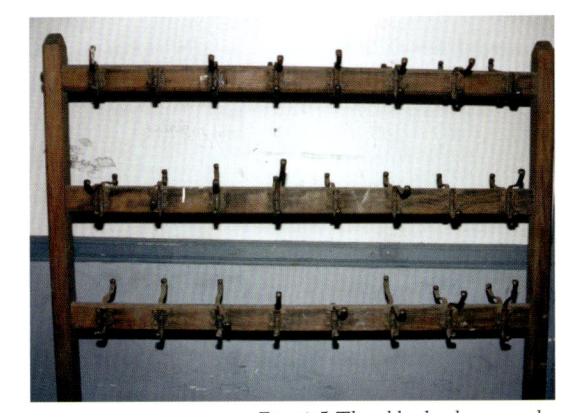

Fig. 4.5 The old school coat-rack
(authors own photo)

---

[50] National archives of Ireland, ED/1/31/No.119.
[51] National archives of Ireland, ED/4/161-162.
[52] National archives of Ireland, ED/121.
[53] Census records (www.census/nationalarchives.ie) (April 2014).
[54] Census records (www.census/nationalarchives.ie) (April 2014).

She had previously been a monitor in Kings Inn St. school in Dublin city and later a substitute in Fairview.[55]

On October 20th 1888 the school was closed due to an infection outbreak, with an instruction not to be reopened until Dr. Fahie certified that any danger of infection ceased to exist.[56]

From October 1885 to August 1888 **James Cowley** and **James Atley** were both monitors in Lusk School, they were paid £6 per annum.[57]

INSPECTORS REPORTS

Extracts from inspector's reports 1873 to 1896:

Males:

1887

Examination for results fees.

76 pupils presented.

Inspectors comments:

1st class; Writing too small and not between ruled lines of the slate. Notation and phrase spelling only middling.

2nd class; phrase spelling should be better.

3rd class; spelling, grammar and geography to be improved.

4th class; grammar and geography are backward.

Mr. Craig, B.A. Inspector

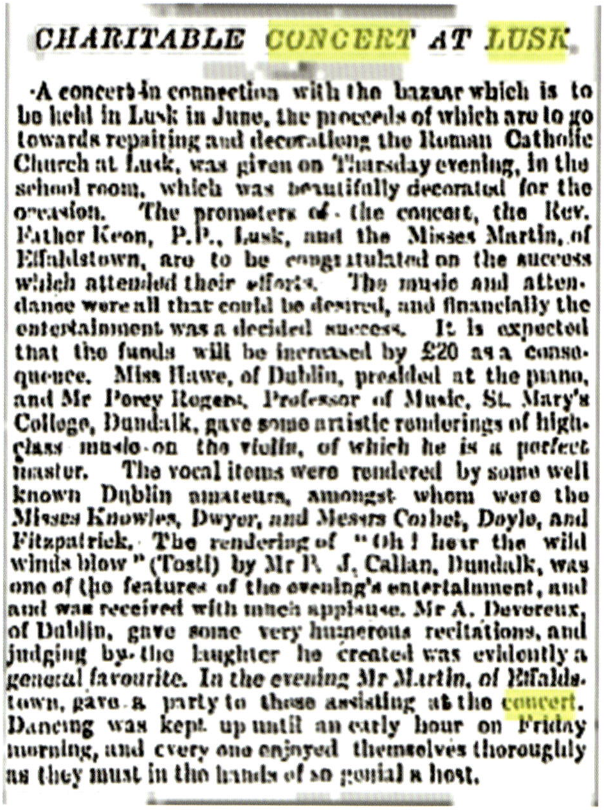

CHARITABLE CONCERT AT LUSK.

A concert in connection with the bazaar which is to be held in Lusk in June, the proceeds of which are to go towards repairing and decorating the Roman Catholic Church at Lusk, was given on Thursday evening, in the school room, which was beautifully decorated for the occasion. The promoters of the concert, the Rev. Father Keon, P.P., Lusk, and the Misses Martin, of Effaldstown, are to be congratulated on the success which attended their efforts. The music and attendance were all that could be desired, and financially the entertainment was a decided success. It is expected that the funds will be increased by £20 as a consequence. Miss Hawe, of Dublin, presided at the piano, and Mr Percy Rogers, Professor of Music, St. Mary's College, Dundalk, gave some artistic renderings of high-class music on the violin, of which he is a perfect master. The vocal items were rendered by some well known Dublin amateurs, amongst whom were the Misses Knowles, Dwyer, and Messrs Corbet, Doyle, and Fitzpatrick. The rendering of "Oh! hear the wild winds blow" (Tosti) by Mr P. J. Callan, Dundalk, was one of the features of the evening's entertainment, and and was received with much applause. Mr A. Devereux, of Dublin, gave some very humorous recitations, and judging by the laughter he created was evidently a general favourite. In the evening Mr Martin, of Effaldstown, gave a party to those assisting at the concert. Dancing was kept up until an early hour on Friday morning, and every one enjoyed themselves thoroughly as they must in the hands of so genial a host.

Fig 4.6
Irish Times, *Jan 24th 1894*

[55] National archives of Ireland, ED/4/1503; ED/4/1372.
[56] National archives of Ireland, ED/2/121/no. 23-24.
[57] National archives of Ireland, ED/4/1503; ED/4/1372.

A New School Building

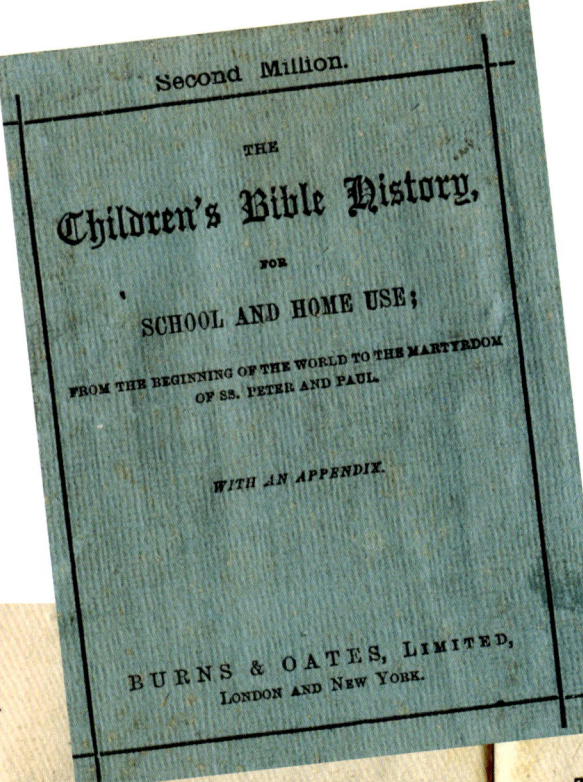

Fig 4.7
Childrens Bible History
(from 1874)
Cover and opening pages.

Second Million.

THE
Children's Bible History,
FOR
SCHOOL AND HOME USE;
FROM THE BEGINNING OF THE WORLD TO THE MARTYRDOM
OF SS. PETER AND PAUL.

WITH AN APPENDIX.

BURNS & OATES, LIMITED,
LONDON AND NEW YORK.

Nihil obstat.
  JOSEPH A. CAN. BANS, S.T.D

Imprimatur.
  ✠ HENRICUS EDUARDUS,
    Archiep. Westmonast.

Die 29 Oct. 1874.

PRINTED IN ENGLAND.

PREFACE

THIS little Manual has been compiled by a Teacher, who has long felt the want of a cheap Bible History to suit the capacity of the elder children in Catholic Elementary Schools.

The language is simple, and the description of the various events is given in mere outline, so that the pupil may, to commence with, acquire a knowledge of the *principal* facts, and thus form a basis for a more extended and detailed knowledge of the subject.

NOTE.—The pages of this book have been re-arranged, and the Parables of our Lord added to the Appendix. They are now *stereotyped*, and are thus secured from further change.

Females:

Jan 1873

Senior pupils should know the explanation of words more accurately.

Oct. 1873

Children well taught, results very favourable. Observed that several pupils in writing from dictation neglected the proper use of capitals.

Nov. 1874

School preparing satisfactorily.

Oct. 1884

Proficiency of junior classes is excellent. Senior classes excellent in reading.
Exercises in other subjects not yet finally corrected. Geography fairly understood.

Oct. 1885

Proficiency very satisfactory in general.

Oct 1887

Inspectors report following the results examination. 'The principal and her assistant are painstaking and efficient and their school is in a very satisfactory state, both as regards the literary proficiency of the pupils generally, as a place of moral discipline'.
Mr. Craig, Inspector.

On January 26th 1894 a report required that a clock, hand basin and towel should be provided in the school.[58]

On Jan 24th 1894 a concert was held in Lusk schoolroom, the proceeds of which were to be devoted to repairing the Roman Catholic Church. There appeared to be some concern regarding whether some rules were broken in using the school premises for a church fund-raising event. The inspector was asked to report whether a violation occurred. The inspector subsequently reports that no such violation occurred.[59]

---

[58] Lusk primary school, school inspector's reports.
[59] *Irish Times* Jan 24th 1894.

CHAPTER 5

Into The 1900's

The Untimely Death of Two Teachers, and the ensuing saga.

On 14th July 1896 **Michael Roche** was appointed assistant teacher in Lusk. Mr. Roche had attended St. Patricks teacher training college, Drumcondra. He was appointed principal of Lusk school in February 1901. His salary was £68 rising to £78 on becoming principal.[60] Mr. Roche, originally from Miltown-Malbay in Co. Clare, became ill in August of 1903, Mr. John Sweeney substituted for Mr. Roche from 31st August until 18th Sept. 1903. William Cotter took over as substitute on 22nd September and remained until 14th November 1903.[61] Mr Cotter himself became ill at that point.[62]

George Carton a local grocer and hardware merchant provided lodgings for the two substitutes at twelve shillings per week.

Due to his illness Mr. Roche had returned to his native Co. Clare. On 5th December 1903 he died from a lung condition,[63] he was thirty-one years of age.

Substitute teachers at the time were not paid by the commissioners of education but rather directly by the teacher for whom they were substituting. The two substitute teachers were being paid £1 per week (20 shillings) for their teaching duties.

When Mr. Roche died some outstanding salary was due to his estate by the office of national education. The outstanding amount due was £13 17s 2d (thirteen pounds, seventeen shillings and two pence).

Michael Roche's next-of-kin, his father Edward Roche, a shop keeper in Miltown-Malbay, Co. Clare, made a claim to the office of national education for the amount outstanding. In the meantime however, Mr. George Carton, a Lusk shopkeeper, had made a claim with the same office for money owed to him by Mr. Roche.

Mr. Carton had provided lodgings for the two substitute teachers for the time they were in Lusk. Mr Carton alleged that he had entered into an agreement with Mr. Roche to keep his substitute teachers

---

[60] National archives of Ireland, ED/4/1372.
[61] National archives of Ireland, ED/9/17749.
[62] National archives of Ireland, ED/4/1372.
[63] General registrations office Dublin, deaths register.

in lodgings for twelve shillings per week. There was now an amount outstanding of £5.17.6 for which George Carton claimed against Mr. Roches estate.

The office of national education were unable to settle payment of outstanding salary to Mr. Roches' father as long as the creditors' claim was outstanding. In a bid to resolve the issue a tripartite series of communication ensued over a number of months between the office of national education, Mr. Roches father Edward Roche, and Mr. George Carton in Lusk.

Mr Edward Roche (Michael Roches father) stated that he would expect the school manager Rev. T. Byrne PP Lusk to compensate Mr. Carton and Mr. Cotter, saying 'his son would have applied for sick leave from the education board but that Fr. Byrne precluded him from doing so, on the basis that he could not close the school and that he (Mr. Roche) should employ a substitute'. Mr Roches father claimed that his son obeyed the manager and that in conscience Fr. Byrne should now pay any money due and not put further demands on his grieving family. Mr Roche further claimed that his sons' health deteriorated due to fatigue and the worry of preparing the children for religious examinations, stating that had he obtained sick leave and come home at the early stage of his illness he would have recovered.

In the meantime and to further compound the problem, Mr. William Cotter, one of the substitutes in question, also died from his illness; he was twenty-two years of age and from near Abbeyfeale, Co. Limerick.

With regard to Mr. Cotter's situation his father explains in a letter to the commissioners for education that he had to convey his son's remains to his homeplace in Abbeyfeale, Co Limerick (Kilconlea, Abbeyfeale, Co. Limerick), at great expense, a distance of almost 200 miles. He sought compensation from the board and from the school management for expenses incurred in transporting his sons remains to Co. Limerick and for any teaching payment outstanding for his time in Lusk school. Mr. Cotter's father was a farmer in Co. Limerick, with a family of ten, William was the eldest, while the youngest was three years of age.

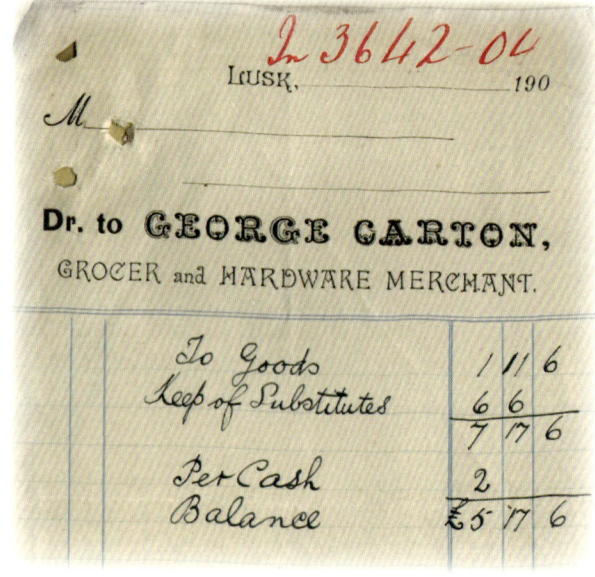

Fig 5.1 original invoice from George Carton

Into The 1900's

There then followed a succession of correspondence between the five parties involved which lasted for a period of twelve months before eventually being resolved.[64]

Michael Roche had a brother Ned Roche who was on the County Clare football team that won the Munster football championship in 1917.[65]

George Carton's shop in Lusk was located where Murrays pub the Top-Shop now stands and will be remembered by Lusk people of the 1930's through the 1960's as Emily Cartons shop.

More teacher appointments

Daniel Murphy was assistant teacher in the school from April 1902, this was during Michael Roche's reign as principal. Immediately prior to this, Mr. Murphy had been in Aughacasla, Camp, Co. Kerry, and before that in Rath, Ballybrittas, Portlaoise. He stayed in Lusk for just six months and was replaced in September by **Patrick O'Shea**, who stayed for one year. Patrick O'Shea was from Bantry, Co. Cork and had been a monitor in Bantry boys national school. Both Mr. Murphy and Mr. O'Shea had attended St. Patricks' teacher training college.[66]

School inspectors report

On March 26th of 1903 a school inspectors report referred to the yard and out-offices being in an unsatisfactory state, the cesspit should be cleaned, the urinal drain put into proper order and surface sweepings piled up in the rear should be removed. The inspector also reported that pupils have a faulty manner of holding pens, and that singing is 'flat'. The manager is informed of these defects and requested to have them remedied without delay. On 8th October the manager was asked to provide a clock.[67]

Richard Hegarty was the assistant teacher from August 1903. He left Lusk in April 1906 to take a teaching appointment in St Peter's school in Roath, near the city of Cardiff in Wales.[68]

James (Séamus) Fenton

James Fenton was appointed to a teaching post in Lusk school in 1904. He was born in 1874 in the parish of Caherdaniel, Co. Kerry; at age fourteen he became a teaching monitor in the local school he

---

[64] National archives of Ireland, ED/9/17749.
[65] Interview with Mr Aidan Carroll of Miltown Malbay, Co. Clare (25th June 2014).
[66] National archives of Ireland, ED/4/802.
[67] National archives of Ireland, ED/2/121/No. 23-24.
[68] National archives of Ireland, ED/4/1503.

had attended as a pupil. Having spent five years as a monitor he entered St. Patricks teacher training college, Drumcondra, Dublin in 1893, where he obtained first place in the entrance examination, and retained first place in his class for the two years he spent there.

His first teaching appointment was in 1895 to the boys national school in Kilbeggan Co. Westmeath where he remained for nine years. While in Kilbeggan he was awarded the Carlisle and Blake prize for teaching practice.[69]

He was appointed principal to Lusk school on 1st May 1904;[70] he was twenty-eight years of age. In July 1904, shortly after coming to Lusk, he married Bridget Judge a native of Co. Westmeath. They were married in the church of St Agnes, Corallstown, just outside Kinnegad. Bridget Judge was also a primary school teacher, living in Kinnegad at the time. She had studied in Our Lady of Mercy teacher training college Baggot St., Dublin, from 1901 to 1902[71]

In 1948 Séamus Fenton published *It All Happened, Reminiscences of Séamus Fenton*.[72]

In chapter VI, of *It All Happened*, entitled; 'Fingal, Its Associations and the Sequel', Séamus Fenton makes various references to his time in Lusk.

The following are extracts from that chapter:

> A teacher, wherever stationed, should learn Historical Geography. The best course I know of is the summer course in Aberystwyth University, conducted when I attended by Drs. Fleure, Hethrington and others; there the proper *methods* are taught and in an interesting manner. If the teacher cannot afford to spend the summer months there, let him read *O'Donovans Letters* and *Dr. Johnston's Journey to the Western Isles of Scotland*, where the latter guides the reader along glen, island and inlet, stopping every now and then to talk about matters of interest. He stresses a canon of general learning that it should be borne in mind by teacher and student: 'whatever makes the past, the distant or the future predominate over the present, advances us in the dignity of thinking beings… To abstract the mind from all local emotion would be impossible if it were endeavoured, and foolish if it were possible.'

He continues:

> Let me now say something about my next school area and its inhabitants: Lusk and the Fingallians. In 1904 I moved to Fingal to take up schoolwork. A very distinct old nation is this "tribe of the foreigners", Fine Gall, doubly so to one who aims at seeing all places through the eyes of the historian.

---

[69] Séamus Fenton, *It All Happened, reminiscences of Séamus Fenton*, (1948), Gill and MacMillan.
[70] National archives of Ireland, ED/4/1372; ED/4/1503.
[71] Census records (www.census/nationalarchives.ie) (June 2015); General registrations office Dublin, marriage register.
[72] Séamus Fenton, *It All Happened, reminiscences of Seamus Fenton*, (1948), Gill and MacMillan.

> In the early days of the Gaelic League the Fingall Feis was of outstanding distinction, and the Ashbourne fight of the local volunteers under Tom Ashe and Dr. Hayes was an event of Easter Week. Lusk and Ratoath, Norse outposts for two centuries after the Danish invasion, are both centres of intense tillage industry, largely inherited from industrious Norwegian forbears. The Lusk pastor in 1904, Fr. O'Byrne, a former Roman student, had the distinction of being the bearer of the Franciscan MSS from Rome to Merchants' Quay. A predecessor, Fr. Tyrrell, was an active member of the Repeal Association, a branch of which he established in the parish. As a traverser he was arrested along with O'Connell [Daniel] in 1843, but died in the early days of the prosecution. Another pastor of Lusk, Fr. Nicholas Farrell, often reminded his hearers that he had the lustre of having prepared the learned Dr. O'Donovan for death in 1861.
>
> Memories of a very eloquent parish priest, Fr. Dan Heffernan, still survive in Lusk. His joyousness made him a favourite all through North Dublin, and many of his remarks from the pulpit have passed into local parlance. Parishioners applying for a post as workers on the Military Farm, previoulsy known as the Prison Farm, always paid him a visit for 'a few lines'. He had a very pleasant note to write, till the suit of Ned Kanute fairly puzzled him. Ned had just completed three years penal servitude for having taken a leading part in a sanguinary faction-fight some miles away. But the resourceful pastor was equal to the dilema. 'Ned Kanute', he wrote, 'I had known for years as an exemplary workman, but I lost sight of him during the past three years, and am now glad…………..'. Ned secured the job.
>
> I talked to old people in Fingall who, though less than twenty miles distant, had never visited the capital. tis a great big cage, my father used to tell us, where, if you once got right into, you'd never get out of, and never be the same again.

During the summer of 1906 Séamus attended a summer school in woodwork and drawing. He was an adovcate for manual training for pupils in primary schools.

He writes:

> In conjunction with the literary feature of their work, all children should receive a training in handwork. A scheme of manual training put forward in 1900 by the Commissioners through the influence of Archbishop Walsh and Dr. Starkie, though intellectually conceived, was not a success. The failure was largely due to the refusal of the Government to make an adequate grant towards building and equipping, as an addition to every school, a suitable class-room for such training. A large number of teachers were trained in Dublin in 1900 by experts from England and Sweden,

at the end of the course a number, including myself, were selected to teach the subject in rural centres.

Under the most expert and skilful teaching, boys will get wearied towards the end of lessons, the under-nurtured before the others. There is one exception to this rule, and that is in the case of woodwork and kindred subjects. At woodwork they never wearied in my experience during class hours: on the contrary, they would beg for the key to the woodwork room in the evening to return and continue the fashioning of the wood models.

Towards the end of their period of functioning, the Commissioners intended to re-introduce the lapsed scheme of 1900. Alfred Purser, Chief Inspector, after a second visit to Sweden urged the introduction of the subject into the Irish Training Colleges. There was much governmental confusion during that period, as the British felt that their own period of functioning in Ireland was coming to an end; and when Dr. Starkie made an appeal to the British Treasury for a substantial grant to build and equip additional class-rooms, the reply was that owing to the imminence of Home Rule in some shape or other, the people of the Green Isle should wait until after that happy change of government, and bear the cost themselves.

As Deputy Chief Inspector of schools, I urged the teaching of the subject in the training colleges, but without effect. I got it as far as the preparatory colleges, Mallow and Glasnevin, but no further. The subject never reached the training colleges.

Some people from Lusk will well recall the late 1950's when the local library hall was fully equipped with woodwork benches and full sets of woodworking hand tools. A woodwork teacher arrived every Tuesday evening to give instruction in woodwork and technical drawing. Originally a Mr. Cronin arrived on his motor scooter each week and later Mr. Maurice Holly took over the classes, he drove to Lusk every week in his Morris Minor car. Classes started after normal school hours, for boys from the primary school. These classes were extremely popular (echoing the sentiments of Séamus Fentons experience described above) with almost every boy from the senior classes in Lusk school attending to learn the rudiments of woodworking and technical drawing. Woodwork classes for the men of the parish were held later the same evening. For certain there are many pieces of work from that time still lingering in family homes or outhouses in Lusk.[73]

---

[73] Authors own memories.

Séamus also strongly championed the monitorial or pupil-teacher system, he states:

> After the treaty, for instance, those of us who had long experience pleaded for a continuation of the pupil-teacher and monitor system, somewhat modified, but we were completely silenced in speech and numbers by those who gave advice that was relished, and those stall-feeding institutions known as preparatory colleges, were established at vast expense. After years of trial, the authorities who had experience of both systems had no doubt as the superiority of the discarded one.
>
> Monitors and pupil-teachers were selected with much care in pre-treaty days by managers, teachers and inspectors, there was competition within the district, the inspectors' district as the unit, and a check by the senior inspector. Then for five years the progress of the young teacher was closely watched, and the very best selected for a two-year course of training. The system worked admirably. The monitorial system was not retained.[74]

Séamus Fenton was actively connected with the national school system from 1888 to 1939. He remained in Lusk school until Februrary 1907, having been promoted to inspector of the national schools system, and later to deputy chief inspector, a position he held until his retirement in 1939.

From the reminscences of Séamus Fenton in *It All Happened* it is evident that he was a wonderful, enthusiastic and forward thinking educator. Lusk school suffered a great loss to the education of its children when Seamus Fenton was promoted to inspector, but the national school system as a whole surely gained.

Séamus Fenton was born and reared in Co. Kerry, and just one year after he left his teaching post in Lusk another great Kerryman arrived to take up teaching duties in the parish, (Corduff school) his name was Thomas Ashe. There surely is something about Kerry men.

Extracts from *It All Happened, Reminiscences of Seamus Fenton*, 1948, published here with the kind permission of original publishers Gill and Macmillan

Mrs. Bridget Fenton, (née Judge, see above), was appointed assistant teacher in Lusk boys school in May 1906, remaining in the position until October 1907, this was the first time in the history of Lusk school that a female teacher was appointed to teach the boys. Mrs Fenton first came to the parish of Lusk as principal teacher of Corduff school on 28th August 1904, following her marriage to Séamus Fenton on 28th July 1904.[75] Immediately prior to this she had been principal in a school in Westmeath. Upon transferring to Lusk school Mrs Fenton was replaced as principal in Corduff school by Mrs

---

[74] Seamus Fenton, *'It All Happened', reminiscences of Seamus Fenton*, (1948), Gill and MacMillan.
[75] National archives of Ireland, ED/4/1503; ED/4/4522; ED/4/1372.

Margaret Owens (née McManus) who remained in that positon until October 1907. Miss Annie Scully was a *locum* principal in Corduff for the following three months until the appointment of Thomas Ashe in March 1908.[76]

John Dowling was a locum teacher in Lusk school from January to March 1904. On May 6th 1904 a letter of complaint was received from Constable Saul, Royal Irish Constabulary, Lusk, relating to John Dowling. Constable Saul claimed that John Dowling left the locality owing him (Constable Saul) £6-12 shillings for lodgings. Constable Saul was seeking the outstanding lodgings fee from school management. He was subsequently informed that the school management does not interfere in private monetary affairs. John Dowling later took up a post as assistant teacher in Balbriggan school.[77] It is not known if the matter between Constable Saul and John Dowling was resolved.

During this period it was quite common to hold various school fund-raising events, and in this regard a bazaar was held in Lusk in 1906 to raise such funds for the school.[78]

James Kelly was a *locum* in the school from March to July 1907, during which time, 25th June to 5th July, the school was closed due to an epidemic.[79]

Thomas O'Connell became principal in March 1907, a native of Co. Kerry, he had been asistant teacher in St. Saviours boys school Denmark St. Dublin and Rathmines boys school before coming to Lusk. His salary at the time was £58, raised to £63 from July 1908, he remained at Lusk school until 1912.[80]

Edward Monks was a monitor in the school for three years, from July 1907 to June 2010, he was paid £10 per annum. He also substituted in Corduff school.[81]

Miss Emily Leonard was a substitute teacher in Lusk girls school during 1906 before being appointed assistant teacher in the Lusk boys in October 1907 on a salary of £44. She was twenty years of age, a native of Rush town and was a teaching monitor in Rush school from the age of thirteen.[82] Miss Leonard remained in Lusk school for a further two years. She got married around 1909/10 becoming Mrs. Emily Martin.[83]

---

[76] National archives of Ireland, ED/4/1503; ED/4/1508.
[77] National archives of Ireland, ED/2/121.
[78] National archives of Ireland, ED/4/1503.
[79] Ibid.
[80] National archives of Ireland, ED/4/1506; ED/4/1507; ED/4/1509; ED/4/1512.
[81] National archives of Ireland, ED/4/1509.
[82] National archives of Ireland, ED/4/1503.
[83] National archives of Ireland, ED/4/1509.

Her first child John was born in late 1910 and they continued to live in Rush town. Emily Leonard's mother was Margaret Leonard. She had an older sister Katie, a younger sister Mary and a younger brother Joseph.[84]

Miss Leonard was replaced by Mr. Peter Leonard as a *locum*. Peter Leonard had been a monitor in nearby Rush school for two years prior to this. He was subsequently appointed assistant teacher in Lusk and remained in the school until 1912. It was noted that Mr. Leonard's reign was not a success and the manager wished to replace him with a qualified assistant female mistress for boys under seven. The manager required an 'efficient female assistant, qualified to play and sing, and impart instruction in manual training to the junior group'.[85]

Peter Leonard was son of Nicholas Leonard a fisherman from the town of Rush, and his wife Mary. He was aged twenty-one when first appointed *locum* in Lusk school.[86]

During 1909 both **Mary Murtagh**, who was also an assistant teacher in Rush, and **Mary Keenan** (*locum*) taught in Lusk girls school for short periods.[87]

'Mrs O'

Mrs. Hannah M. O'Sullivan was appointed assistant teacher to Lusk girls school in March 1909. In October of the same year she was made principal, replacing Miss Margaret Coleman who had been teaching in the school since 1897.[88]

Mrs. Hannah O'Sullivan had been principal in Hedgestown school immediately prior to her appointment as assistant to Lusk school[89] (Hedgestown is one of the two other schools, along with Corduff, in the parish of Lusk).

Originally from near Caherdaniel, Co. Kerry, two of her sisters, Mary and Annie were also national school teachers.[90] She originally came to Lusk as Miss Hannah Fenton (brother of Séamus Fenton,

Fig. 5.2 Mrs O'Sullivan
photo courtesy of Mrs Emer Johnson (Taylor)

---

[84] Census records (www.census/nationalarchives.ie) (April 2014).
[85] National archives of Ireland, ED/9/22631.
[86] Census records (www.census/nationalarchives.ie) (April 2014).
[87] National archives of Ireland, ED/4/1509.
[88] National archives of Ireland, ED/4/1509.
[89] Ibid; national archives of Ireland, ED/4/1503.
[90] Census records (www.census/nationalarchives.ie) (May 2015).

Lusk school 1904-1907). She was principal teacher in Corduff school in December 1903, remaining in Corduff until August 1904 when she transferred to Hedgestown as principal following the retirement of Miss Anne Ryan.[91]

Hannah Fenton was a graduate of Our Lady of Mercy (OLM) teacher training college (for females) in Baggot St. Dublin, from 1900 to 1902.[92]

OLM Baggot St. was later transferred to Carysford, Blackrock, Co. Dublin and became known as Carysford College.

In 1908 Hannah Fenton married Bartholomew O'Sullivan, he was also from near Caherdaniel, Co. Kerry. PP Rev. Thomas Byrne married them in Lusk on November 18th 1908.[93] They later had two daughters Eilis and Maureen. Eilis married Mark Taylor of the Swords Taylor family.
Mrs. O'Sullivan remained in Lusk school until retirement in 1941, thirty two years service in Lusk school and a total of 38 years in Lusk parish schools, including her time in Corduff and Hedgestown schools. She is still remembered by many of the old folk in the village and was affectionately known simply as 'Mrs. O'.

Mrs O'Sullivan died in 1973 aged ninety-one and is laid to rest in Lusk cemetery along with her husband Bart and daughter Maureen.

Application for funding for teachers' residence

In a letter dated March 21st 1910 sent by the school manager to the board referring to Lusk school being one room 36ft. x 15ft. providing accommodation for seventy-seven children and another room 18ft. x 10ft. that is used as a residence for a teacher. This room contains a fireplace and provides space for eighteen children. It is apparent from this letter that one of the teachers was living in the schoolhouse. The school manager Rev. Thomas Byrne made an application for a loan to provide a teachers' residence. The application was referred to the Board of Public Works for favourable consideration. Fr. Byrne requested commencement at once, the building of a teachers' residence.

This has not been forthcoming as quickly as he would have liked and he further writes; 'that the building be commenced at once as the teacher is obliged to live at Rush three miles from his work (he has to walk the three miles morning and evening in severe weather) which is detrimental to the interests of this school'. The teacher living in Rush at the time was Mr. Thomas O'Connell.

---

[91] National archives of Ireland, ED/4/1372.
[92] National archives of Ireland, ED/4/1503.
[93] General registrations office Dublin, marriages register.

The inspectors' report of September 4th 1912 states:

Site measurements are 84ft. 7inches x 61ft. 2inches, nicely situated and equal in area to the neighbouring plot on which a neat Carnegie Library has been built. Ground is valuable in Lusk, the proximity of the village to the railway station and its comparitive nearness to Dublin tend to keep the price high. Even when set for grazing I understand the land fetches £5 per acre per term, it is correspondingly expensive to purchase.

The parish priest was requested to seek the purchase of additional land adjacent or behind the said site, but the PP said 'he couldn't get it for love nor money'.

It was suggested that the four to five acres on which the PP's residence is located could be offered for a teachers residence. However the PP said 'he could not without the sanction of his ecclesastical superiors and the parishioners give for a site any portion which goes with his residence. It has always been for the PP and must remain so, whether its extent was five or fifty acres. A residence placed on his land would to some extent interfere with his privacy'.

Details of the loan application were:

Estimated cost of building £250
Amount of loan £250
It was proposed to adopt one of the Board of Works designs, Design No. 1.
Size of site, about 60 x 80ft.
The proposed site is a commons and free from rent. The owner from whom the site is being purchased requires a small strip for entrance to his field. It was suggested to the Board of Works that the site be accepted. It had been suggested some time previously to provide a site for the teachers residence on the school grounds. However this was deemed unsuitable due to its close proximity to the school privies and the graveyard, and the limited space of the site.

On January 29th 1913 the commissioners of public works sanctioned a loan of £250 to provide a residence for a national school teacher in Lusk.[94] The house was built soon afterwards, adjacent to the Carnegie library and was in use by a teacher of the school until the 1970's, and still in use today as a private residence.

---

[94] National archives of Ireland, ED/9/15495.

Thomas Devine

In August 1912 Thomas Devine was appointed principal on a salary of £135. Tom Devine was a native of Kilmihil, Co. Clare, where he was a pupil in Cooraclare national school. He was born 19th October 1863.[95] In September 1884 age twenty he entered St Patricks teacher training college Dublin, graduating in July 1886.[96] He later graduated with a BA Degree-Mathematics (Royal University of Ireland)[97] and was probably one of very few primary school teachers to hold such a qualification at that time. In 1901 Tom Devine was teaching in the primary school in the parish of Ballyphilip, Portaferry, Co. Down.[98]

In 1911 he was professor of mathematics in Mount St. Joseph (Cistercian College) boarding school in Tipperary.[99]

Thomas Devine was a member of Mount St. Joseph College staff from the time the college opened in 1905 and remained on the teaching staff of the college until 1911.[100]

The following is an excerpt from *Cad Bliain Faoi Rath*, an historical publication produced in 2005 to commemorate the centenary of Mount St. Joseph secondary school.

> Mr Thomas Devine was one of three lay teachers employed on our opening in 1905. He taught Irish and Mathematics. Mr. Devine wore no gown, he didn't even wear a hat. His forte was Irish. A hard worker himself, he made us work too and succeeded in making us take a keen interest in the Irish language. In those days he was usually known as "Cad e sin?" But in later years, on his showing a strong predilection for the heroine of "Bean an Leasa" he was generally known as "Fear an Leasa" – a sobriquet he himself greatly enjoyed and highly appreciated.[101]

He returned to primary school teaching to take up the appointment of principal in Lusk school in 1912, where he remained until his retirement on 30th September 1928, at the age of sixty-five years.

Mr. Devine was the first resident of the teachers house, referred to above, built in 1913.[102]

---

[95] National archives of Ireland, ED/12/14826.
[96] St. Patricks' teacher training college, Drumcondra, Dublin, p7 1883 -1914, college register.
[97] Royal University of Ireland (RUI was superseded by the National University of Ireland and Queens University Belfast under the Irish Universities Act, 1908); National archives of Ireland, ED/4/794; census records, (www.census/nationalarchives.ie) (April 2014).
[98] Census records 1901, (www.census/nationalarchives.ie) (April 2014).
[99] Census records 1911, (www.census/nationalarchives.ie) (Dec. 2014).
[100] Mount St. Joseph college, Roscrea, (college records).
[101] Mount St. Joseph college, Roscrea, *Cead Bliain Faoi Rath*, originally from an article written by Mr. Liam S. Maher (RIP), English Teacher, Cistercian College (Mount St. Joseph) 1950 to 1987, and attributed to Mr. John Ryan, student of Mount St. Joseph 1905 to 1910, who later entered the Priesthood.

Sara Mulligan was assistant teacher for the boys from September 1912 to Februrary 1915. She was a native of County Sligo and had attended Our Lady of Mercy teacher training college, Baggot St. Dublin.[103] Prior to her time in Lusk school she had been in Kilkenny,[104] and from Lusk she went to Cabinteely school.

Sara Mulligan, along with Hannah Fenton (Mrs. O'Sulivan) from Co. Kerry, and Bridget Judge (Mrs Fenton) from Co. Westmeath, and who later became Hannah O'Sullivans' sister-in-law, had each been students in Our Lady of Mercy teacher training college at the same time, and later, the three of them were teachers in Lusk school.

James Monks was a monitor from July 1914, when he was seventeen years old, to June 1917. Over this period his pay went from £10 to £20 per annum.[106]

Elizabeth McCaffrey was born in Co. Dublin and as a child she moved to Co. Cavan, her father Hugh McCaffrey was an RIC officer, and later a publican in Swanlinbar. Miss McCaffrey was assistant teacher in Emyvale Co. Monaghan up to December 1909.[107] In January 1910, aged twenty-two years, she came to teach in Lusk girls school. Her salary was later raised to £51, to £58-10 in March 1914 and by December 1917 was £88. Miss McCaffrey remained in the position until March 1918. She was immediately replaced by **Katie Kavanagh**, whose salary was £72, rising to £76 later in the same year. Katie Kavanagh stayed for only one year, leaving Lusk school to take a teaching position in Clane, Co. Kildare.[108]

Ellen Long (known as Nellie) was appointed as assistant teacher in the boys school in Februrary 1915. Miss Longs salary was £44, rising to £51 in February 1915. She had been a monitor in Rush school and later an assistant in St Vincents boys school North William St. Dublin for five years prior to her Lusk appointment. Miss Long remained in Lusk school until November 1925. In December 1925 she transferred to Rush boys school.[109]

---

[102] Valuations office Dublin, valuations records for Lusk.
[103] National archives of Ireland, ED/4/1518.
[104] www.census/nationalarchives.ie (June 2015).
[105] National archives of Ireland, ED/4/1518.
[106] National archives of Ireland, ED/4/1518; ED/4/1521; ED/4/2121; ED/4/2125; ED/4/2132; ED/4/2137.
[107] National archives of Ireland, ED/4/2132; www.census/nationalarchives.ie (August 2015).
[108] Ibid.
[109] Ibid.

INSPECTORS REPORTS
Extracts from Inspector's Reports: 1902 to 1913[110]

Boys School
Oct. 1902

Reading	Fair
Writing	Middling
Spelling	Fair
Grammar	Good
Composition	Middling
Kindergarten and Manual Instruction	–
Drawing	Middling
Needlework	–
Singing	Fair
School Discipline and Physical Drill	Fair

Inspector's further comment:

> The instruction and training of infants need more systematic attention. All the written work of the school should be done with more care. Ionic solfa charts should be provided. Teachers should plan out their work systematically and keep progress records. There were no 'readers' for sale. Teacher informed me that pupils supply their own pens, copy-books, exercise books, etc., purchased in the village.
>
> Mr. O'Connor, Inspector.

Oct. 1903

> The proficiency of the pupils at present very unsatisfactory. The school seems to have made no progress since last annual inspection except in Reading and Spelling. The timetable needs revision and provision made for Manual Instruction Object Lessons.
>
> I made various suggestions to the teachers with a view to remedy the defects in the proficiency, and I believe the Assistant Mr. Hegarty, will do his best to act on them. There is little hope that the Principal will be able to resume duty.
>
> The report was signed by Mr. P.J. Honan, Sub-Inspector.

---
[110] Lusk primary school, school inspectors' reports.

Into The 1900's

The reference here to the Principal being 'to resume duty', would appear to refer to Mr. Michael Roche who had been on sick leave for some time and referred to earlier in this publication. Although it would appear the inspectors reference to this event was somewhat out of date given that Mr. Roche had in fact died the previous January, although it should be said that this would have been the first school inspection since Mr. Roche's passing.

Oct.1904

The inspection report for the following year was much more favourable than the 1903 report. Senior Inspector Mr. C Smith said:

'The school is at present excellently well conducted. The principal is enthusiastic, earnest and skillful. The assistant works hard but his work needs a good deal of finish and polish. The demeanor of the children testifies to the laying on solid foundations of habits of study, application and self-restraint, while their personal neatness and that of the school-room tell favourably of the work done by Mr. Fenton since his appointment'.

Nov. 1905

Lusk boys school continues to be conducted in a very satisfactory manner and bears favourable evidence to the skillful and attentive manner in which the members of staff discharge their duties. Order and discipline are well maintained. The accounts are properly kept.

Mr. C. Smith, Inspector.

Sept. 1906

Mr. G. Bateman, inspector, in his report stated:

The general state of the school is satisfactory and evidences care and skill on the part of the staff. The only subject in which a high proficiency was not reached is in Penmanship of the senior boys.

Mr. G. Bateman, Inspector.

Oct. 1907

During the hours that constitute an attendance, the principal should be continuously and actively engaged in teaching, he cannot devote any portion of such time to the writing out of the rolls for the next quarter, he should also give criticism lessons regularly to the paid monitor, and at his examination in June test the boys in every subject. The school is, generally speaking, in a good state, the only subject in which any marked weakness was shown was the arithmetic of the fourth and fifth standards. Oral expression ought to be cultivated. Song books should be used by pupils.

The number of attendances made by pupils during the year 1906-07 had not been entered in the register. Though there are five Protestants on rolls, the religious denomination of the pupils had not been entered for the quarter ended 30th September 1907.

Mr. G. Bateman, Inspector.

Sept. 1908

The principal gave well thought out history lesson, and generally speaking his work was of a solid character. The pupils write neatly, but they have stiffness of attitude which will prevent them from being ready penmen. In Elementary Science, the results of the pupils experiments should be properly recorded, and the subjects chosen for Object Lessons, such as admit the provision of specimens for each child. The pupils are quiet and attentive, but they lack readiness and quickness, and they do not answer fully and clearly as is desirable. The shoots should be freed from grass.

Dr. Batemen, Inspector.

May 1911

The Principal is now doing his work in a thorough, whole-hearted manner, and on the whole with marked success. He ought however, to improve the spelling of the Third Standard, impart instruction in Elementary Science to all the Fourth Standard pupils, and give due attention to ear tests in Singing. The Assistants teaching is only of fair quality. The shoots to be cleared.

Mr Bateman, Inspector.

Apr. 1913

Good progress is being made by the majority of the Seventh standard pupils, but the general instructions given to standard three to five proved only fairly effective; indeed in some subjects, it fell below this level. The assistant is earnest and methodical, and promises to be a success; she will however need to give increased attention to junior drawing and to revision of the written work. The out office pits should be emptied; the urinal freed; the internal walls of both the school and offices distempered or lime-washed and the external walls of the building and the boundary walls cement washed or otherwise cleaned. The classroom ought to be supplied with dual desks. A few slates are needed for the roof of the offices, and a little glazing in the main room.

Dr. Bateman, Inspector.

Dec. 1913

Good progress is being made in singing. Elementary science is carefully executed; but the instruction given to the pupils in third and fifth standards in reading, history and geography proved only fairly effective. Written English work in the fifth standard was only of a moderate character, but it was satisfactory in the seventh standard. The manager proposes at an early date to put the school house in thorough order; and to equip the classroom with dual desks. Special stress should be laid on the importance of daily cleaning of the teeth.

Of fourteen pupils enrolled in the fourth and fifth standards on 1st July last, none appear to have been promoted.

Dr. G. Bateman, Inspector.

Girls School

October 1902

Inspectors are required to rate the standard of the pupils expressed by one of the following: Excellent, Good, Fair, None.

On this inspection the overall rating given was: 'Good'

Reading	Good
Writing	Very Good
Spelling	Good
Grammar	Fair
Composition	Fair
Kindergarten and Manual Instruction	Fair
Drawing	Good
Needlework	Fair
Signing	Good
School Discipline and Physical Drill	Good

Mr. O'Connor, Inspector.

October 1903

The pupils are punctual. Discipline and order are good and the children with a few exceptions are clean and tidy.

The teachers take suggestions in a good spirit and are thankful for such hints as may aid them to improve their methods and proficiency of the pupils. A progress record will be kept in future. The tone of the school is good.

Mr. P.J. Honan, Sub-Inspector.

October 1904

Lusk Girls School continues to be conducted in a satisfactory manner and evidences careful and skillful work on the part of the staff. Arithmetic will call for more intelligent treatment in the senior classes and the junior classes should be trained to go through their school duties with less noise. The accounts are correct. The school-room and premises were commendably neat.

Mr. C. Smith, Senior Inspector.

November 1905

The general proficiency of Lusk Girls School is satisfactory, and shows that the members of the staff work hard and zealously in the discharge of their duties. Arithmetic and object lessons called for increased attention. A small effort has been made in the direction of cookery – this is a trend in the right direction. Order and discipline are well maintained. The accounts are correct. The premises are neatly kept.

Mr. C. Smith, Inspector.

September 1906

On the whole English receives careful attention, but increased attention should be given to easy analysis, and to Etymology and Syntax, particularly in so far as they bear on the correction of errors made by the pupils. The freehand drawing done deserves commendation, but in the senior classes it should be supplemented by a course of easy Geometrical Drawing. It will be necessary to give instruction in Geography and Arithmetic according to the suggestions in the notes for Teachers. Singing is evidently a favourite subject and is successfully taught.

Mr. G. Bateman, Inspector.

October 1907

Though the want of a classroom hinders progress, the school is in most respects in a satisfactory state. Oral expression however should be diligently cultivated and a real effort made to cultivate the reasoning powers of the girls who are slow in Arithmetic. As dotted paper when used too long has a cramping effect, Second Standard ought to draw at least for the greater part of the year on plain paper. Callisthenic exercises ought to be done…… Mr. G. Bateman, Inspector.

Strike action at the School

In 1914 parents engaged in strike action and kept children away from school in protest. Pupils remained away from school for a short period of time owing to local disagreement connected to use of the school for first-aid classes. Fr. Byrne PP refused to allow the school to be used for nursery classes.[111]

Mrs. Ellen Rooney, of Rathenny, Lusk, in correspondence to the Commissioners of Education points out that the school manager refused to allow parents the use of the school for nursing classes for local mothers.

The commissioners responded saying they have no role in the matter, control and use of the school before or after school hours is left to the manager.

Fig. 5.3
Copy of original envelope containing letter from Commissioners for Education to Mrs Rooney.
Reproduced with kind permission of the National Archives of Ireland

A report appeared in the *Drogheda Independent* on Nov. 7th 1914 with the heading 'School Childrens Strike':

> 'A strike of the children attending Lusk national school occurred last Wednesday. The cause of the strike is extremely controversial'.

In a letter to education commissioners dated 7th Nov. 1914 from Bridget Doyle, Commons, Lusk, states:

> Fearing you might be under a wrong impression why the children have been taken from Lusk school. I have taken them and intend keeping them away until we get our equal rights from Fr. Byrne. We have the library (referring to the nearby Carnegie library) closed against us for our Gaelic classes,

---
[111] National archives of Ireland, ED/9/24870.

we have been begging for a nursing class for the past three months. We then asked for the school, it was refused also. Fr. Byrne has used the school for his own first-aid class, he has used the library for running rifle practice and drill for his volunteers, we are denied of everything so are determined to keep the children at home until we have our own rights. The crowd around Fr. Byrne can have every privilage though they are only a small section of the parish.[112]

From other corrspondence it would appear there was an element of politics attached to this issue. There had been an election for a 'rural district councillor' and Mr. Rooney, son of the Mrs Ellen Rooney, was a defeated candidate. He attributed his defeat to the PP. Fr. Byrne who wished to set up his own First-Aid class in Lusk in connection with the volunteer movement. Fr. Byrne announced this one Sunday morning inviting all to become members irrespective of local politics. He stated that on Sunday evening Mrs. Rooney started a first-aid class on her own account. Fr. Byrnes class was held in the Lusk library which on the night was besiged by Mrs. Rooneys' followers whereupon the library committee decided to refuse the use of this room for any classes of the kind. Fr. Byrne moved his class to the school room and refused to allow Mrs Rooneys class to use it. As a result, some of the parents kept their children away from school, about 40% of the pupils were affected. The inspector felt that the manager had done no wrong and that he could hardly be expected to allow his school to be used by persons who defy his authority and flout his control, more especially as these persons are perfectly at liberty to attend the classes being held and run by Fr. Byrne.[113]

List of Books approved by the Commissioners of National Education July 1917[114]
- *Stories That Never Grow Old*
- *Twenty Thousand Leagues Under the Sea (for 4th and lower standards)*
- *A Flock of Flour*
- *The Wood Without an End*
- *Black Beauty*
- *History of Europe from Waterloo to the Great War*
- *The Right Road Series; Book II and Book III*
- *The Homestead Readers, Junior Book*

All of the above books were published by The Education Company of Ireland

---

[112] National archives of Ireland, ED/9/24870.
[113] National archives of Ireland, ED/9/24870.
[114] National archives of Ireland, ED/11/36/2.

Into The 1900's

- *Queer Things*
- *The Story of the Year*
- *Geography for Junior Grade*
- *Green Fairy Tales*
- *The Children of the New Forest*

Published by Messers Fallon Bros.

The following list were Approved Texts for Teachers use only.
Temperance Subjects:
The Teachers guide to the Government Temperance Syllabus, (Uncon Publ. Co. London)
- *Alcohol and the Human Body*
- *Lessons and Experiments on Scientific Hygiene and Temperance*

Published by McMillan and Co. Ltd. London.

- *Syllabus of Lessons on Temperance (Published by the Board of Education, England)*:
- *Specimen Temperance Lessons for Schools*
- *The A, B, C of Temperance*

Published by The General Assembly's Committee on Temperance.

On the sanctioning of the above books for teachers the commissioners stated:

> All these are useful books……….., number. 438 especially so *Lessons and Experiments on Scientific Hygiene and Temperance*, but they are books for the teacher , not for the pupil. That is, they are not suitable for use by pupils as reading books on 'temperance'. As a basis for the teachers' lessons on temperance they are recommended for inclusion on the boards list.

CHAPTER 6

'When One-Hundred years is Aft' and Gone'

It was now almost one-hundred years since the first school in Lusk was established.

Pupil Attendance Record – The First 100 years

The average pupil attendance over the whole one-hundred year period was sixty boys and fifty-six girls. Although complete data is not available for the number of pupils on the roll, there are some records indicating that the actual numbers on the rolls far exceeded the average attendance. For instance, from 1855 to 1866 the average number of boys on the roll was seventy-five, with the highest number attending at eighty-four and the lowest at fifty-one for the period. The average attendance for the same period was 50% of the number on the roll, with the highest attendance at 76% and the lowest 47%.

Over a three year period, 1866-69, in the girls school, the average number on the roll was seventy-three, with average attendance of 45%.

In the first forty years the number of boys attending exceeded that of girls by approximately 25%. For the next twenty-five years the number of girls attending exceeded boys by approximately 15%. From 1897 to 1923 the ratio of boys to girls was virtually fifty/fifty.

There was a notable decline in the number of children attending the Lusk school during the famine years, a drop indeed of approximately 50%, with numbers starting to rise again from the 1860's onwards. *(Appendix 1, Chart 1)*.

The main factor, most likely, was the fact that between 1841 and 1851 almost 800 people died in the Balrothery Union workhouse, many of those were children. Other children, along with adults, were sent to Australia and Quebec in Canada, under the government-sponsored scheme to assist emigration. It is not inconceivable that many children from the locality and outside the workhouse suffered similarly. During this period the population in the Lusk electoral district dropped by 12%.[115] The second contributing factor may have been the formal recognition by the Commissioners of Education and the subsequent opening of another school in the parish at Corduff, in 1844. This is likely to have taken at least some potential pupils from the Lusk village school (although there had been pay schools

---

[115] Sinead Collins, *Balrothery poor law union, county Dublin, 1839-1851* (Maynooth studies in local history), 2005.

in both Corduff and Ballough at the time of the Irish Education Survey 1824-25, with fifteen and sixteen pupils respectively).[116]

It can be seen that the number of pupils in Lusk started to rise again post famine *(Appendix 1, Chart 1)* indicating that famine deaths, and emigration arising from the famine was by far the greatest contributing factor.

Teacher Salaries

At the beginning of the formal national education system in Lusk in 1832 the teachers' salary was £12 for males and £6 for females. By the end of the century the salary for males had increased barely threefold, while females salary almost equaled that of males. *(See Appendix 3, Chart 9)*. However, the figures shown in the chart take some degree of salary incremental credit into account and it is most likely there was still some considerable differential between male and female teacher salaries. Following the turn of the century teachers salaries approximately doubled, with a differential clearly evident between males and females pay. Around about 1913-14 there was in fact a salary reduction introduced. Salaries started to rise again in 1917 through to the end of the first one hundred years when the male principal was paid £430 and the female principal £340, both of these figures were at the top of the salary scale.[117] These figures represent an increase by a factor of thirty-six for males and fifty-six for females over the one hundred year period.

Through the 1800's teachers were not particularly well paid, their wages being about equal to a labourers pay and about one-third that of a tradesman.

In 1874 a gents' winter overcoat cost fifty-five shillings. The price of a newspaper was typically one penny, much cheaper than in earlier years, mainly due to increased newspaper circulation and readership.[118]

A total of thirty seven teachers were involved in the teaching of boys in the school over the first one-hundred year period, only three of these were female teachers. For the teaching of girls there was a total of twenty-one teachers for girls for the same period, all of these teachers were female. *(See Appendix 4)*

The primary school manager was always the parish priest. In Lusk, a total of eleven parish priests played a part through the first one-hundred years.

---

[116] Dublin city archives/gilbert library, commissioners of Irish education inquiry 1824-25, house of commons parliamentary papers.
[117] National archives of Ireland, ED/4/1516.
[118] *Irish Times*, July 1874.

Thomas Devine was still principal in the boys school in 1919, a position he held until his retirement in 1928. Ellen Long was still the assistant teacher and she remained until 1923.

Annie Doran came in as assistant teacher in 1919, stayed until March 1921. She was succeeded (in Lusk school) by her sister **Mary Doran**, who in 1923 married local man Michael Seaver. Mary Doran and Annie were from Moate, Co. Westmeath. Before coming to Lusk school Mrs. Seaver (Doran) had previously been teaching in Ring school, near Balbriggan, she remained teaching in Lusk school until 1929. She returned to live in Moate Co. Westmeath along with her husband Michael Seaver and took a teaching post in nearby Tubber Co. Offaly, cycling the journey each day. She remained in Tubber until she retired in the 1960's.[119] Mary Doran had attended Our Lady of Mercy teacher training college in Baggot St. Dublin. Annie Doran had been a Monitor in St Brigids school, Moate, Co. Westmeath. Following her time in Lusk she returned to teach in Moate boys school.[120]

Fig. 6.1
Mary Doran-Seaver
Photo courtesy of Pat Seaver

From the official recognition of the school in 1832, through the first twenty-five years of the school's existence there was a considerable turnover of teachers. For the first thirty or so years a total of nine female teachers, for girls, passed through the school, ranging from one year to five years service, until Mary Gaynor joined the school in 1855 and stayed for thirty-nine years. Meanwhile in the boys' school, for the first forty years, to 1873, there had been eleven male teachers, also ranging in service from one to five years.

In stark contrast, when the new school building opened in 1874 John Donnelly took charge of the boys, while Bríd Connor became assistant in the girls school, their teaching service lasted twenty-eight and twenty-nine years respectively.

Both John Donnelly and Bríd Connor were natives of Lusk.[121]

---

[119] Patrick Seaver, grandson of Mary and Michael Seaver.
[120] National archives of Ireland, ED/4/2136; Dept. education and skills, records management, school roll no's
[121] Genealogy records (http://dublinnorth.rootsireland.ie) (May 2014).

Mrs Mansfield

On December 1st 1925 Mary Elizabeth (Maureen) Maguire (Mrs. Mansfield) joined the teaching staff of the boys school, replacing Ellen Long. She was twenty years of age at the time and Lusk was most likely her first teaching post having attended Our Lady of Mercy teacher training college, Baggot St. Dublin through 1923-25.[122]

She remained in Lusk school until 5th May 1930, when she took up the position of principal in Hedgestown school.[123]

Maureen Maguire was born in her mothers home town of Castlecomer, Co. Kilkenny.

Her family later lived in Co. Galway where Maureen attended primary school. She was a monitor in the school up to June 1923.[124]

In September 1928, during her time in Lusk school, she married Skerries man Thomas Mansfield.[125] Their two sons Basil and Leo attended Lusk school during the 1940's.[126] There were five other children all born in Lusk except the youngest.

Mrs Mansfield remained in Lusk school until 5th May 1930, immediately transferring to Hedgestown school as principal following the resignation of James Monks, principal of Hedgestown to that time.[127] She remained in Hedgestown until 1946, transferring with her husband and young family to Inishboffin island off Co. Galway where she taught in the primary school on the island for the next two years. For the remainder of her career she worked in a number of primary schools including, Gabhlán, Connemara, Finglas in Dublin, St Laurence O'Tooles, Seville Place Dublin city, and Scoil Bhríde in Ranelagh Dublin.[128]

Mrs Mansfield died in July 1986 aged 81 and is laid to rest on Inishboffin Island.[129]

Fig 6.2
Mrs Mansfield as a young woman and in her later years.
Photo courtesy of Mrs Barbara Gibbons (Mansfield)

---

[122] National archives of Ireland, ED/4/2131; ED4/2142.
[123] National archives of Ireland, ED/4/2131; ED4/2142.
[124] National archives of Ireland, ED/12/10833; Interview with Mrs Barbara Gibbons of Co. Wicklow (29th June 2015).
[125] www.geni.com, (June 2015).
[126] Lusk primary school, school registers.
[128] National archives of Ireland, ED/4/2131.
[128] Interview with Mrs Barbara Gibbons of Co. Wicklow (29th June 2015).
[129] Ibid.

Miss Mary Kelly was assistant teacher in the girls school from March 1929, remaining for just one year. She had transferred to Lusk from Hedgestown school where she had been teaching from December 1925.

Fig 6.3 — Girls Class c.1920
Front Row L-R: *Katie Carton, Tessie McGee, Maureen Hand, ?unknown, Nellie Deane, Maureen O'Sullivan, Sheila Fay, Brid Hand, Maureen Sherwin.*
2nd Row: *Teresa Mills, May Russell, Minnie Daly, Lizzie Dennis, Kitty O'Reilly, ?unknown, Kathleen McNally, ?unknown, Gretta Owens, May Fay, Nancy McGee, Nancy Collins*
3rd Row: *Eilish O'Sullivan or Mary Sweetman, ?unknown, Kate Hand, Nancy Skelly, Alice Groves, Molly Connolly, Maggie Clarke, May Gosson, ?unknown, Nellie Magee.*
Back Row: *May McLoughlin or Alice Dennis, Nellie McNally, Bridie Dennis, Maureen Sherwin, Maggie Connolly, Lizzie Cruise, Dora Cruise, Bridie O'Reilly, Mary Owens, Alice Dixon, Alice Clarke.*

Fig 6.4 Junior boys 1920
Front Row: L-R: *John Egan, Richard Derham, Jack Malone, Eamon Monks, Bob Daly (behind), Tom Malone, Dickie Bentley, Christy Russell, Jack McKenna, Richie Deane, Jack Dennis.*
Middle Row: *Owen Bentley, Richard McNally, Billy Williams, James Gallagher, Myles Morgan, Tom Fay, Bill Malone, Willie Russell, Seamus Cowley.*
Back Row: *Miss Ellen Long (Teacher), Joe Sherwin, Christy McNally, Mick Gosson, Jem Bentley, Eugene Sherwin, Tommy Skelly, Tommy Gosson, Joe Carton, Paddy Russell, Nick Daly.*

*Fig. 6.5
Senior boys class 1920
Photo courtesy of Pat Kelly*
Front Row, L-R: *Brendan Monks, Bob Keane, Joseph Doyle, James Daly, Nick Sherwin, George Hogan, John Fay, Billy Magee.*
Middle Row: *Joseph (or Peter) Malone, Nick Doyle, Charlie Hurley, Riobard Hand, Joseph Magee, Thomas O'Brien, Christy Deane, John Barrett.*
Back Row: *Christy Magee, Alphonsus Brown, Peter Gosson, Charles Brown, Seamus Monks, Arthur Davis, Bernard Donnelly, Peter McCann, John O'Brien.*

*Fig. 6.6 Boys Class, c.1923
Unfortunately not many of the names are available, apart from;* **Back Row:** *1st Left is Seamus Cowley, 2nd is Riobaird Hand and 4th is Christy Magee.*
Middle Row: *4th from left Richard McNally,*
Front Row: *3rd from left Briain Donnelly, 4th Peter O'Brien, 5th Christy McNally. These boys would have started school somewhere between 1914 and 1918. A look at the list of pupil names in Appendix 5 may be of some help to anyone trying to identify an ancestor.*

(Photo courtesy of Billy Sherry)

Fig. 6.7
Girls Class 1925
Photo courtesy of Pat Kelly
Front Row, L-R:2nd Row: Agnes Connor, Maureen Sherwin, Sheila Owens, Theresa Devine, Nellie Maypother, May Maypother, Bridget Donnelly, Nellie Deane, Madge Browne, Monica Davis, Peggy Devine, Marcella McNally.
3rd Row: Kathleen McNally, Nancy Skelly, Molly Connolly, Minnie Daly, Greta Owens, Mary Sweetman, Kathleen Smyth, Mary McLoughlin, Judy Maguire, Lizzie Cruise, May Gosson, May Russell, Alice Dixon.
Back Row: Dolly Owens, Dora Cruise, Maggie Devine, Alice Dennis, Eileen Monks, Sheila Fay, Maureen O'Sullivan, Chrissie Seaver, Nancy Monks, May Fay, Annie McGee, Alice Groves.

Fig 6.8
Lusk School Boys c.1925 (Ranging in age from 5 years to 11 years)
Back Row, L-R: Jack Dennis, Paddy Cruise, Richie Deane, Mick Gosson, Christy McNally, Jem Browne, Peter O'Brien, Willie Wade.
Centre Row: Mikey Skelly, Joe Deane, Joe Sherwin, Michael McGee, Tommy Skelly, Tommy Gosson, Tommy Jenkinson, Christy (Kit) Russell, Mick Seaver, Paddy Gallagher, Bob Daly, Jem Bentley.
Front Row: Mikey Bentley, Frank Fay, John McGee, Paddy Fay, Joe (Eugene) O'Brien, Fred O'Brien, Pat Magee, Jack Browne, Jemmy Russell, Liam Cowley, Matt McCann, Joe Dennis, Paddy Seaver.

Fig. 6.9
L-R: Jack Browne, Jemmy Russell and Joe Dennis, 2009. The three are also in the above picture Fig. 6.5 in the front row, 85 years earlier.

Laurence Dunne

Larry Dunne served in Lusk School from 1st October 1928. He remained in Lusk school to January 1966. Mr. Dunne was born (Jan 1901) and reared in Rush to Laurence Dunne Senior, a seaman by profession, and Margaret Dunne (formerly Margaret Leonard). Larry had a twin brother William who died before the age of two years. He also had an older brother Patrick, and four sisters.[130] Having been a monitor in Rush primary school he entered St. Patricks teacher-training college, Dublin in September 1919, aged nineteen, graduating in 1921.[131] On completing his teacher training in St. Patricks college he substituted in Lusk school for Miss Long for one week in September 1921.[132] In November 1921 he took a position as assistant teacher in Artane industrial school where he served until March 1924.[133] From there he went as assistant teacher to Rutland St. boys school in Dublin City where he remained to September 1928. At this point he came to Lusk school as principal, replacing Mr Tom Devine. Larry held the post of principal in Lusk boys for over thirty-seven years.[134]

---

[130] Census records (www.census/nationalarchives.ie) (Dec. 2014).
[132] St Patricks' teacher training college, drumcondra, Dublin, p.19 of the 1914 – 1960, college register.
[133] National archives of Ireland, ED/4/2125; Dept. education and skills, records management, school roll no's.
[133] National archives of Ireland, ED/12/8989.
[134] National archives of Ireland, ED/12/20185.

On October 28th 1928, less than one month following his appointment as principal in Lusk, Larry married Mary Dillon, in St. Patricks church Skerries where Mary was living at the time.[135] Mary Dillon was also a national school teacher and a graduate of Our Lady of Mercy teacher training college Baggot St. Dublin. They took up residence in the teachers' house on The Green opposite the church, where Tom Devine had also lived during his time.[136] They lived there until about 1940, before moving to Rush.

Larry was a grey-hound racing enthusiast as well as a keen golfer and one of the founding members of Rush golf club.[137]

Many former pupils of Larry Dunne will recall the songs he taught to the senior boys in his classes such as the Irish ballad 'Boolavouge' recalling the story of Fr. Murphy and the events in Wexford during the 1798 Rising.

The first verse of Boolavouge runs:

> At Boolavouge as the sun was setting
> O'er the bright May meadows of Shelmalier,
> A rebel hand set the heather blazing
> And brought the neighbours from far and near.

Another favourite song that Larry regularly had the boys singing was the old marching song 'Step Together'.

The first verse:

> Step together, boldy tread,
> Firm each foot, erect each head,
> Fixed in front be every glance,
> Forward at the word advance,
> Serried files that foes may dread,
> Like the deer on mountain heather,
> Tread light,
> Left right,
> Steady boys and step together.

---

[135] General registrations office Dublin, marriage records.
[136] National archives of Ireland, ED/12/20185.
[137] Interview with David Dunne of Co. Louth, (March 19th 2015).

And yet another of his favourites, 'The Ballad of Kevin Barry', recalling the execution of Kevin Barry in 1920:

> In Mountjoy jail one Monday morning,
> High upon the gallows tree,
> Kevin Barry gave his young life for the cause of liberty,
> Just a lad of eighteen Summers,
> Still there's no one can deny,
> As he walked to death that morning,
> He proudly held his head on high.

Larry Dunne was exactly one year older than Kevin Barry when Barry himself was executed in 1920. Larry was attending St Patricks' teacher training college Drumcondra during this period, while at the same time Kevin Barry was a medical student in UCD on the other side of the city. Because of the age closeness of the two young men, and both being young college students at the time, it may be that Larry Dunne had a certain empathy with Kevin Barry, and hence attempted to pass that down to his pupils through the songs.

Fig. 6.10 Larry Dunne (Courtesy of David Dunne)

Mary Dunne (née Dillon) was born February 1900 in Co. Roscommon where her mother, Jane Dillon (née Morris) was a national school teacher.[138] She attended Our Lady of Mercy teacher training college Dublin, 1919 to 1921. She first came to the North Co. Dublin area as an assistant teacher to Loughshinny school where she spent seven years from October 1922 to December 1929,[139] and was living in Skerries when she married Larry Dunne in 1928. From January to May 1930 she was assistant teacher in Rush girls school.[140]

She first came to Lusk school in May 1930 as assistant teacher in the boys school, where she remained until December 1938. In January 1939 she went to St. Peter and Pauls girls school in Balbriggan for a

Fig 6.11 Mrs. Mary Dunne (Courtesy of David Dunne)

---
[138] General registrations office, Dublin, birth records; census records (www.census.ie) (15/05/2015).
[139] National archives of Ireland, ED/4/2137.
[140] General registrations office Dublin, marriage records.

short period and then returned to Rush girls school until July 1941, before coming back to Lusk this time as principal of the girls school, replacing Mrs. O'Sullivan, (Mrs. O').

Mrs. Mary Dunne remained as principal of Lusk girls school until mid 1960's.[141] She died in September 1965 aged 65 years. Larry Dunne died February 1972, aged 71 years. They are both interred in Whitestown cemetery, Rush.

Fig. 6.12
Boys with teacher Larry Dunne c. 1930/31
Ranging in age from 8 to 14 years.
Front Row, L-R; Art O'Brien, John Carton, Enda Monks, Tom Boylan, Padraic Kelly, Jack Kavanagh, Mick Boylan, John (pipes) Bentley, Matt McCann.
Middle Row: Paddy Skelly, Mikey Neary*, Jack Savage, Joe (Eugene) O'Brien, Paddy Fay, Joe Dennis, Jemmy Russell, unknown, Willie Hoey.
Back Row: Paddy Seaver, John O'Brien, Mikey Bentley, Liam Cowley, Thomas Redmond, Paddy Cruise, Jack Browne, Larry Dunne (Teacher)
*(It has been suggested that this is Paddy Redmond)

Fig. 6.13
Front Row, L-R: Tommy Kavanagh, Seamus Skelly, Paddy McGirl, Larry Boylan, David Owens.
2nd Row: Paddy Boylan, Larry Connolly, George Davis, Mick Dennis, Jackie Kelly, James Maypother, Brendan O'Connor, Peter Carton.
3rd Row: Mick Neary, Johnny Ferguson, Joe Connolly, Harry Edwards, Richard Devine, Raymond or Teddy Whelan, Nicky Carton.
Back Row: Willie Jenkinson, Nick Connor, Aidan Devine, Oliver Bentley, Mick Hoey, Seamie McNally, Sean Broe, Larry Dunne (Teacher).

---

141   National archives of Ireland, ED/4/2141; ED/4/2146; ED/4/2156.

An old Lusk poem (*Courtesy of Seamie McNally*)

The Three Old Characters referred to in this poem:
1. Larry Dunne was the school teacher
2. Nicky Rooney the Farmer
3. Charles McDaid the Garda Sergeant.

The Lusk Billiard Hall:

The Lusk billiard hall is a place of renown,
It stands snug and tidy in the midst of the town,
If you want to be a member its welcome you'll be,
You just walk right in and stump up your fee,
If you're fond of the cards sure its 'solo' they play,
You can take up a cue and skit your pennies away,
But now take my advice and don't go there at all,
For you'll get a suck-in in the Lusk billiard hall,
There you'll meet Nicky Rooney both decent and gay,
He lives a mile from the village, out Quickpenny way,
He comes in in his car or a bike he would push,
Just to talk about the carrots Larry Dunne grows in Rush,
Now the sergeant himself he turns up every night,
And if there's a row he's the first in the fight,
I hear now he's driving a pony and trap,
And he's scouring the village in search of 'oul scrap,
If you've any 'oul iron or pieces of tin,
Just drop him a card and he's sure to call in,
If you want him at night you'll just have to call,
For he's sure to be found in the Lusk billiard hall.

Schools Folklore Project

In 1937 the Irish Folklore Commission along with the Department of Education and the National Teachers Organisation initiated a scheme for primary school children to collect and document folklore and local history. Children in many of the schools throughout the country were involved in collecting folklore material in their locality. The children were encouraged to go out and write stories relayed to them by parents, grandparents and other older people in the community. This collection became known as the 'Schools Manuscript Collection' and the original written material of the children is archived under the National Folklore Collection at University College Dublin.

Lusk primary school under the principals in charge at the time, Mr. Larry Dunne (principal, boys school) and Mrs. Hannah O'Sullivan, (principal, girls school) was involved in the project. As a result we now have available to us some very valuable historic written records from the work produced by the children.

Some of the children involved in the Folklore Project at the time include:

> Maura McCann, Maureen Devine, Gretta McCann, Alice Hoey, May McGuigan, Phyllis O'Connor, Pauline Maypother, Maura McNally, Ellie Kavanagh, Rose Oglesby, Mollie Brogan, John (Jackie) Brogan, Tommy Groves, Christy Maypother, Patrick Boylan, John (Jackie) Kelly, Michael (Mick) Dennis and Brendan Connor.

The following are some examples of the original stories recorded and written by the school children. (Reproduced with kind permission of Folklore Dept. UCD)

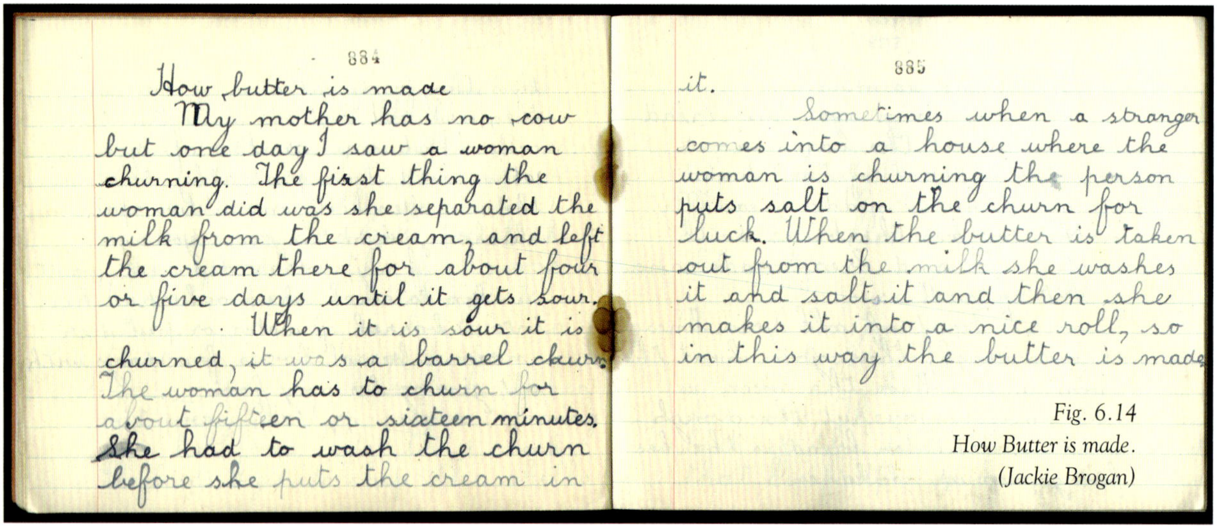

884

How butter is made

My mother has no cow but one day I saw a woman churning. The first thing the woman did was she separated the milk from the cream, and left the cream there for about four or five days until it gets sour.

When it is sour it is churned, it was a barrel churn. The woman has to churn for about fifteen or sixteen minutes. She had to wash the churn before she puts the cream in

885

it.

Sometimes when a stranger comes into a house where the woman is churning the person puts salt on the churn for luck. When the butter is taken out from the milk she washes it and salt it and then she makes it into a nice roll, so in this way the butter is made

Fig. 6.14
How Butter is made.
(Jackie Brogan)

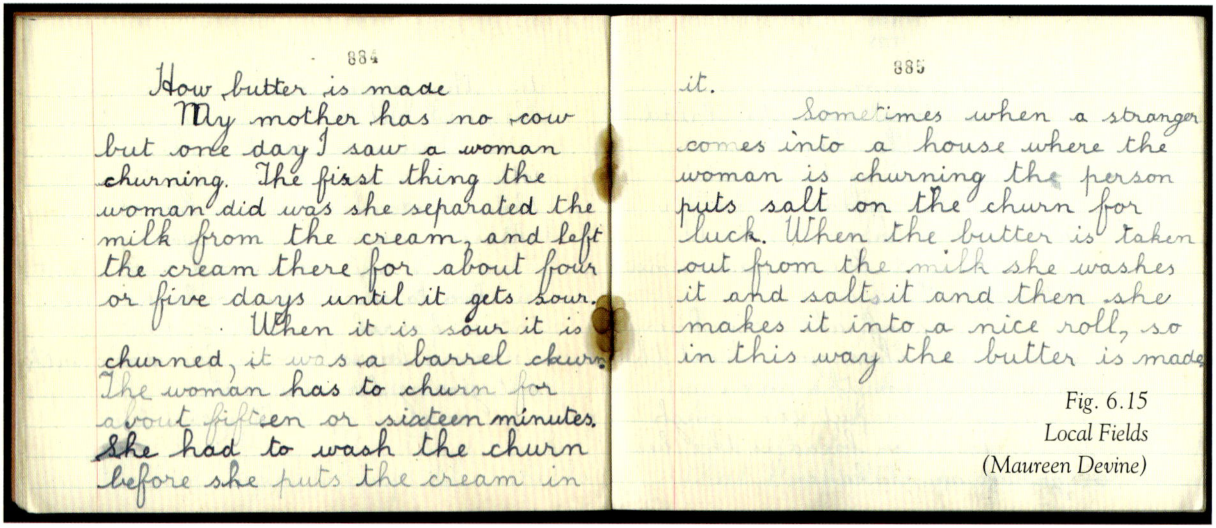

884

How butter is made

My mother has no cow but one day I saw a woman churning. The first thing the woman did was she separated the milk from the cream, and left the cream there for about four or five days until it gets sour.

When it is sour it is churned, it was a barrel churn. The woman has to churn for about fifteen or sixteen minutes. She had to wash the churn before she puts the cream in

885

it.

Sometimes when a stranger comes into a house where the woman is churning the person puts salt on the churn for luck. When the butter is taken out from the milk she washes it and salt it and then she makes it into a nice roll, so in this way the butter is made

Fig. 6.15
Local Fields
(Maureen Devine)

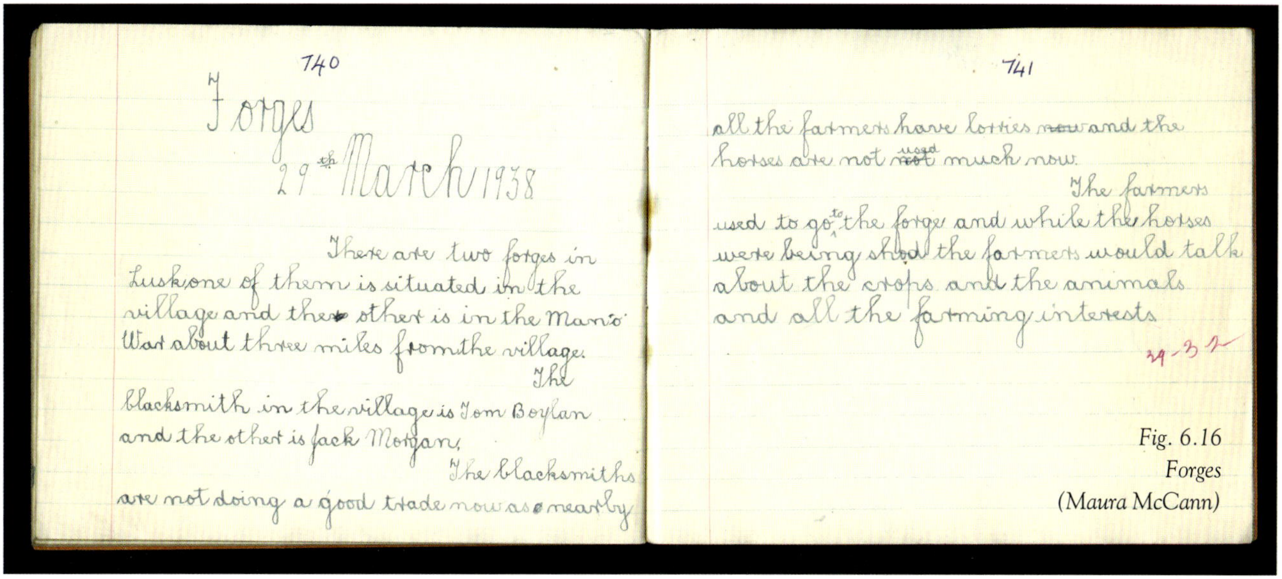

740

Forges

29th March 1938

There are two forges in Lusk one of them is situated in the village and the other is in the Man o' War about three miles from the village. The blacksmith in the village is Tom Boylan and the other is Jack Morgan. The blacksmiths are not doing a good trade now as nearly

741

all the farmers have lorries ~~now~~ and the horses are not used ~~not~~ much now. The farmers used to go to the forge and while the horses were being shod the farmers would talk about the crops and the animals and all the farming interests.

29-3-?

Fig. 6.16
Forges
(Maura McCann)

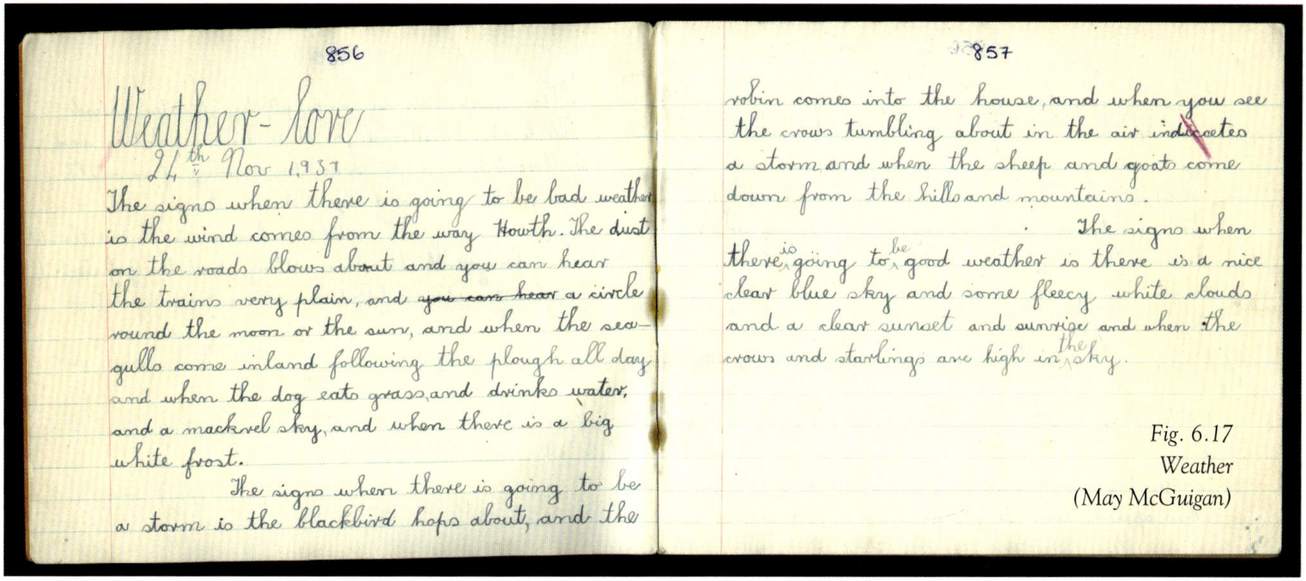

856

Weather-lore

24th Nov 1937

The signs when there is going to be bad weather is the wind comes from the way Howth. The dust on the roads blows about and you can hear the trains very plain, and ~~you can hear~~ a circle round the moon or the sun, and when the sea-gulls come inland following the plough all day and when the dog eats grass, and drinks water, and a mackrel sky, and when there is a big white frost.

The signs when there is going to be a storm is the blackbird hops about, and the

857

robin comes into the house, and when you see the crows tumbling about in the air indicates a storm and when the sheep and goats come down from the hills and mountains.

The signs when there is going to be good weather is there is a nice clear blue sky and some fleecy white clouds and a clear sunset and sunrise and when the crows and starlings are high in the sky.

Fig. 6.17
Weather
(May McGuigan)

Fig. 6.18
Front cover, May McGuigans copy book.

Fig. 6.19
Original school copybook,
front and back cover

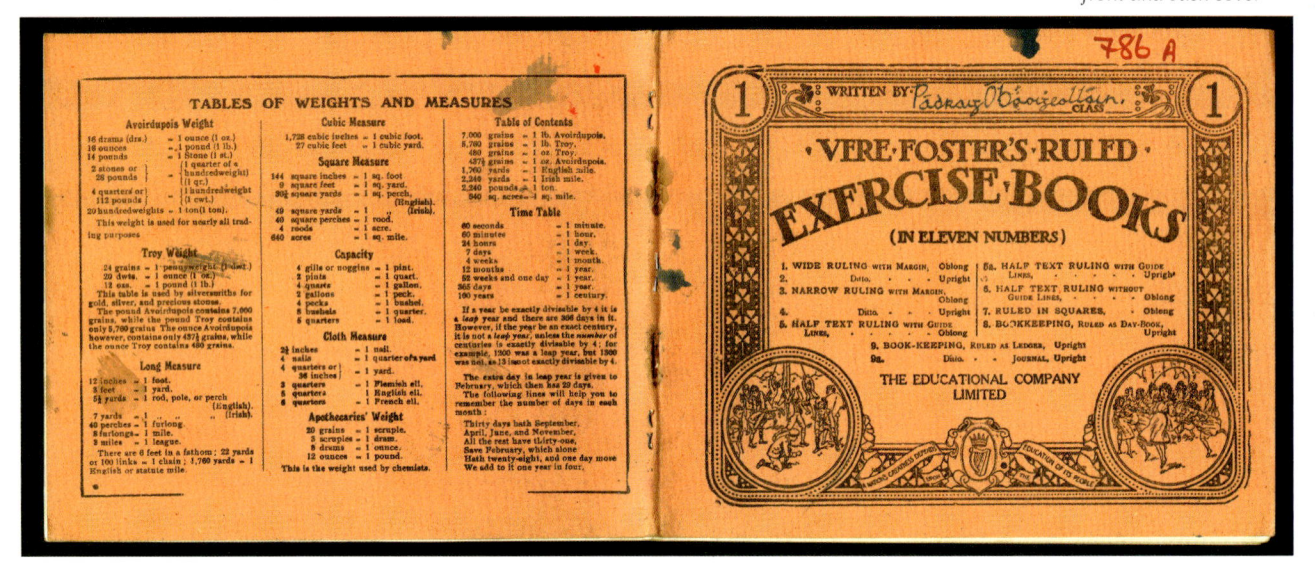

The following are some further examples of the stories recorded by Lusk school children for this folklore project, transcribed directly from the original copy books.

Local Crafts. 1st Dec. 1937, (Maura McCann, 5th Class)

There were not very many crafts or trades carried on in this district long ago, except basket-making, harness –making, nail-making, thatching, carpentry, coach-building and stone-cutting.

The only trades that are not carried out now are nail-making and coach-building. Christy Rooney of the Man O' War used to build the coaches that travelled from Dublin to Belfast. Harness-making is carried on still but the farmers say they are not making them as the well as in the olden days. James Cowley is a harness-maker in Lusk and he has a good trade as he is the only one in Lusk and all the farmers go to him.

There are a lot of carpenters in Lusk now compared to long ago. Tommy Halpin was a travelling carpenter. They used to go around and stay in the houses for about a month making tables and other things and repairing the houses.

Basket-making is very common now as well as in the old days. There are two good basket-makers in Lusk now, namely, Thomas and Jack Dennis. They make them out of sallies and then sell them to the farmers who use them for giving turnips to the cattle in Winter and for picking potatoes into them in the Summer.

There is very little nail-making now, long ago men used to make them and walk five or six miles to sell them. We have two blacksmiths in Lusk. One of them lives where the inn or hotel was in the Man O' War and the other man lives in the village.

Local Heroes. January 1938, (Crostóir Mac Potar)/(Christy Maypother)

There were many heroes in Lusk long ago. John Rooney was a famous hurdler and Mark Taylor was a famous footballer and champion jumper.

Patrick White was the best runner in Ireland, he ran from Balbriggan to Dublin.

Edward Hayden was a good swimmer; he could swim from Rogerstown to Donabate smoking a pipe. John Smith was a good swimmer also; he could swim a quarry backwards and forwards.

Willie Bentley was a good wrestler and Thomas Monks and Edward Connor were wrestlers also.

Local Cures: 17th Nov. 1937, by Tommy Groves.

Long ago when there were no doctors people made there own medicine and cures.

Bread soda was the cure for a burn. Cow-dung was the cure for any gathering or swelling. Paraffin oil was the cure for a scald, cold tea is the cure for stys on the eyes, goose-grease is the cure for cracks in the hands. A poultice of sugar and soap for a thorn in the finger. Raw beef is the cure for a black eye, vinegar for a headache, mustard is the cure for a tooth-ache, boiled celery and salt is the cure for boils.

Raw onions is the cure for chilblains, 'Blessed Cream' is the cure for erysipelas.

Hot castor oil is the cure for earache, bread soda and sugar is the cure for the heart-burn. Washing soda was the cure for warts. Butter and soot was the cure for a whittle. Soot and burned straw for 'the pip'.

A few other cures recorded by other school children include:
- Forge water is used for curing a wart.
- Sulphur ointment cures 'ring worm'.
- Bulkey-shans cure a disease on the legs called 'fellon'.
- Carry a potato in your pocket to ward off rheumatism.
- Whooping Cough: Put the affected person under a donkey three times.
- Put a snail to a wart to get rid of it. (Presumably to get rid of the wart, not the snail!)

Local Industries: (Tommy Groves)

There were not many industries about our district. It is said that there was a brewery at Brown's on the road to Corduff. This brewery used to supply the Covent in Grace Dieu with ale.

There was supposed to be a tan yard over at Rooneys of Raheny.

In former years there was a brick works in Jones field at a place called Loughbarn near the Man of War.

Thatching: 2nd March 1938, (Seán O'Ceallaigh)/(Jackie Kelly)

In olden times most of the houses were covered with thatch, that is a covering of straw. It is not everyone who can do this and a man who could thatch well earns very good money.

The tools used by the thatcher are: the slice, the rake and a large knife. Before thatching, the thatcher must prepare the straw. Wheaten straw is generally used because it is the best. Then it is pulled to take the short straw out of it. Then he wets it to make it soft; salt water is the best to wet (the) straw because it kills the seeds of any weeds that may be in the straw. When the straw is ready it is tied in handy bunches. Then the thatcher gets a ladder and goes up on the house. He tears away some of the old thatch first. Then he gets a handful of straw called a 'wangle'; he knots one end of the straw and pushes it into the old thatch by means of the slice. He does the thatching course-by-course, he puts three wangles in every course. When he has the thatch on, he beats it and combs it with a rake. He pegs it down with wire, in some parts of the country they tie the thatch down with sally rods.

There are a few good thatchers in this place (Lusk), their names are Paddy Donnelly, Thomas Masterson and James Carton, they get about eight or ten shillings a day.[142]

Primary School Certificate

The Department of Education first introduced the Primary Certificate in 1929. Children in sixth class, before completing the primary cycle sat an examination in Irish, English, History, Geography and Mathematics, and for girls Needlework was also examined. Initially the primary certificate examination was optional. In the late 1940's a compulsory examination was introduced for all sixth class pupils. The number of subjects was reduced to three at this point, Irish, English and Arithmetic. The Primary Cert was finally abolished in 1967.

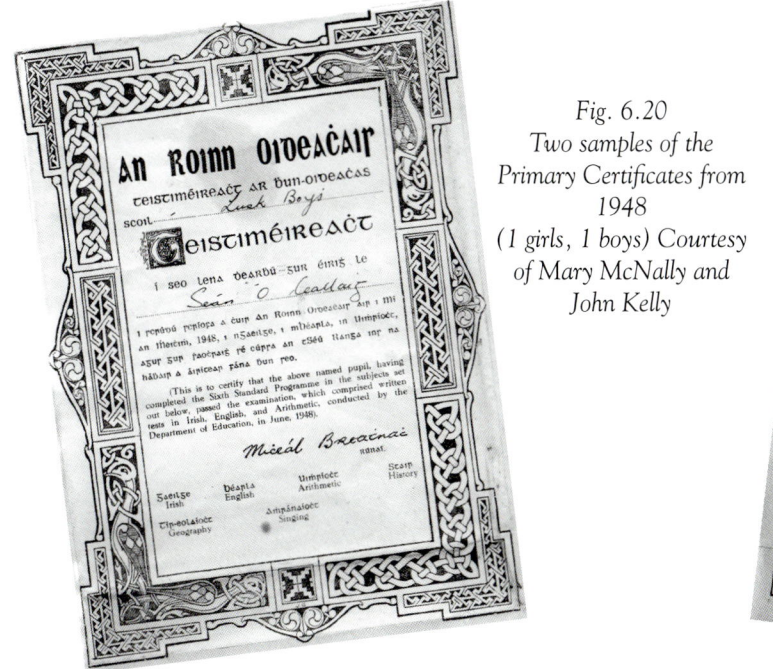

Fig. 6.20
Two samples of the Primary Certificates from 1948
(1 girls, 1 boys) Courtesy of Mary McNally and John Kelly

---

[142] University college Dublin, schools manuscript collection.

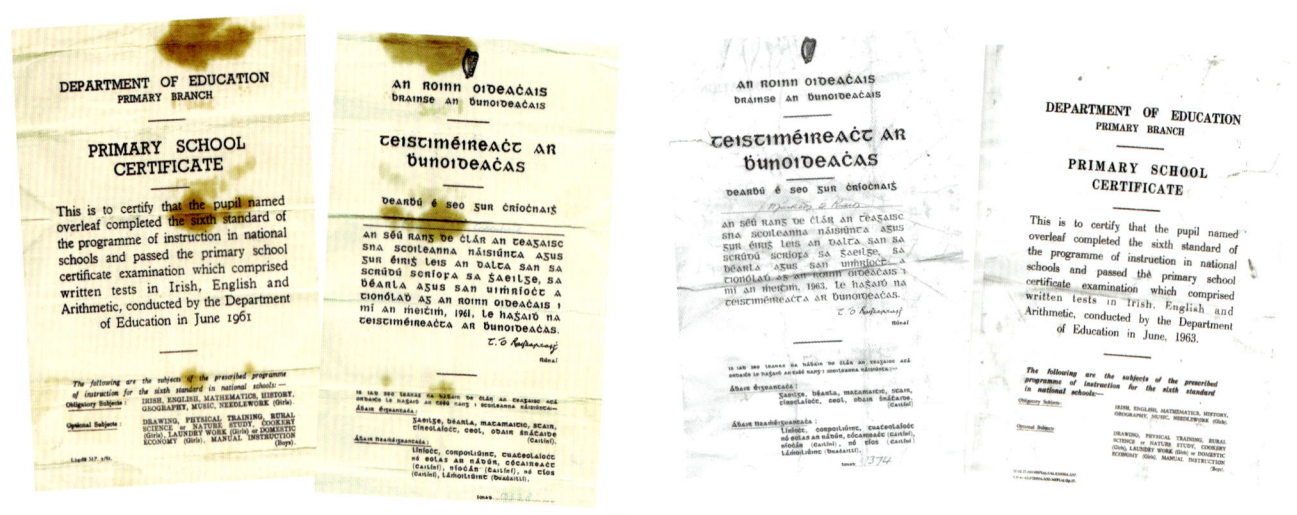

Fig. 6.21
A sample of a boys and a girls Primary Certificate from 1962
Courtesy of Joan Donnelly (O'Connor) and Martin Ryan

Primary School Readers 1940's

1940's primary school Gaelic essay readers.
Courtesy of Mrs Mary McNally
(Translations courtesy of Ms. Susan Morgan)

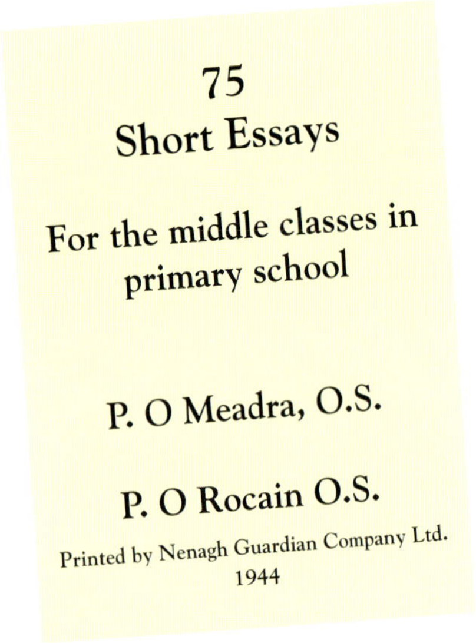

Fig. 6.22
1940's primary school reader

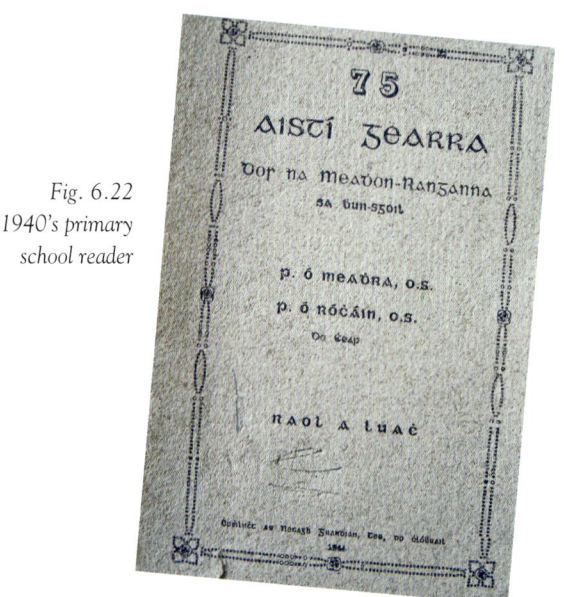

The Post Office

I often go on a message to the post Office. I went there yesterday to get a postal order. There was a queue of people in there before me.

There were three clerks behind the counter. One of them was selling stamps and weighing parcels. Another was taking telegrams. The third was speaking on the phone. Telegram boys were coming and going.

Up I went to the counter. I asked for the postal order and got it. I thanked the clerk and out I went.

Exercise:

Conversation between a post office clerk and a boy looking for a postal order.

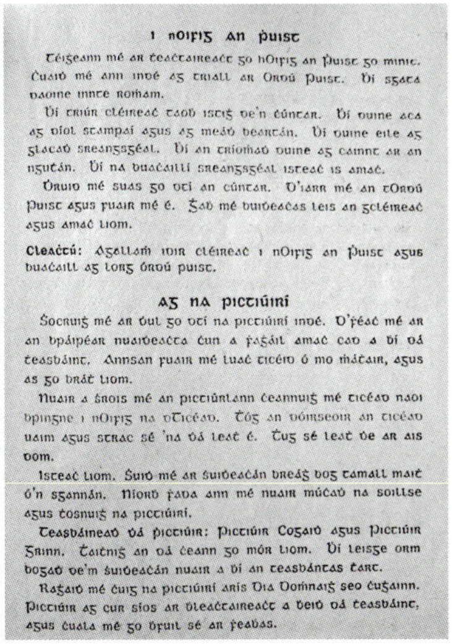

I nOifig an Ṗuist

Téiġeann mé ar ṫeaċtaireaċt go hOifig an Ṗuist go minic. Ċuaiḋ mé ann inḋé ag triall ar Ordú Puist. Ḃí sgata daoine inntí romham.

Ḃí triúr cléireaċ taoḃ istiġ de'n ċúntar. Ḃí duine aca ag díol stampaí agus ag meaḋ beartán. Ḃí duine eile ag glacaḋ sreangsgéal. Ḃí an tríoṁaḋ duine ag caint ar an nguthán. Ḃí na buaċaillí sreangsgéal isteaċ is amaċ.

Ḃruiḋ mé suas go dtí an cúntar. D'iarr mé an tOrdú Puist agus fuair mé é. Ġaḃ mé buiḋeaċas leis an gcléireaċ agus amaċ liom.

Cleaċtú: Agallaṁ idir cléireaċ i nOifig an Ṗuist agus buaċaill ag lorg órdú puist.

Ag na Pictiúirí

Ṡocruiġ mé ar ḋul go dtí na pictiúirí inḋé. D'ḟéaċ mé ar an bpáipéar nuaiḋeaċta ċun a ḟaġáil amaċ cad a ḃí dá ṫeasbáint. Annsan fuair mé luaċ ticéid ó mo ṁáṫair, agus as go bráṫ liom.

Nuair a ṡrois mé an pictiúrlann ċeannuiġ mé ticéad naoi bpingne i nOifig na dTicéad. Ṫóg an dóirseoir an ticéad uaim agus strac sé 'na dá leaṫ é. Ṫug sé leaṫ ḋe ar ais dom.

Isteaċ liom. Ṡuiḋ mé ar ṡuiḋeaċán breáġ bog tamall maiṫ ó'n sgannán. Níorḃ fada ann mé nuair múċaḋ na soillse agus ṫosnuiġ na pictiúirí.

Teasbáineaḋ dá ṗictiúir: Pictiúir Cogaiḋ agus Pictiúir Grinn. Ṫaitniġ an dá ċeann go mór liom. Ḃí leisge orm bogaḋ de'm ṡuiḋeaċán nuair a ḃí an teasbántas ṫart.

Raġaiḋ mé ċuig na pictiúirí arís Dia Doṁnaiġ seo ċugainn. Pictiúir ag cur síos ar ḃleaċtaireaċt a ḃeiḋ dá ṫeasbáint, agus ċuala mé go ḃfuil sé ar feabas.

Fig. 6.23

At the Pictures

I decided to go to the pictures yesterday. I looked at the newspaper to find out what was showing. Then I got the price of a ticket from my mother and off I went happily.

When I reached the cinema I bought a ticket for ninepence in the ticket office. The doorman took the ticket from me and tore it in two. He gave me half back.

In I went. I sat on a lovely soft seat for a while before the film. It wasn't long before the lights were turned out and the pictures started.

Two pictures were shown. A war picture and a funny picture. I really liked the two of them. I was lazy to leave my seat when the show was over. I will go to the pictures again next Sunday. A detective will be showing and I heard it is brilliant.

My Cat

We have a big black cat at home. Seabhac (Hawk) is his name. We gave him that name because his mother was always after birds. Seabhac is one year old now. He is dappled and he is big and strong and agile. Nature is repeating itself as he is always chasing the birds too.

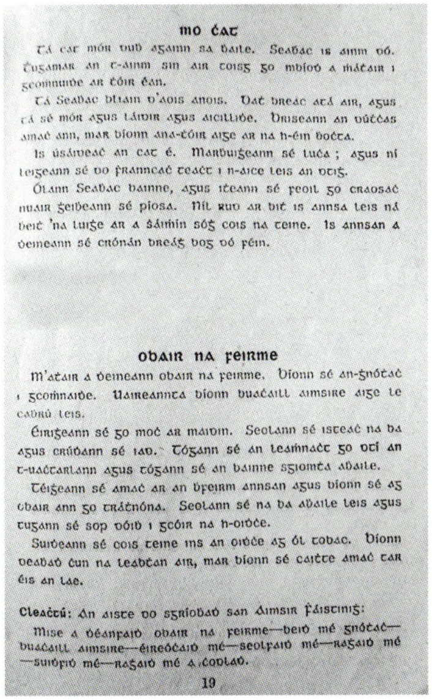

Mo Ċat

Tá cat mór dubh againn sa ḃaile. Seaḃac is ainm dó. Ṫugamar an t-ainm sin air toisg go mbíoḋ a ṁáṫair i gcoṁnuiḋe ar ṫóir éan.

Tá Seaḃac bliain d'aois anois. Daṫ breac atá air, agus tá sé mór agus láidir agus aicillíḋe. Briseann an dúċas amaċ ann, mar bíonn ana-ṫóir aige ar na h-éin ḃoċta.

Is úsáideaċ an cat é. Marḃuiġeann sé luċa; agus ní leigeann sé do ḟranncaċ teaċt i n-aice leis an dtiġ.

Ólann Seaḃac bainne, agus iṫeann sé feoil go craosaċ nuair ġeiḃeann sé píosa. Níl rud ar biṫ is annsa leis ná beiṫ 'na luiġe ar a ṡáiṁín sóg cois na teine. Is annsan a ḋeineann sé crónán breáġ bog dó féin.

Obair na Feirme

M'aṫair a ḋeineann obair na feirme. Bíonn sé an-ġnóṫaċ i gcoṁnaiḋe. Uaireannta bíonn buaċaill aimsire aige le caḃrú leis.

Éiriġeann sé go moċ ar maidin. Seolann sé isteaċ na ba agus crúḋann sé iad. Tógann sé an leaṁnaċt go dtí an t-uaċtarlann agus tógann sé an bainne sgioṁṫa abaile.

Téiġeann sé amaċ ar an bfeirm annsan agus bíonn sé ag obair ann go tráṫnóna. Seolann sé na ba abaile leis agus tugann sé sop dóiḃ i gcóir na h-oiḋċe.

Suiḋeann sé cois teine ins an oiḋċe ag ól tobac. Bíonn deabaḋ ċun na leabṫan air, mar bíonn sé caiṫte amaċ tar éis an lae.

Cleaċtú: An aiste do sgríoḃaḋ san Aimsir Ḟáistiniġ:

Mise a ḋéanfaiḋ obair na feirme—beiḋ mé gnóṫaċ—buaċaill aimsire—éireóċaiḋ mé—seolfaiḋ mé—raġaiḋ mé—suiḋfiḋ mé—raġaiḋ mé a ċodlaḋ.

19

Fig. 6.24

He is a useful cat. He kills the mice and he keeps the rats away from the house. Seabhac drinks milk and he eats meat greedily when he gets a piece. There is nothing he likes more than to lie contentedly by the fire. Its there he purrs nice and softly to himself.

Farm Work

My father works on the farm. He is always very busy. Sometimes he has a farmhand to help him. He rises early in the morning. He sends in the cows and he milks them. He takes the new milk to the dairy and takes the skimmed milk home.

He goes out on to the farm then and works for the afternoon. He takes the cows home with him and gives them hay for the night.

He sits by the fire in the evening smoking his tobacco. He hastens to bed then as he is spun out after the day.

Exercise:
Write an essay in the future tense. I will do the farm work – I will be a busy farm boy – I will rise – I will go – I will sit – I will go to sleep.

Miss Moloney

Kathleen Moloney was junior assistant mistress in the Lusk girls school from September 1931 and formally appointed assistant teacher in January 1937, a post she held until September 1960. She had previously been a substitute teacher in Ballivor, Co. Meath to July 1930, and in Hedgestown school Lusk from July 1930 to September 1931.[143]

Although born in Dublin she was reared in her mothers home place, the small village of Galmoy, Co. Kilkenny.

During her time in Lusk school she lived in Dublin city and travelled to and from Lusk every day by bus and became a familiar figure walking briskly and with a friendly smile from the bus to the school and back each day. She was fond of walking and regularly walked from Dublin city centre where she lived, to meet her friends in Rathfarnham, south Dublin and walked back again. Miss Moloney died in 1988 at the age of 83 having lived with and been cared for in her latter years by her niece in Coolock Dublin.[144]

---

[143] National archives of Ireland, ED/4/2141; ED/4/2146; ED/4/2180; ED/4/2174; ED/4/2174; ED/4/2199. ED/4/2142.
[144] Interview with Mrs Ann Cullen of Dublin (May 20th 2015).

Miss Moloney taught the female junior classes in Lusk school for almost thirty years and is remembered with great affection and fondness by all the pupils of the time. Following a period of leave of absence from Lusk school to look after her elderly aunt. Miss Moloney returned to Lusk but this time to Corduff school in the same parish where she remained until her retirement. Miss Moloney, along with Mrs O'Sullivan were the only teachers to have served in all three schools in Lusk parish.

Fig. 6.25
Kathleen Moloney in her younger years

Fig. 6.26
Kathleen Moloney
Photos, courtesy of Mrs. Anne Cullen

Mrs. Annie (Nan) Dunne

Mrs. Dunne will be well remembered by boys who went to the school through the 1940's to 1960's. A native of Swinford, Co. Mayo where her family had a combined store consisting of hardware, groceries and pub. The eldest of a large family, her maiden name was Durkin. In 1932 she married Edward (Ned) Dunne whose family where from Portarlington, Co. Laois.[145] He was principal teacher in Corduff school from 1934.

Annie Dunne attended Craiglockhart Teacher Training College, Edinburgh, Scotland from 1927 to 1929, her specialist subjects being 'Drawing and Music'.[146] She taught in a primary school in Scotland from 1929 to 1931,[147]. On returning to Ireland she took a teaching post in Kings Inn St. Convent, Dublin (Irish Sisters of Charity) where she remained for one year to September 1932, and later in Clonshaugh, (Raheny, Dublin) primary school where she spent six years to December 1938.[148]

Mrs. Annie Dunne was appointed to Lusk school as Junior Assistant Mistress in January 1939. She was subsequently appointed assistant teacher in Lusk from January 1941[149] and continued in that post

---

[145] Interview with Mrs Deirdre Steale-Dunne of Dublin (3rd June 2015).
[146] Society of the Sacred Heart, Irish/Scottish provincial-archives, Mount Anville, Dublin.
[147] National archives of Ireland, administration of national schools, ED/2.
[148] National archives of Ireland, ED/4/2141.
[149] Ibid.

as teacher of junior boys until 1965/66. Following the death of Mrs Mary Dunne (principal of the girls school and no relation) in September 1965, Mrs Annie Dunne took over teaching the senior girls and in early 1966 she was appointed principal of the girls school.[150]

She died in December 1981 and rests along with her husband Ned in the cemetery attached to the Lusk RC Church.

Former pupils of Mrs Dunne in Lusk school recall her taking out the tuning-fork and striking it off the desk to get everyone in tune before commencement of the singing class. Others recall her playing the accordion in the school.

The song that Mrs. Dunne had her junior boys regularly perform and sing out loudly was the old scouting song called 'The Happy Wanderer'.

I love to go a wandering,
Along the mountain track,
And as I go, I love to sing,
My knapsack on my back,

(*chorus*)

Val-de-ri, val-de,ra,
Val-de-ri, val-de-ra, ha, ha, ha, ha, ha, ha,
Val-de-ri, val-de,ra,
My knapsack on my back.
I wave my hand to all I meet,
And they wave back to me,
And blackbirds call so loud and sweet ,
From every greenwood tree,

(*chorus*)

Oh, may I go a wandering,
until the day I die,
Oh, may I always laugh and sing,
Beneath Gods clear blue sky.

Fig. 6.27
Mrs Annie Dunne

Fig. 6.28
A young Miss Annie Durkin, during her college days.

Photos courtesy of Mrs Deirdre Steale (Dunne)

---

[150] National archives of Ireland, ED/4/2141.

Measles, Mumps and Scarlet Fever

The dreaded children's diseases of those days resulted in the school being closed for short periods. From 1st October to 3rd November 1939 the school was closed due to an epidemic of measles. Further school closures occurred from 26th to 31st March 1942, an epidemic of scarlet fever, and 17th to 24th April 1942 and 9th to 19th June 1942 due to an epidemic of mumps on both occasions.[151] From 6th to 17th July 1942 an extra vacation was granted for 'farm work'.[152]

PP requests Nuns to take over the Girls School

In 1941 on the retirement of Mrs. O'Sullivan, principal of the girls school, the Parish Priest at the time, Fr. James McMahon, requested permission from the Archbishop to have the girls school taken over by the Sisters of The Holy Faith, Skerries. He had spoken with the Mother General of the Holy Faith Order in Glasnevin, who expressed a willingness to take over Lusk school. However the Archbishop's reply was negative, stating, 'these Sisters had never taken over a school that had previously been in the hands of lay teachers', further stating: 'there is not adequate provision for teaching Sisters who would have to travel from Skerries each day'.[153] And so Fr. McMahon's plan was knocked on the head. It was at this time that Mrs. Mary Dunne was appointed principal of the girls school, having previously been assistant teacher in the boys school.

Fig. 6.29
Girls class c. 1945
Front Row: *L-R: Kathleen Grimes, Josie Peters, Nancy Bentley, Maureen Kavanagh, Eileen Kelly, Evelyn Kelly, Maureen Clarke, Eileen O'Connor*
Middle Row: *Rose Kelly, Maureen McDonnell, Mary Matthews, Kathleen Gough, Madge Carroll, Mary Hogan, Lucy Tyrrell, Harriet Sweetman.*
Back Row: *Eileen O'Malley, Kay Kavanagh, Brid Clare, Maura Dennis, Berrie Clare, Christina Gaffney, Eileen Gaffney.*
Photo courtesy of Mrs Mary McNally (Hogan)

---

[151] National archives of Ireland, commissioners of education registers, ED/2.
[152] National archives of Ireland, commissioners of education registers, ED/2.
[153] Dublin diocesan archive, Clonliffe, correspondence re Lusk school.

Fig. 6.30
Girls Class c.1947-48
Back Row (l-r):
Noeleen Donnelly, Nan Kavanagh, Gertie Rogan, Maureen Hynes, Nellie McCann, Roseleen Gaffney, Mary Gaffney, Lal Oglesby.
Middle Row: *Babs Connor, Ursula Fennell, Margaret McNally, Helen Bentley, Greta Monks, Maura Connor, Breda Sherry, Rita Brown, Bernie Rogan, Rita Grimes.*
Front Row: *unknown, unknown, Angela Knott, Greta Wright, Betty Brown, Angela McNally, Lona Neary, Aileen Hurley, Kathleen Hurley, Rita Daly, Mary Fitzgerald, Breda Brogan.*
(Photo courtesy of Billy Sherry)

PAST PUPILS ACCOUNTS 1920'S-40'S
Maureen McCarthy (nee McCann) RIP
An account of school days and general memories of growing up in Lusk.

Introduction by Mrs. Pat Kelly
In 1962 I married a Lusk man and came to live on the Main St. of Lusk. Maureen McCarthy was a close and interesting neighbour.

As a Londoner my understanding of Irish life was somewhat vague. I was most grateful to Maureen for her wise direction and general information. We remained good friends and I asked her if she would write a short account of her life and times in Lusk.

I was very happy and privileged with the account written by a most generous and bright lady.

Pat Kelly

The following is the story written by Maureen McCarthy (McCann) RIP, in 1999.
(Text in brackets by the author)

I was born in Lusk on 5th December 1924 to Matthew and Elizabeth McCann in a house which is now the Bookies shop, (latterly a launderette, located adjacent to where Cost Cutters shop and the Post

Office is currently located). My grandmother Mary McCann bought the house we currently live in for my father when he got married.

Mrs. Thorne (who lived at the bottom of Trean Hill), was the midwife in Lusk and Dr. Cooney was the local doctor. Nearly all the children were born in their own homes in those days.

My first recollection of childhood was starting school at four years of age. Kitty Daly brought me to school. I cried all the time of my first day at school. It was a Miss Kelly from Donabate who was teaching the junior classes. Mrs. O'Sullivan was the principal teacher. After Miss Kelly we had a Miss Moloney, a young teacher, we thought she was lovely because Miss Kelly was a bit stern and distant (or so we thought) and Miss Moloney related more to our age group.

I went to school each day with Ellie Kavanagh (now Ellie McDonnell, married to Nick McDonnell) and Betty Murray. Betty Murray died young, from diphtheria. Five people in the parish at the time died from this disease and some of us were inoculated as prevention. The dispensary (as the clinic was then called, where the inoculations were carried out) was located where Katie Hunt's shop was later sited. I remember the vaccination to this day; I thought it was dreadful.

Schooldays were the usual routine, we did cookery one year and laundry another year, for two hours each week. On a wet day Mrs. O'Sullivan always read some part of a book for us, or if she had been to a film she would tell us the story. One thing she often did was read 'Roddy the Rover" from the *Irish Press* (newspaper) which she always brought to school.

At the time it was all fires in the school (for heating) and each in turn had to go out to gather sticks, a chore most children loved as it meant time off from classes. Two girls would have charge of lighting the fire each week and dusting and cleaning the desks and getting flowers and doing the altar (decorating the altar); the altar almost always had flowers. At appropriate seasons our teacher would make wines at home so we had to gather elderberries, dandelion roots and parsnips for her.

The catechism exam was one thing we dreaded. Our teachers always wanted 'specially distinguished' and nearly always got it. We had to endure catechism all day for a while before the examination.

We then had preparation for communion and confirmation. We only had the morning off on our first communion day, I remember going back to school for the second half of the day.

I remember the Eucharist Congress in 1932. It was a wonderful spell of sunny, dry weather. It was held in the Phoenix Park. I didn't go because I was too young. I remember the women's and men's sodalities all went (to the Eucharist Congress) they travelled in George McNallys truck (and other trucks) and brought stools or forms (to sit on).

The three of us (my sisters and I) made our confirmation together, it was held only every three years, the numbers wouldn't warrant an annual service. Eileen, my sister was the youngest, and too young at the time for confirmation but was told if she knew her catechism she could make it (her confirmation) that was how it happened.

Fr. John McMahon was the parish priest back then and he loved processions. We had them (processions) at the forty-hours (adoration) on the Sunday and again on the Tuesday, along with a high Mass on the same days. I was in the choir then as were my other sisters and we knew all the Latin phraseology that was used then. We had processions every Sunday in May, at Corpus Christi and on 15th August (feast of the Assumption). The girls used their white communion dresses for their processions. I remember the processions going all the way to the square (in Lusk) where a small altar was erected for benediction, proceeding down the back road, up the post office road, or front road as we used to call it. Everyone had to clean up their house fronts (for the event), it is a pity its not here today for that reason. In my time, Fr. Joseph Union was the curate and he loved music. He built up a great choir and he was very stern with them. Theresa Fulham (she was Theresa Jenkinson then) was the organist. There was a four-part choir; Fr. Union entered them in the Feis Ceol and they won the cup that year.

We had Irish dancing classes in the barn at Harford's farm. Clarke-Barry was the name of the people teaching the dancing.

When I was fourteen I finished school in Lusk and went to St. Mary's, Kings Inn Street. I had to do my primary certificate when I was there, as it wasn't done in Lusk at the time. When the results were announced I came first out of forty-two children and of course the old nun wasn't too pleased that a girl from another school was ahead of all of hers.

In the summer time in Lusk we had the Carrie-May shows (travelling show) they had a great variety of plays. The used to set up in the parochial field, where the scout hall and priests' house is now located. The parish priest always had cows and young cattle in this field. The farmers used leave hay and oats on the green for the parish priests stock for winter. There were also bazaars held in this field, with a big marquee erected where the best bands available were hired for a céilidhe once a week, all to make money for the parish, which it certainly did.

When I finished school I went to work in G.L. McGowan Solicitors office in Balbriggan for holiday work. I cycled to and from Balbriggan each day. I later got a job with David Allen billposting firm at thirty shillings a week, considered good money at the time; most office jobs were paying from fifteen shillings to £1, (twenty shillings equals £1).

We used to cycle to football matches in Balbriggan, Skerries, Rolestown, Swords and occasionally into Dublin city and we thought nothing of the journey. We often went to another football match after tea and finally to a dance in the Palladium in Rush later in the evening. Everyone travelled everywhere together in groups on bicycles. We never thought of drink or drugs. Tea, sandwiches, cake and minerals were all that was appreciated in those days. Girls or young people did not go to public houses.

There were two forges in the parish, Boylans at the back of the old post office was one and the other was Morgans of the Man-O-War. All ploughing was done by horses, all transport by horse or train. I remember a horse and dray coming from the brewery in Skerries to the pubs in Lusk, the driver wore a black hard hat and long coat.

After the war was over (Second World War, 1939 to 1945) people started to get cars; it didn't matter the condition of the car as long as the wheels went round and got you from place to place.

That's all I can think of now. Our lives almost always revolved around church ceremonies, our parents were so strict in our upbringing they had the idea that so long as it was connected with the church it was all right.

Maureen McCarthy (written in 1999)

Maureen started in Lusk school, junior infants, on 15th April 1929. She departed this world in March 2008 aged 83 years.

Memories by Rose Kelly

How delighted I am to have been asked to pen some memories of my childhood in Lusk. I rose to the challenge and delved into my memory box. I well remember my first day at school; my father took me on his bicycle, it was pouring rain. I sheltered under his rain cape. When I arrived at the school a number of first day students were greeted by a gentle and kind teacher named Miss Moloney who travelled from Dublin each day to teach in our school. I soon made a friend on my first day, she was Maureen McDonnell. We were two of a kind, naughty. We remained friends until I left Lusk some years later to work in England. In my class were Mary Matthews, Kathleen Gough, Berry Clare, Maureen Clarke, Eileen O'Connor (Vale), Harriet Sweetman, Ursula Fennell, May Brady, Mary Hart, Kathleen Grimes and Mary Hogan. How I loved being in that class and may I gently say we were not all perfect. Eventually we moved to a higher class, to Mrs. Dunne. Now this lady was a different and more serious teacher who was determined to bring out the best in us by whatever means necessary. If Dunne can't do, it can't be done was her mantra. On one occasion one of us students, how I loved the word 'student', it had a certain ring to it that I loved, were kept in after school for talking in class and I made the observation to my friends that she (the teacher) was a mean and flat-nosed lady, how awful of me. One of my friends went and told her what I had said. I was asked to remain behind after our punishment was meted out to us. Later I was asked by my teacher why I said those awful words and I did admit to saying it but I also said the other girls agreed with me. I did however get along quite well with Mrs. Dunne and often had a little chat over lunch.

Sunday was a special day in our village. Everyone went to Mass and I remember attending Mass on one Easter when Easter dues were collected and I really thought it strange that the priest called out the names of people who donated money (parish dues), beginning with the person who donated the most and down the ladder to the last person who donated the least.

Lusk was a small village where the inhabitants went about their lives in a civil and pleasant manner and everyone knew each other. The core of the village was Katie Hunt's shop where many discussions took place and of course Murray's pub.

We felt very secure in the knowledge that we had a very alert and industrious sleuth; 'no crime while I am on duty' was his attitude, thank you Garda McDonnell. We were also blessed with a young Garda who dutifully kept the pubs closing time in order by having the doors locked, but forgetting to come out himself. Opposite Murray's pub was a little shop owned by Kellys and outside was the bus stop. Two young men (no names mentioned) liked to have a lie in now and again and the bus driver waited for them. Worthy of mention is a well-known and popular gentleman, who else but James (Jemmy) Rogan and his lovely family. His wife Sinéad was a lovely lady with a perpetual smile and may I say there was a lot of talent in that family, one daughter called Nina was a budding thespian whose performances delighted the village folk. The venue for the concerts was the local library. I don't know why it was called the library as I never saw any books in it; however we did enjoy the performances of our local theatre group, which included John (Pipes) Bentley, Rose and Nan Oglesby. Of course Nina Rogan (now Nina Flynn) was such a confidant little girl and did her signing and dance routine to perfection. Then come the children of Newhaggard of whom I am one, we had a different kind of talent, prospecting to the fields and helping ourselves to vegetables, washing them in the river before eating them. We played in Morgan's field (Bridestree) called 'the Slang', one of our group of five or six brought a saw to take home firewood for his mother. He decided to climb a large tree under which a stream flowed. Sitting on the outer side of the bough he began sawing, next we knew he was floating in the stream with the bough and branches on top of him. Luckily, Tommy Fulham came to the rescue.

We took it all in our stride not realising the dangers we managed to get ourselves in to. It was our God-given right to be stupid at times. Those times were special to us as we lived in a healthy environment.

One of the highlights of our time was the yearly visit of the O'Reilly theatre group (a travelling theatre show). We loved to sit in awe at the performances of this family. One of my favourite was 'Murder in the Red Barn'. We all knew the acts off by heart, as it was the same every year. Another event was Duffy's Circus, as if we didn't have enough of our own. We enjoyed all the visits of the entertainment groups.

Our beautiful landmark in Lusk is the 'round tower' and may I say how much I love the (attached) Church building and the history associated with it which was never brought to our attention when I attended school in Lusk. Many thanks to my sister-in-law Pat Kelly for your knowledge and interest in our village that embraced you many years ago, we are pleased to have you in our family, Pat.

We had some beautiful houses in Lusk, one of which was Mrs. Morgan's (Bridestree), a thatched house with chocolate-box appearance. One Saturday I went to Morgan's to collect eggs only to be confronted by flames billowing from the house; it burnt to the ground, so sad to see it go. Another beautiful house was on Ballaely Lane where two old ladies domiciled, Miss Reid, the owner, a posh lady by our standards and her companion, a thatched house in beautiful grounds. We went there to buy apples but never asked questions. We were never gossips in Lusk, just 'information specialists'. This house also caught fire and was gutted. I remember seeing a piano on the lawn after the fire and began playing it. Miss Reid came out and asked if I would like the piano as having lost the house she didn't want it. I said yes, not thinking how I would get it home or where it would fit in our little house; next thing a truck came into the yard, loaded the piano along with some beautiful French furniture and off it went. Miss Reid was nowhere to be seen and I was not a happy girl.

I always felt there was some distinction in the village the 'haves' and the 'have-nots' and may I say I felt quite happy that the 'have-nots' were so happy with their lot; 'what we have is not necessarily what we are'.

These are my memories of my time growing up and living in Lusk, my village it will always be. It was my interaction with my village people that moulded me into the person I am today. Many thanks to Lusk and my people.

With fond memories.

Rose Kelly-Knight, Perth, Australia

Rose Kelly lived at Newhaggard and started school in Lusk, junior infants, on 20th May 1940.

School Days – 1940's
By John Kelly – Lusk

The first journey to school was on the cross bar of my fathers bicycle. The rain pattering down on the oil skin cape under which you sheltered, the swishing of the wheels on the road, and wondering, fearful, wondering.

Mrs. Dunne, Nan or Nancy in her youth, was to be known by many variations of those names, as she was a very serious lady, short of humour and very long on discipline. Later on, the lads would say you could catch a cold from her icy gaze.

The preparation for first Holy Communion seemed to go on for years. The sense of sin was so developed that you felt guilty even thinking about sin, or even just thinking. What an effort of determination and imagination to have something worthwhile to tell on your first visit to that mysterious dark confessional.

Kindly Mrs. Bentley made the ring of blue and white flowers to go around the bottom of the candle which you held. The flickering flame fascinated, the devil at home in fire and smoke.

Some years on, into the big class, bigger room, bigger teacher, Mr Dunne was his name, no relation to the first lady, we hoped. He had a glinting look and an unusual ability to know who was going to say something before they even began.

His first name was Larry and his favourite position was at the high desk, paper opened in front and his watch opened also.

Over time, a selection of sticks or canes were a part of applied discipline; one item never to be forgotten was a shortened billiard cue. A blow on the hand of this could bring much weeping and gnashing of teeth. When lovely Larry slapped you from behind his desk it wasn't too bad, the flicker of the smile in the corner of his eye took some of the harm out of it.

As a result of throwing inkballs, Richard Peters was invited to the desk for a slap-happy exercise by the teacher. Richard found it difficult to keep his hand steady under the quivering cue. A contest of minds went on between him and Larry the longer it went on the redder the teachers' face and neck, the whiter his knuckles; down came the cue like a rocket. Alas the hand was quickly withdrawn and the poor watch smashed in bits. After that bit of excitement it was hard to remember anything further.

Most recollections on changes within ones lifetime begin with comparisons of childhood, then and now. In the 1940's, fear played an important part in Irish life for young and old Lusk people were no different. From early on, family discipline was firm; the police, the school teacher, the priest and the doctor were all held in awe and more than a little fear. Nowadays children are much more at ease with everybody and school is fairly enjoyable. In my time at national school religion was the big subject; mortal sin was associated with failure. The preparation for Confirmation was very intense. At the latter part of the school day, having studied two or three chapters of the catechism, a circle was formed, with our teacher facing the pupils, cane in hand. The questions came loud and clear, the answers muttered mumbo-jumbo. The teacher's displeasure with our efforts was registered with brisk whistling strokes of the cane in hand. The teacher called it 'a tip of the fairy'. It was a curious way in which to learn to love God, or respect your fellow man.

John Kelly started in Lusk School in April 1940.

Poems from Lusk Schooldays, 1940's, recalled by Ms. Christina Conroy (Gaffney)

POEMS FOR INFANTS AND FIRST CLASS

Dear Granny

Dear Granny dear I hope you're well,
I've got a lot of things to tell.
Last night I saw a thin new moon,
It's going to be my birthday soon.
I meant to write you long a go,
But then I didn't write and so,
I'm writing now to ask you if,
Your knee still hurts and still is stiff.

I've got three dolls dressed all in green,
But not one like the doll I've seen.
In Mr Carroll's corner shop, when I go by I always
    stop,
And look inside to see it there,
It's got such lovely golden hair.
If it were mine I'd love it so,
and take great care of it you know.
And do you know what I would do?
I'd call it Mary after you.

Dear Granny dear I hope you're well,
I haven't any more to tell.
Did you like dolls and ever see,
A corner shop and feel like me?
Of course long its ago I mean,
With lots of love from your Noreen.

The Moon
The moon has a face like the clock in the hall,
It shines like thieves on the garden wall,
On streets and fields and harbour quays,
And birdies asleep in the forks of the trees.

The squalling cat and the squeaking mouse,
The howling dog by the door of the house,
The bat that lies in bed till noon,
All love to be out by the light of the moon.

But all the things that belong to the day,
Cuddle to sleep to be out of her way,
And flowers and children close their eyes,
Till up in the morning the sun shall rise.

POEMS FOR THIRD CLASS

Trees (by Joyce Kilmer)
I wish that I could ever see,
A poem as lovely as a tree.

A tree who's hungry mouth is pressed,
Against the sweet earths flowing breast,

A tree that looks at God all day,
And lifts her leafy arms to pray,

A tree that may in Summer wear,
A nest of robins in her hair,

Upon who's bosom snow has lain,
Who intimately lives with rain,

Poems are made for fools like me,
But only God can make a tree.

The Peddlers' Caravan
I wish I lived in a caravan,
With a horse to drive like the peddler man,
Where he comes from nobody knows,
Or where he goes to but on he goes.

His caravan has windows two,
And a chimney of tin that the smoke comes through.
He has a wife and a baby brown
And they go driving from town to town.

Chairs to mend and delph to sell,
He clashes his basins like a bell,
Tea-cups and saucers ranged in order,
Plates with the alphabet round the border.

The road is wide and the sea is green,
But his house is like a bathing machine,
The world is round and he can ride,
Rumble and splash to the other side.

With a peddler man I'd like to roam,
And write a book when I come home,
All the people would read my book,
Just like the Travels of Captain Cook.

Christina Gaffney started in Lusk School in September 1938. She first learned these poems from her junior-class teacher Miss Kathleen Moloney, and wishes to dedicate this section to Miss Moloney.

'When One-Hundred years is Aft' and Gone' 87

Fig. 6.34 Girls c.1952
Front Row: *l-r Rita Daly, Nellie McCann, Betty Browne, Mona Donnelly, Breda Sherry.*
Back Row: *Ursula Fennel, Rita Browne, Breda Brogan, Maura O'Connor, Mary Gaffney, Greta Monks.*
Photo courtesy of Mrs Nellie Moore

CHAPTER 7

The 1955 School Building

During the early 1950's the two-storey 1874 school building had become unfit for purpose, and a plan to build a new school on a nearby site was initiated by the then Parish Priest, Rev. Fr. Vincent Steen.

The school was to be have four classrooms, two for girls, one room for junior classes, and one for senior classes, and two rooms for the boys, juniors and seniors. Junior classes were: junior infants, senior infants, first class and second class. Senior classes were, third, fourth, fifth and sixth classes.

There were four teachers in the school, each teacher had four classes (grades) in the one classroom.

The new school would cater for 130 pupils in total (boys and girls). It would not cater for any greater number of pupils than the 1874 building, so it would seem that space was not the main requirement for building a new school. Most likely it was sanitation, heating, children's play areas and other facilities that needed to be brought up to modern requirements at the time.

In July 1954 a notice was placed in the *Irish Builder and Engineer* inviting tenders for the construction of the proposed new school in Lusk. In late November or early December 1954 the Commissioners of Public Works accepted a tender from J.J. Tynan (Builders) Blackrock Co. Dublin for the construction of the new school. There is no record available of the tender value, however from examination of contracts awarded for similar sized schools, of similar design, and within a radius of approximately twenty miles of Lusk, and in the same year, indicates that the cost of building the school was in the region of £8000.[154] A number of local people were employed by the contractor for the duration of the project, including Jack Connor and Bobby Groves from

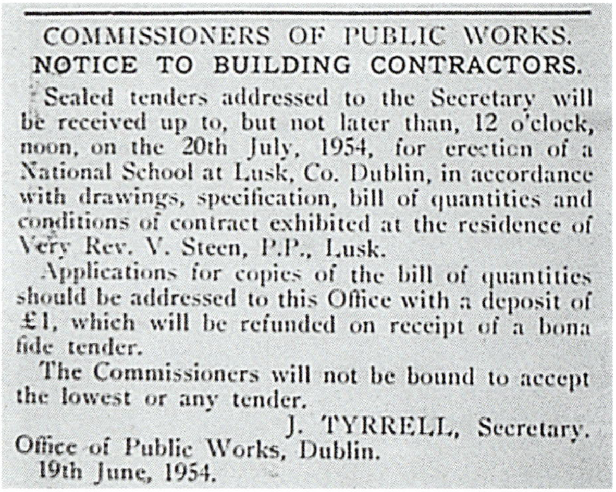

COMMISSIONERS OF PUBLIC WORKS.
NOTICE TO BUILDING CONTRACTORS.

Sealed tenders addressed to the Secretary will be received up to, but not later than, 12 o'clock, noon, on the 20th July, 1954, for erection of a National School at Lusk, Co. Dublin, in accordance with drawings, specification, bill of quantities and conditions of contract exhibited at the residence of Very Rev. V. Steen, P.P., Lusk.

Applications for copies of the bill of quantities should be addressed to this Office with a deposit of £1, which will be refunded on receipt of a bona fide tender.

The Commissioners will not be bound to accept the lowest or any tender.

J. TYRRELL, Secretary.
Office of Public Works, Dublin.
19th June, 1954.

Fig. 7.1
Invitation to Tender for Construction of Lusk Primary School.
(Irish Builder and Engineer)

154 Architectural archives, Irish builder and engineer June 1954.

Lusk, Paddy Cappock from Skerries, as builders labourers'. Noel Cappock from Skerries was the carpenter, and local blocklayer Mattie Devine built all the walls. Matties' pay for the blockwork was £1-7-6 (one pound, seven shillings and six pence) per one hundred blocks laid.[155]

During the same period of time the price of concrete blocks was in the region of £34 per thousand, while cement was £5 4s 6d per ton (five pounds, four shillings and six pence).

Wage rates in 1954 were in the order of 3 shillings 10½ pence per hour, for skilled workers and 3 shillings, 5 pence for labourers. That equates to about £7–15s and £6–15s respectively per week, for a 44-hour week.

The official opening of the school took place on January 30th 1956.

The new school was officially recognised from 9th January 1956 and was allocated a new role number; 17961E from this time. The last pupils to be registered in the 'old school' were Ann Russell, Attracta Scally, Ann-Marie Bentley, Eileen Hanberry, Joe Hand and Gerry Monks, all in September 1955.

The first pupils to be registered in the 'new school' were Dora Dennis, Teresa Llewellan, John Daly and Michael Seaver, all in January 1956.[158]

Fig. 7.2
The 1955 School

Fig. 7.3
The 1955 School Name Plate

Official Opening of the 1955 School Building, January 30th 1956
Throughout the mid 1950's a comprehensive programme of school building was undertaken by the Department of Education. In November 1955 the following report was published in *Irish Builder and Engineer*.

---
[155] Conversation with Mattie Devine of Lusk, (28th April 2015).
[156] Architectural archives, *Irish builder and engineer* Dec 4th 1954.
[157] National archives of Ireland, ED/4/2198.
[158] Lusk primary school, School Registers.

NEW SCHOOL BLESSED

Most Rev. Dr. McQuaid arriving at Lusk, to perform the blessing ceremony following the opening of the new National School.

The Archbishop of Dublin, Most Rev. Dr. McQuaid, blessed the new National School at Lusk, which was opened by Mr. L. Murray, Secretary, Department of Education, representing the Minister for Education.

The new school, which will accommodate 130 pupils, replaces a school which was built in 1874.

The attendance included: Very Rev. J. Canon Purfield, P.P., V.F., Rolestown; Very Rev. S. Marley, P.P., Donabate; Very Rev. P. O'Flynn, P.P., Balbriggan; Mr. P. Burke, T.D., and Mr. E. Rooney, T.D.

Fig. 7.4 The Altar Boy carrying the Cross is 13 year old Macullin Gaffney (Irish Independent, Jan 31st 1956)

Dr. McQuaid blesses new school

Fig. 7.5 Irish Press, Jan 31st 1956

Replaces a building 82 years old

IRISH PRESS Reporter

THE Archbishop of Dublin, Most Rev. J. C. McQuaid, D.D., yesterday blessed the new national school at Lusk.

The school, which will accommodate 130, replaces one built in 1874.

The school was opened later by Mr. L. Murray, secretary, Department of Education, representing the Minister.

The Archbishop was assisted by Very Rev. V. Steen, P.P., Lusk, and Very Rev. J. Matthews, P.P., Donabate.

Later he presided at Mass in St. Macullin's Church, celebrated by Rev. C. Herlihy, C.C.

A guard of honour of children lined the path leading to the main entrance as the Archbishop arrived.

At a function held later his Grace congratulated the parish priest and the parishioners.

It was not enough, he said, to have a school that was good in its form and materials. It was the spirit of the school that was most important. It was the spirit that would control the parish in the years to come, said Dr. McQuaid.

Mr. Murray said that the Department could do a certain amount in providing schools. But it was mainly up to the people themselves.

Fr. Steen said that while a grant had been made available from the Department, the parishioners had promptly and willingly raised their share.

School Building in the Republic of Ireland

In the annual report of the Department of education it was stated that buildings erected during the year provided for 42,035 pupils of national schools. There were 247 new schools, 39 enlargements and 1,168 improvements, at a total cost of £4,785,013, of which £690,695 was the amount of local contributions. The schools, it was stated, were planned in conformity with modern ideas in school architecture, were attractive in design and had up-to-date heating facilities.

The 1955 School Building

In December 1960 a report indicates Lusk school having a complement of 120 Pupils (sixty boys, sixty girls) and four Teachers.

Expenses incurred for year ending June 1961 include:

Heating:	£10 7s 3d	Insurance:	£11 10s 4d
Cleaning:	£4 10s 4d	Repairs:	£5 5s 8d

For year ending 30th June 1965 the average number of pupils were 58 Boys and 48 Girls. In 1970 the average enrolment was 151.[159] This indicated the beginning of the population rise in Lusk.

Fig. 7.6 Girls junior to senior classes 1955
Front Row: *L-R: Kathleen Kiernan, Esther Bentley, Mary Hurley, Marcella Peters, Margaret Doyle, Dymphna Donnelly, Rita Clarke, Marie Neary, Jennie Boyle, Maureen Skelly, Eimer Clare, Mary Browne.*
2nd Row: *Ailish Cowley, Maureen Knott, Margaret Kiernan, Ann Jenkinson, Patricia Daly, Kathleen Boyle, Margaret Dennis, Dorothy Cruise, Barbara Neary, Eithne Browne.*
3rd Row: *Patricia (or Jean) Doyle, Siobhan Rogan, Joan Connor, Gillie Peters, Rose McDonnell, Kathleen Russell, Margaret Carton, Kitty Byrne, Breda Bentley, Joyce O'Brien, Maureen Ryan, Vera Ryan, Una Ryan.*
4th Row: *Colette Donnelly, Marie McNally, Philomena Derham, Margaret Jenkinson, Eimer Oglesby, Chrissie Clarke, Teresa Gough, Breda Hurley, Marie Daly, Ann Boyle, Brenda Wall, Maree Cruise, Bernie Dennis.*
Back Row: *Madge Kavanagh, Maura Murphy, Lona Neary, Betty Grimes, Marion Donnelly, Teresa Clarke, Maura Connor, Maud Bentley, Betty Daly, Pearl Sherry, Betty Donnelly, Mary Clarke. This is the last group of girls in the old 1874 building before moving into the new 1955 school building.*

---

[159] Dublin diocesan archive, Lusk school/architects report, 1965.

Fig. 7.7 Confirmation 1955
Front Row: *L-R: Thomas Hayden, John Carton, Brendan Delaney, Gerry Dennis, J Brady, Michael Cruise, Brian Peters Peters, Joe Moore, Dessie Harford, Seamus Carton, Brendan Monks, Breffni (Terry) Gough, Cyril Delaney, Richard McLoughlin, Noel Doyle.*
Back Row: *Dickie Clare, Brian Barrett, Michael Russell, Willie Moore, Macullin Gaffney, John Kerrigan, Sean Wall, Richard Peters, Denis Neary, Mark Taylor, Christopher (Kit) McCann, Pat Connor, Johnny Dennis, Michael Hanberry, Padraic Cruise, Gerry Clarke, Kevin Daly, Georgie Bentley, J. Brady.*

The above Confirmation group consists of boys from all three schools in the parish. Confirmation was held only every three years, consequently there were pupils from 4th, 5th and 6th classes making confirmation at the same time.

Following the opening of the new school in 1955, the 1874 building was always referred to locally as simply 'The Old School'. In the 1960's it was used as a meeting place for many local clubs and activities including the local youth club, the Round Towers GAA club (for committee meetings) also the boys' club run by Mr. Gerry Wynne and others. The Parish draw (Silver Circle) was held in the 'old school' every Monday night. It was also used as a cinema. Pictures (movies) were shown every Sunday afternoon and Sunday evening, organised by Fr. Mahon, the Parish Curate at the time, with Peter McNally or Gerry Wynne operating the projector.

Fr. Mahon also used the upstairs rooms for the training of altar boys during the late 1950's early 60's. The premises was later used for bingo sessions and many other activities and meetings besides. In the mid 1960's the Black Raven Pipe Band obtained the use of the upstairs rooms for practice and still use the premises to the present time.

In the 1970's, due to overcrowding in the 1955 school building, the 'old school' premises, along with the library hall, was once again called into use on a temporary basis, as a school house, while the first additions were being put to the four-room 1955 building. From that period on and with the continuing rise in population in the locality, additional classrooms continued to be added where today (2015) the school has 30 classrooms and 45 teachers, catering for in excess of 800 pupils. In September 2015 it is expected that 112 new pupils will register in infant class.

At the time of writing, plans are in place for complete new schools, a junior school and a senior school, to replace the 1955 school building and to cater for the increasing number of pupils in the locality.

School discipline in times past

For many pupils in the earlier years schools were often not particularly pleasant places compared to the learning experience that pupils have in schools today. In earlier years, and even not too long ago, pupils were seated at their desks and expected to remain seated for the duration of the school day except for a short break in the morning and at lunchtime. Relationships between teacher and pupil were more often than not one of fear, with little or no jovial or good-humoured interaction in many cases. Corporal punishment, generally in the form of caning, and other demeaning methods such as ear-pulling, poking, slapping and so on was dished out to pupils in primary schools as a means of discipline. Many people of today, who attended school up to the 1960's will well remember being on the receiving end of various forms of punishment through their school days.

Some particular teachers were considered to be, to say the least, harsh with their pupils, the bata often being delivered in abundance, imbuing the wrath of many in the process. Some were even very heavy smokers and smoked cigarettes even all through class times, a practice that todays' generation would find completely incredulous.

Parents rarely intervened and had very little interaction with the teachers once the child was registered in infant class. The teachers and the school manager controlled all aspects of running the school and the disciplinary actions meted out was considered the norm, and it happened with regularity in most if not all schools, although it must be said there were some teachers who were particularly soft on corporal punishment and had a very good relationship with their pupils, and then there were those who dished it out with great severity. It was no wonder that so many boys and girls could not wait to get out of school.

It has to be said that the use of corporal punishment was supported by the Education Board. However, many people who were at school during the era of corporal punishment may be surprised to learn of the following instructions issued by the Office of National Education at the time regarding the 'infliction of corporal punishment';

- Corporal punishment should be inflicted only for grave transgression, never for failure of lessons.
- The Principal Teacher only should inflict punishment. An interval of at least ten minutes should elapse between the offence and the punishment.

- Only a light cane or rod may be used for the purposes of inflicting the corporal punishment:
- No teacher should carry about a cane or other instrument of punishment.
- Frequent recourse to corporal punishment will be considered by the Commissioners as indicating bad tone and ineffective discipline.

Many pupils from those days may only wish that the Commissioners of Education had enforced their own rules.

Corporal punishment was officially banned in 1982 when the Minister of Education issued the following circular:

> The Minister for Education in pursuance of the Government commitment to the abolition of corporal punishment in schools, has, following consultations with representatives of Teacher and Managerial Organisations, amended Rule 130 of the Rules for National Schools to read as follows:-
>
> *School Discipline*
> 130 (1) Teachers should have a lively regard for the improvement and general welfare of their pupils, treat them with kindness combined with firmness and should aim at governing them through their affections and reason and not by harshness and severity. Ridicule, sarcasm or remarks likely to undermine a pupil's self confidence should not be used in any circumstances.
>
> (2) The use of corporal punishment is forbidden.
>
> (3) Any teacher who contravenes sections (1) or (2) of this rule will be regarded as guilty of conduct unbefitting a teacher and will be subject to severe disciplinary action.
> This amendment will have effect from 1st February, 1982.

In 1996 the use of corporal punishment in schools became a criminal offence.

Pupils in primary schools today have a more comfortable relationship with their teachers. The classroom today is a much happier and safer environment than in earlier years, where pupils interact with each other and their teachers as part of the learning experience. Parents today play a significant part in running of the school through involvement with boards of management and many other extra-curricular activities. Many primary schools, including Lusk School, engage their pupils in learning activities such as a school garden, a range of music and sporting activities, green activities, a student council and many other activities besides, where pupils learn in a fun, safe and happy atmosphere.

CHAPTER 8

Where Pupils lived

During the 1800's most Lusk pupils addresses were listed as either; Lusk or North Commons, as simple as that. From a total of 568 pupils names available from 1800's 63% are stated as having an address of simply Lusk, while 17% have an address of North Commons or Commons, and 3% lived in Tyrellestown. A smaller number of children were from: Quickpenny (8), Newhaggard (7), Military Farm (6), Man O' War (6), Railway Station, Ballealy and Corduff (4 pupils each), Rahenny, and Rogerstown (3 children each from these locations).[160]

From 1900 to 1970 a total of 1586 (819 boys and 767 girls) pupils are listed in the school records for this period. Of this number 46% of the pupils addresses once again were simply referred to as Lusk. Only 7% were from Commons/North Commons, compared to the 17% in the 1800's. This may be due to the fact that the townland of Great-Common extends into the upper part of Lusk village (from the Post Office Road upwards beyond The Green and out the Skerries Road to the area currently referred to as The Commons). The address of people living in this area at the time was Commons or North Commons, while nowadays such locations would have a more defined address such as, The Green or Post Office Rd, Skerries Rd., Station Rd. etc.

The Green first appeared as an address (in school records) in 1937, Station Rd. and Dublin Rd. from 1937 and 1938 (previous to this, Station Rd. was referred to as Railway Rd. or Rush Rd.), The Square in 1941, Post Office Rd and Skerries Rd. in 1945, while Main St. didn't appear as an address until 1946.

Twenty-three children who were living in the former old Balrothery Union were attending school in Lusk (in the 1840's this building had been the Balrothery Union workhouse). From 1928 to 1935 the Balrothery Union building was under the control of the local authority/district council, and was used to temporarily house families from the locality.[161]

In the 1800's only seven children in the school were listed as having an address at Newhaggard and three children from Rogerstown. From 1900 to 1970, sixty-nine children from Newhaggard and over ninety children from Rogerstown, including 30 children, (from 12 families) with an address as railway

---
[160] Lusk primary school, School Registers.
[161] Ibid.

station, (their fathers were all employed on the railway) were attending Lusk school.[162] A number of children living at Rogerstown attended school in Rush rather than Lusk during this period.

The Remount Farm
Remount depot in Lusk was one of four such bases of the British army for the training of military horses, the other three were in Britain. From the early 1890's the British cavalry established the base in Lusk and it became known as the military farm and later as the government farm. Although to Lusk people later on it was simply referred to as 'the farm'. The site of Remount farm at Lusk had earlier in the 1800's been a convict prison farm. From 1914 following the outbreak of the World War One Lusk remount farm became an important location. It was here that horses were trained for the battlefields of the Great War.[163] Nearby Rogerstown estuary was used extensively for training and the close proximity of the railway station facilitated the transportation to the North Wall for shipping the horses abroad. The farm gave considerable employment in Lusk during its period of existence, and many children of military officers and other personnel attended school in Lusk over the period of its thirty years existence.

From 1891 to 1921 twenty-eight families of military personnel were living on the Remount Farm sending fifty-five children, twenty-three boys and thirty-two girls, to Lusk school. The husbands/fathers of the families were mostly soldiers from Britain. They had come to Lusk as part of the military and were all living in or near the remount farm. Many of the children were born in Lusk and some remained on afterwards and married locally. As well as soldiers other occupations were to be found on the military farm, such as: blacksmiths, bookkeepers, grooms and canteen personnel.[164] Surnames of families living on Remount Farm included: Baker, Bambrick, Booth, Bird, Brake, Brinn, Cotton, Deane, Dixon, Foster, Hall, Harper, Hogg, Jolly, Myles/Miles, Peacock, Privett, Simmons, Smeed, Snodden, Thacher.

---

[162] Lusk primary school, School Registers.
[163] *Land of the horse*, magazine published in association with the RDS, remembering the Irish war horse, p18-19, 2014.
[164] Lusk primary school, School Registers.

CHAPTER 9

Into the 1960's

Mr and Mrs Doherty

In 1966 on the retirement of Mr. Larry Dunne, Mr Daniel Doherty a native of Donegal, was appointed principal while his wife Patricia Doherty was appointed assistant teacher in the boys school. Mrs Annie Dunne who had for quite a number of years at this stage been assistant teacher in the boys school was transferred to the girls section following the recent death of Mrs. Mary Dunne.

At this stage Lusk school was still a four-teacher, four-classroom school like it had been throughout its history.

Mr Doherty was born in New York in 1922, returning with his family to Dungloe, Co. Donegal during the great depression in America.[165] In 1943 he graduated from St. Patricks teacher training

Fig. 9.1
Michael Browne, Kenneth Knott and Fintan Sherry, outside the school door, c1965

Fig. 9.2 1965/66
Front Row, L-R: *Paddy Seaver, Tom Jenkinson, Martin Skelly, Martin Donnelly, Eugene Clarke, John Skelly, Christy Boylan, Colman Dunne (Sub-Teacher).*
Back Row: *Michael Browne, Gerry Russell, Christy Russell, Maurice Connor, Fintan Sherry, John Hughes, Cathal Hurley, Liam Boylan, Leo Sheridan.*

---
[165] Correspondence with Moya Doherty (April 21st 2015).

college, Dublin. Mrs Doherty attended Carysfort teacher training college graduating in 1948.[166] Prior to being appointed to Lusk Mr Doherty was principal in St. Marys primary school Pettigo, Co. Donegal while his wife Patricia was teaching in nearby Lettercarn national school.[167]

Mr. and Mrs. Doherty are the parents of Moya Doherty of Riverdance fame. Moya along with her two older sisters and two younger brothers were pupils in Lusk school during this period.

Mr. Doherty left Lusk school in 1975 to take the position of principal in the senior school Clontarf, while Mrs. Doherty was appointed principal of the junior school in the new emerging development at Darndale, north Dublin.[168]

Fig. 9.3
Mr. and Mrs Doherty

Fig. 9.4 Confirmation 1967
Front Row, L-R: *Stephen White, Leo Sheridan, Gerry Cowley, Noel Walsh, Cathal Hurley.*
Back Row: *Brendan Arnold, James Rooney, Christy Russell, Gerry Russell, Liam Boylan, Damien Sheridan, Maurice Connor.*

Fig. 9.5 Confirmation 1970
L-R: *Joe Devine, Martin Dennis, Tom Jenkinson, Gay Russell, Noel Cowley, Thomas Russell*

---

[166] Dublin diocesan archives, Clonliffe, letter from Rev. Fr. Vaughan PP Lusk.
[167] Correspondence with Moya Doherty (April 21st 2015).
[168] Ibid.

Fig. 9.6 1971 class
Front Row, L-R: *Edie Gordon, Betty Sheridan, Bernie McGee, Rosaleen Monks, Breed O'Rourke, Marian Bentley, Bernadette Browne, Catherine Browne.*
Back Row: *Martin Boylan, Thomas Russell, Ian Bennett, Joey Russell, Willie Jenkinson.*

Fig. 9.7 1973 class
Front Row, L-R: *Robert McGuinness, Nuala McNally, Margaret Harford, Olive Harford, Frances Harford, Catherine Skelly, Brendan Sweetman.*
Back Row: *Dermot Devine, Mark Bentley, Michael Devine, Sean Doherty, Brendan Ryan, Alan Sweetman, Noel Bennett.*

Mr Des O'Leary

Mr O'Leary was appointed principal to Lusk school in 1975 replacing Mr Doherty. By this time there were six teachers in the school. Mr O'Leary is a native of Co. Mayo and immediately prior to his appointment to Lusk had been teaching in St. Canices primary school, Finglas. During his tenure in Lusk he applied considerable vitality and enthusiasm to his role. He introduced the annual children's concerts, the gatherings of parents and friends in the school following First Communions and Confirmations, and, along with teacher Mr Paddy Fay, fostered participation of the school children in various sporting activities including athletics. His good humour, friendly attitude and encouragement of pupils both inside and outside of school hours is well remembered and appreciated by former pupils and colleagues alike.

Des O'Leary himself recalls the period of time when Oberstown school had recently opened, complete with a fine swimming pool. The manager of the said school offered the use of the swimming pool to Lusk school. Des O'Leary jumped at the offer; his main problem however was transporting the children the couple of miles out to Oberstown. Not to be deterred, he duly called on the services of one Billy Sweetman who kindly supplied his lorry, and this mode of transport was used to get the kids to the swimming pool on a regular basis. Mr O'Leary was also instrumental in getting local parents involved in extra-curricular activities for the children, including knitting, sewing, art, football, athletics, and so on. At one point due to his encouragement up to thirty parents were coming into the school to impart various skills to female and male pupils alike.

Mr O'Leary subsequently spent thirty-three years as principal in Lusk school.

Mr. O'Leary was principal until his retirement in 2007, whereupon the current principal Mr. Paul Comiskey was appointed to the position.

Fig. 9.10 Mr. Des O'Leary Principal Lusk Primary School 1975 - 2007

Fig 9.8 A large gathering of former pupils attended a reunion in Lusk soccer clubhouse in 1988.

*Fig. 9.9 On one of those many occasions when Des O'Leary had the support of the ladies for yet another event, with the obligatory tea and cakes. **L-R:** Des O'Leary, Marie Clinton, Pearl Finnegan, May Llewellyn, Kathleen Browne, Maura O'Hara, Anne-Marie Finnegan, Brenda Jenkinson, Marguerite Finnegan*

The First Housing Developments in the Village

From 1970's onwards, new housing developments began to emerge for the first time in Lusk village. Kelly Park, Ash Grove and Orlynn Park being the most prominent, and the first pupils to go to the school from the new developments began to emerge.

From 1971 to 1992 approximately 1260 pupils registered in Lusk school. During this period 26% of the pupils (registering) were from Orlynn Park, while 16% were from Kelly Park and Ash Grove.

Less than 5% had 'The Commons' or 'Commons' as their address. Unlike in earlier years the address 'North Commons' or 'Great Common' was no longer being used.

In the 1960's

Lusk Primary School Athletes Shine in Major Sport Competition
(Fingal Independent July 3rd 1992)

Celebrations held in Lusk over triumph

YOUNG athletes from Lusk National School had an extra special reason to celebrate last week. Not only were they breaking up for the long-awaited Summer holidays but they were also celebrating some fantastic victories in the finals of the Dublin Inter-Primary School Athletics Competition.

Sixth class teacher Mr. Paddy Fay is the co-ordinator of the school's annual entry into this popular athletics meet. Over 40 schools compete in each of the four original sections and it is a tremendous honour for athletes to even reach the finals, let alone win medals and trophies.

Lusk National School was proud to have no less than 36 athletes, both boys and girls, competing in the finals in Santry. They duly brought home gold, silver and bronze medals and three of the top overall awards in the contest.

Fifth class student Brendan Clare, the son of Sean and Brid Clare, won the coveted President's Medal, which is awarded on a points system taking in three events.

Brendan, from the Green, Lusk, was following neatly in the equally fast footsteps of his older brother John who won that same medal for the school in 1981.

Eleven-year-old Brendan earned the medal for his first place successes in the under 12 100m, under 12 hurdles and his second place success in the under 12 relay team. That relay team also included Kevin Brogan, Desmond O'Laoghaire, Alan Teeling and sub Paul Ryan.

Brendan was also repeating the success of fellow student John Carroll, who brought that medal back to Lusk last year. John was just one point behind Brendan in this year's contest.

John came second in the under 13 100m this year and also earned a silver in the under 13 high jump.

The girls' equivalent of the President's Medal is the Lord Mayor's medal. This year no less than four talented athletes had equal points and the medal was presented to each of them - and they are all from Fingal!

Two students from Realt na Mara, Skerries, and two Lusk National School students took the honours. Julie Kearns (12) and Marguerite Finnegan (13), both sixth class pupils in Lusk, each earned the top points.

Their win was particularly appropriate as their mothers Catherine Kearns and Pearl Finnegan have been towers of strength in helping Mr. Fay organise the annual entry into the games.

Julie's brother David is another star athlete. Fifteen year old David recently won the All-Ireland schools' athletics in the under 17 400m hurdles.

Marguerite won first place in both the under 13 and a half high jump and 100m. Julie won third place in the under 12 long jump and first place in the hurdles. She was also on the relay team which came second.

That relay team also included Jacqueline Synnott, Kara Foran and Donna McKeon.

In the boys' athletics the under 13 and a half relay team scooped the gold medal. The team included Stephen Farrell, Peter Winters, John Carroll and Jason McGee, with sub Dave Farrell.

Tribute has been paid to Jason McGee who stepped successfully into the runners of Dave Farrell, who had to withdraw from the team after receiving a back injury in the heats. Jason not only equalled the team's pace but gained yardage for them in the finals.

Yet more individual medals was brought home in triumph by Elaine McCormack, who scooped the gold medal in the under 11 high jump, and Marc Butterly, who won the gold in the under 13 and a half 800m.

The success of Lusk National School athletes in this annual competition is almost a local tradition at this stage and is a tribute to both the talent of the pupils and the dedication of Mr. Fay.

A former sprint champion himself, Mr. Fay is a staff coach with BLE and greatly enjoys encouraging the students in their athletic endeavours.

Fig. 9.10
Lusk Primary School Pupils, Athletics Competitors 1992
(Newspaper cutting courtesy of Pearl Finnegan, and reproduced with permission of Fingal Independent)

CHAPTER 10

Pupil Numbers

Summary of pupil numbers over the one-hundred year period 1892 to 1992

Year	Number of Pupils Registered		Total
	Boys	Girls	
1892 - 1899	65	127	192
1900 - 1970	753	767	1520
1971 - 1992	649	614	1263
Total	1467	1508	2975

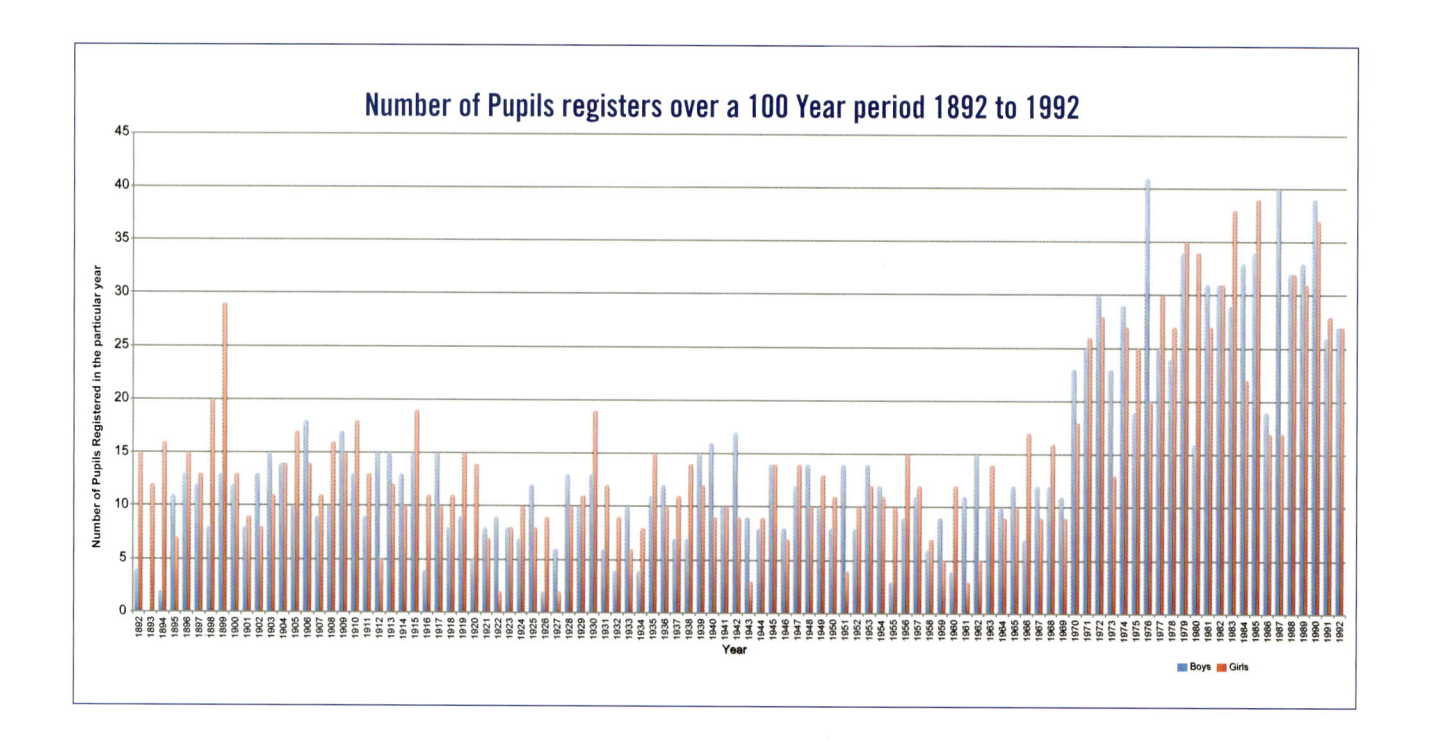

Number of Pupils registers over a 100 Year period 1892 to 1992

Pupil Numbers

Number of Pupils registered each Year from 1892 to 1942

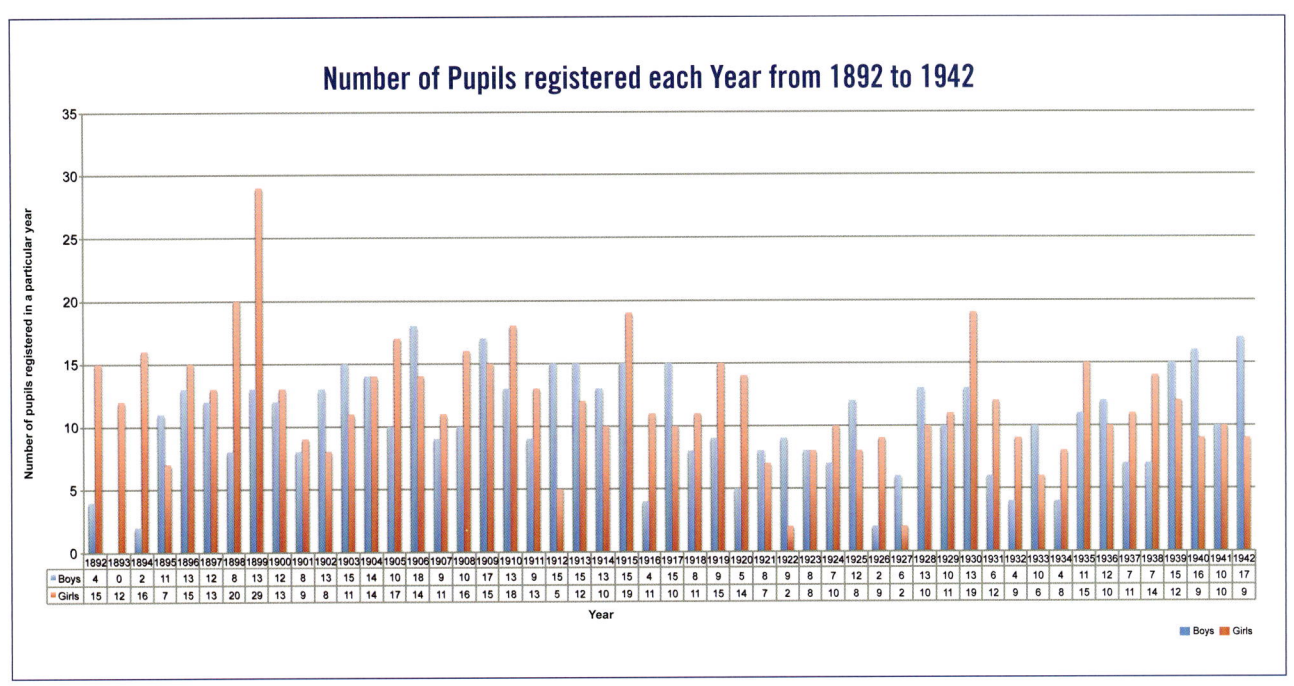

Year	Boys	Girls
1892	4	15
1893	0	12
1894	2	16
1895	11	7
1896	13	15
1897	12	13
1898	8	20
1899	13	29
1900	12	13
1901	8	9
1902	13	8
1903	15	11
1904	14	14
1905	10	17
1906	18	14
1907	9	11
1908	17	15
1909	13	18
1910	9	13
1911	15	5
1912	15	12
1913	15	10
1914	4	19
1915	15	11
1916	8	15
1917	9	14
1918	5	7
1919	8	2
1920	9	8
1921	8	10
1922	7	8
1923	12	9
1924	2	2
1925	6	10
1926	13	11
1927	10	19
1928	13	12
1929	6	9
1930	4	6
1931	10	8
1932	4	15
1933	11	10
1934	12	11
1935	7	14
1936	7	12
1937	15	9
1938	16	10
1939	10	9
1940	17	9

Number of Pupils Registered each year from 1943 to 1992

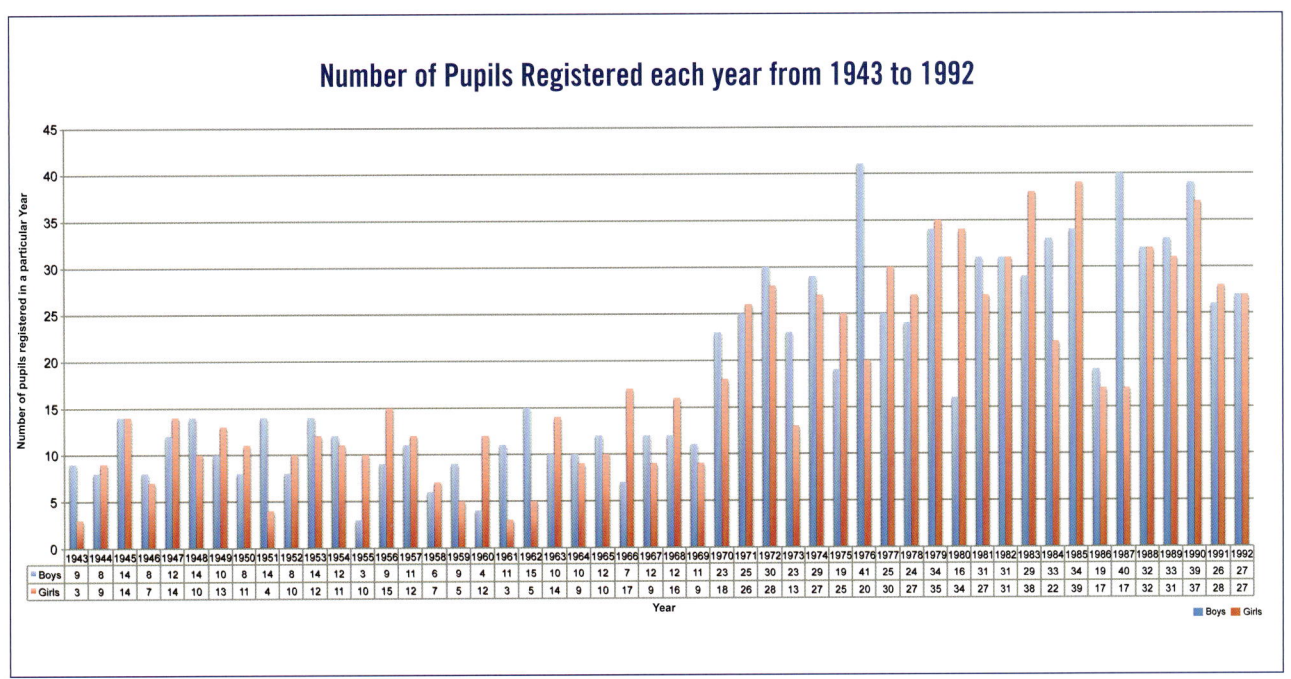

Year	Boys	Girls
1943	9	3
1944	8	9
1945	14	14
1946	8	7
1947	12	14
1948	14	10
1949	10	13
1950	8	11
1951	14	4
1952	8	10
1953	14	12
1954	12	11
1955	3	10
1956	9	15
1957	11	12
1958	6	7
1959	9	5
1960	4	12
1961	11	3
1962	15	5
1963	10	14
1964	10	9
1965	12	10
1966	7	17
1967	12	9
1968	12	16
1969	11	9
1970	23	18
1971	25	26
1972	30	28
1973	23	13
1974	29	27
1975	19	25
1976	41	20
1977	25	30
1978	24	27
1979	34	35
1980	16	34
1981	31	27
1982	31	31
1983	29	38
1984	33	22
1985	34	39
1986	19	17
1987	40	17
1988	32	32
1989	33	31
1990	39	37
1991	26	28
1992	27	27

CHAPTER 11

Parents of School Pupils and their Occupations (Through 1800's/early 1900's)

Through the 1800's most of the fathers of school pupils were either farmers or labourers. Approximately 41% of all the pupils' parent (usually the father) were labourers, while 27% were farmers.

When labourers and farmers are taken together these two occupations accounted for approximately 73% of the total. Other occupations, in smaller numbers, in the locality at the time included; stewarts/herds, constables, blacksmiths, carpenters, warders, grocers, dealers, masons and tailors.

From 1900 through to 1970 42% of occupations were labourers, while those who were farmers had reduced to just 11%. Other occupations during this period included: soldiers (mostly based on the Military Farm (Remount Farm), railway workers, gardeners/market gardeners, harness-maker and mental hospital attendants (St. Itas Portrane)

Some of the less common occupations were: carrier/haulier, car-man/car owner, cycle-agent, drayman, showman, a postman (referred to some instances as a letter-carrier), a retired circus performer, a bus conductor, and in the 1940's, there is one man listed as a jockey.

From 1960 to 1980 labourers accounted for only 7% of the occupations. Other occupations beginning to emerge for the first time included: mechanic, Aer-Lingus employee, C.I.E. employee, ESB employee, pilot, secondary school teacher, accountant, electrician, banker, TV engineer, welder and hairdresser.

The figures above refer only to the occupations of parents of those who had children in the school. Never the less it does give a reasonable indication of the range, frequency and changes occurring with occupations in the locality generally.

Also, the figures will be somewhat distorted given that the occupations of some of the fathers will have more than one child in the school. However bearing these points in mind the analysis gives a reasonably valid overview of the situation that existed for the period.[169]

---

[169] Lusk primary school, school registers.

CHAPTER 12

Surnames and First Names

The most frequently occurring school-children surnames

Through the **1800's** the top ten most frequently occurring surnames of children registering in the school were:

	Top 10 Boys Surnames	Top 10 Girls Surnames	Top 10 Boys and Girls combined
1	Dennis	Donnelly	Dennis
2	Daly	Dennis	Clarke
3	Skelly/Scally	Clarke	Sweetman
4	Cruise	Devine	Daly
5	Sweetman	Sweetman	Skelly/Scally
6	Hogan	Kelly	Magee/McGee
7	Magee/McGee	Daly	Cruise
8	Bentley	Magee/McGee	Donnelly
9	Clarke	Connor/O'Connor	Devine
10	Peters	McNally	Bentley

One-Hundred Years of Boys Surnames. (1892 to 1992)

When did particular Surnames first appear as pupils in the school, and when did the same surname last appear in school records?

The following details may be useful to people tracing their family history in the locality. It should be borne in mind however that the names relate only to children attending the school, and it is the year that the child started school, not the year the child finished school. It may also be the case that some family names were in the locality before and after the year given in the table below, due to their children having finished school. Also, it is worth remembering that any particular surname listed may or may not be from the same family. In most cases the family name extending over the particular span

From **1900 to 1960** the top ten most frequently occurring surnames were:

	Top 10 Boys Surnames	Top 10 Girls Surnames	Top 10 Boys and Girls combined
1	Clarke	Connor/O'Connor	Magee/McGee
2	Dennis	Donnelly	Clarke
3	Magee/McGee	Magee/McGee	Dennis
4	Daly	Devine	Daly
5	Sweetman	Jenkinson	Connor/O'Connor
6	Bentley	Kelly	Donnelly
7	Hogan	Clarke	Kelly
8	McCann	Dennis	Bentley
9	McNally	McNally	Sweetman
10	Peters	Neary, and O'Brien	O'Brien

of years shown will in fact be from the same family or extended family, but in some cases the names will be from families with no direct connection to each other.

Never the less the information may serve as a starting point for anyone doing family history research, or add to information that a family may already have.

Not all family names that attended the school are captured in this list; readers should refer to the names in Appendix 5 for the full list of family names.

One-Hundred Years of Boys Surnames. (1892 to 1992)

Boys Surnames 1892-1992	The year when the name first appeared in school records	The year when the name last appeared in school records
Bentley	1915	1979
Brogan	1897	1984
Carton	1892	1977
Clare	1946	1984
Clarke	1896	1982
Connolly	1892	1930
Connor/O'Connor	1906	1991
Cowley	1911	1984

Boys Surnames 1892-1992	The year when the name first appeared in school records	The year when the name last appeared in school records
Cruise	1897	1992
Daly	1903	1992
Dennis	1896	1991
Devine	1897	1992
Donnelly	1895	1894
Doyle	1897	1991
Fay	1896	1993
Grimes	1906	1977
Hoey	1891	1970
Hogan	1905	1989
Hughes	1904	1988
Jenkinson	1892	1963
Kelly	1892	1993
Kiernan	1895	1904
Magee/McGee	1913	1965
Masterson	1899	1906
Maypother	1895	1933
McCann	1897	1973
McNally	1900	1991
Monks	1896	1990
Moore	1897	1985
Murtagh	1902	1987
Neary	1929	1982
O'Brien	1914	1974
Peters	1903	1981
Russell	1911	1992
Seaver	1895	1971
Sherry	1912	1984
Skelly/Scally	1917	1992
Sweetman	1889	1976
Teeling	1898	1992

One-Hundred-and-Twenty Years of Girls Surnames. (1872 to 1992)

Girls Surnames 1872-1992	The year when the name first appeared in school register	The year when the name last appeared in school register
Donnelly	1868	1991
Dennis	1862	1985
Clarke	1876	1991
Devine	1876	1980
Sweetman	1863	1988
Kelly	1868	1981
Daly	1873	1989
Magee/McGee	1869	1984
Connor/O'Connor	1867	1990
McNally	1873	1986
Skelly/Scally	1869	1992
Carton	1872	1979
Jenkinson	1891	1979
Bentley	1873	1984
Cruise	1874	1991
Connolly	1868	1918
Hughes	1871	1991
Kiernan	1871	1954
Maypother	1878	1936
McCann	1873	1976
Brogan	1875	1981
Doyle	1875	1982
Murtagh	1867	1902
Moore	1882	1978
O'Brien	1914	1984
Neary	1929	1973
Russell	1871	1986
Seaver	1873	1973

First Names and Surnames

Girls Surnames 1872-1992	The year when the name first appeared in school register	The year when the name last appeared in school register
Sherry	1874	1986
Grimes	1904	1973
Fay	1883	1990
Monks	1895	1980
Clare	1933	1992
Cowley	1878	1991
Hoey	1873	1972
Masterson	1872	1894
Hogan	1905	1988
Peters	1939	1990
Teeling	1874	1991

Most frequently occurring Boys First Names 1892-1899

Approximately 67 Boys names appear in school records from 1892 to 1899. (There are no boys names available before 1892). Of the 67 names only 15 different 'first names' are used. The most popular being **John,** followed in popularity as shown opposite.

One of each of the names listed below was also in use:
  Peter
  Austin
  Nicholas
  Harold
  Matthew
  Hugh
  Charles

Boys First Names
John
Thomas
Patrick
James
Richard
Joseph
Michael
William

Almost 60% of the boys were named either; John, Thomas, Patrick or James.

Most frequently occurring Girls First Names 1862-1899

Maggie was in popular use from 1890's to 1920's

A total of 497 girls are listed as having registered in the school through the 1800's. (Most of the girls names are from 1872 onwards, (there are a small number from the 1860's). The top ten names (opposite right) represent 73% of all first names through this period of time.

50% of all girls were called either: Mary, Mary-Jane, Margaret/Maggie, Elly/Ellen, or Annie/Anne.

A small number of the following names appear for this period also:

Ada	Dorothy	Letita
Alice	Emily	Louisa
Alicia	Esther	Maria
Angela	Hannah	Rose
Beatrice	Helena	Sarah
Charlotte	Isabella	Susan
Christina	Julia	Teresa
Davidina	Kathleen	

Girls First Names
Mary/ Mary-Jane
Bridget
Kate/Catherine
Margaret/Maggie
Elly/Ellen
Annie/Anne
Eliza
Mary-Anne
Jane
Frances

FIRST-NAMES 1900 TO 1960

Top Twenty Boys Names 1900 to 1960

John/Jack	Christopher/Chris/Christy	Francis
Thomas	Sean	Robert
Patrick/Padraig	Richard	Nicholas
James	Seamus	Bernard
Michael	Peter	Edward
Joseph	George	Charles
William	Martin	

First Names and Surnames

Top Twenty Girls Names 1900 to 1960

Mary/Maire/May/Mai	
Kathleen	In use up to 1960
Margaret/Maggie	There were no Maggies registered in the school after 1929
Bridget/Bridgid/Brigid/Bride/Breed	
Anna/Ann/Annie/Nancy	
Eileen	
Alice	
Kate/Katie/Kitty/Kittie/Cait	
Maureen	
Teresa	
Rosie/Rose/Rosanna/Rosaleen	
Christina	
Elizabeth/Betty	
Lilly/Lillie/Lillian	
Patricia	
Joan/Jean	
Lizzie	There were no Lizzies registered in the school after 1920
Catherine/Kathryn	
Gertrude/Gertie/Gretta	
Maura	

CONCLUSION

Having set out to investigate and record the development of primary education in the village of Lusk what has emerged in the process is an indication of the changing face and influences of the social and economic landscape of the locality through the nineteenth and twentieth centuries.

From the early days of hedge schools, a school house of mud walls and thatched roof, to the establishment of formal national education, through the famine years of the mid nineteenth century, to the technological age of the late twentieth century, Lusk school and education generally in the locality has embraced all the changes and grown with the developing needs and demands that modern education brings.

Over one-hundred individual teachers were employed and contributed to the education of approximately 4,500 pupils in Lusk school through the 170 years that has been the subject of research produced in this publication. Some of those teachers were local people who themselves had been pupils in Lusk school. Many came from other counties all over Ireland. Some came for short periods and left while others stayed for quite some time, settled and raised their families in Lusk, while others simply moved on when their work was done. All of them in some manner or form brought their own social, intellectual, physical and moral influences to bear on the formation and development of young minds.

Whether by choice or necessary emigration, hundreds of former pupils of Lusk school can now be found in many lands throughout the world and it is almost without question that Lusk village and Lusk school will always be in their hearts.

It is a fervent hope that the contents of this book will not only inform and enlighten but also provide the opportunity to recall many memories of school times in Lusk and perhaps inspire others to explore the past for the benefit of the future.

To all those who have gone through the school doors, pupils and teachers alike, who helped shape what is The History of Lusk School, *go raimh maith agat.*

REGISTER OF Lusk Male NATIONAL

113

APPENDICES

Appendix 1, 2, 3, 4 and 5[170]

Date of Entrance.	Register Number.		Pupils' Name in Full.	Date of Pupil's Birth.	Religious Denomination as stated by Parent or Guardian.	Residence.	Position or Occupation of Parent or Guardian.
1.92	360	1	Connolly Richard		R.C	Collinstown	Farmer
5.92	373	2	Carton Joseph	15.10.87	R.C	Lusk	Grocer
7.92	375	3	Kelly Richard		R.C	"	Farmer
10.92	378	4	Jenkinson James	16.10.87	R.C	Newhaggard	Steward
12.89	364	5	Sweetman Thomas		R.C	Lusk	Labourer

Name of Pupil.	Year ending	No. of Attendances made in the Year.	Class in which Enrolled.	Precise Date of Admission to that Class.	Class in which Examined.	Results of Examination.									Extra Branches.
						Reading, &c.	Writing.	Arithmetic.	Spelling.	Grammar.	Geography.	Agriculture.	Needlework.	Vocal Music	
1 Richard Connolly	30.10.02	85	6th	12.99	6th										
	30.9.04														
	30.9.05														

---

[170] National archives of Ireland, Appendix 1, 2, 3 and 4 below are derived from an amalgam of reference sources including the following: file No. ED/4/ 1, 2, 3, 4, 5, 6, 54, 56, 60, 63, 66, 69, 72, 75, 78, 81, 151, 152, 153, 155-7, 158-160, 161-162, 786, 788, 789, 792, 790, 791, 794, 795, 796, 797, 800, 801, 802, 1372, 1373, 1503, 1506, 1507, 1509, 1512, 1515-1516, 1518, 1521, 2121, 2125, 2131, 2136, 2141, 2146 (Note, all of the above numbers are prefixed by file no. ED/4). Appendix 5, pupils names were recorded from Lusk school registers.

| 30.10.02 | 151 | 6th | 12.99 | 6th |

APPENDIX 1

Pupil Attendance

Chart 1

Average Pupil Attendance Through the 1800's

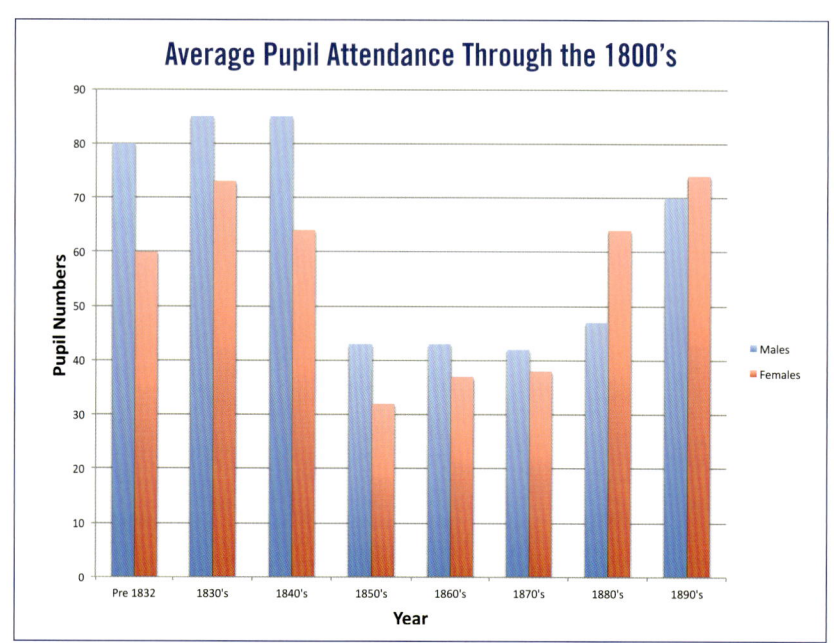

Chart 2

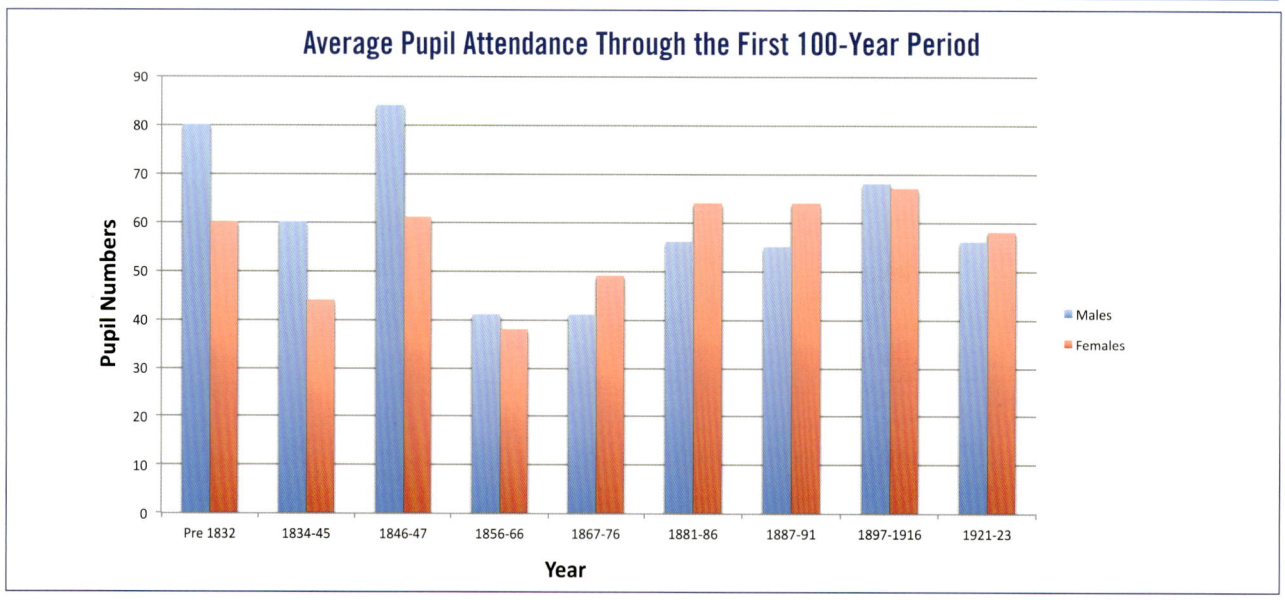

Average Pupil Attendance Through the First 100-Year Period

Appendices

Chart 3

Average Pupil Attendance - 1900 to 1965

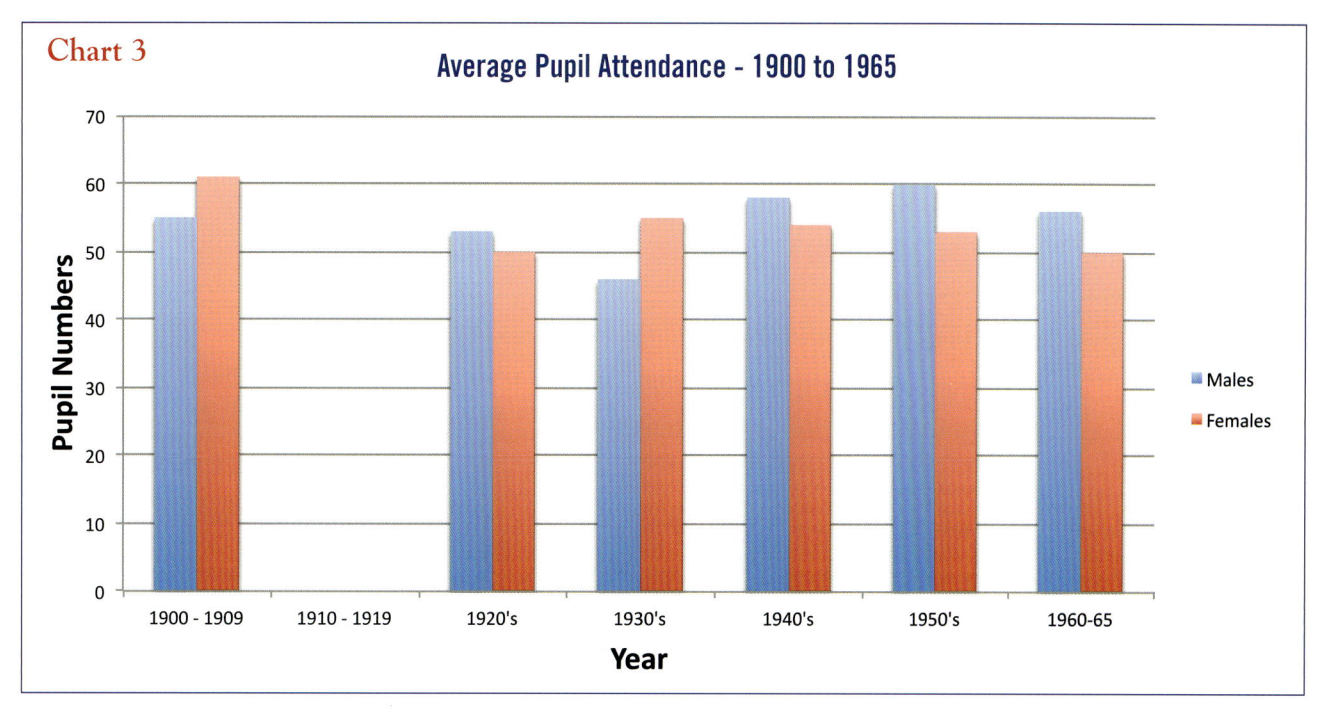

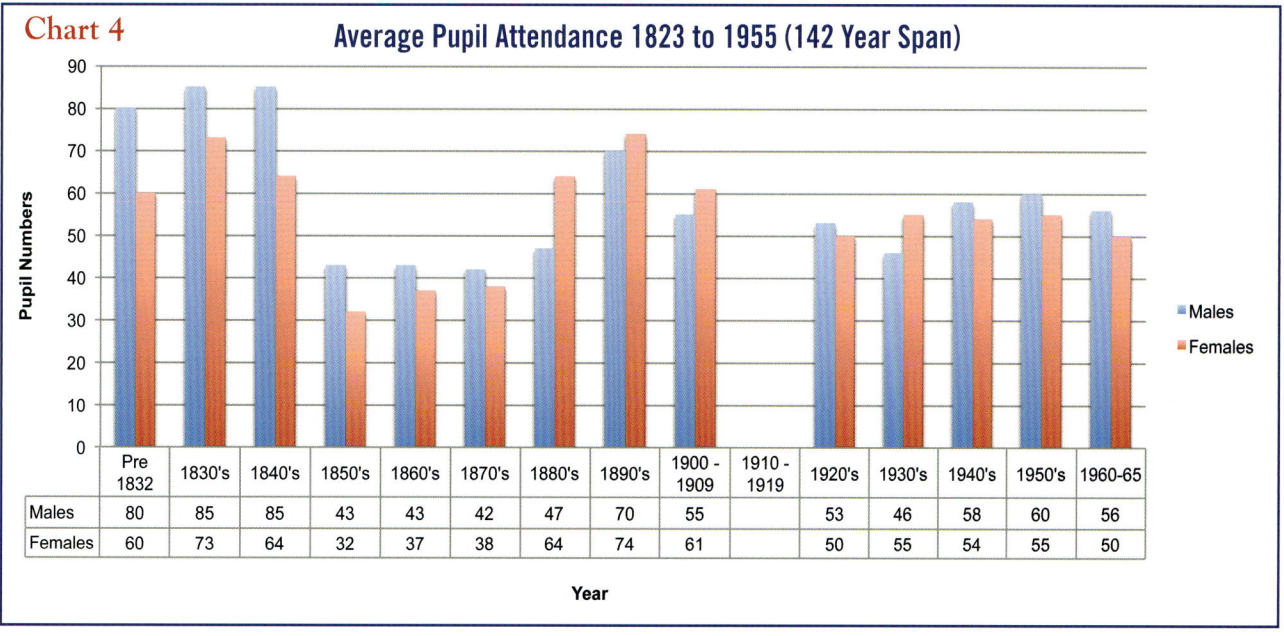

Chart 4

Average Pupil Attendance 1823 to 1955 (142 Year Span)

Year	Pre 1832	1830's	1840's	1850's	1860's	1870's	1880's	1890's	1900 - 1909	1910 - 1919	1920's	1930's	1940's	1950's	1960-65
Males	80	85	85	43	43	42	47	70	55		53	46	58	60	56
Females	60	73	64	32	37	38	64	74	61		50	55	54	55	50

Note: Where gaps appear in the above chart it simply means that figures are not available in the records for that period.

Through the 1800's the average number of pupils in the school was 116, the highest numbers recorded was during 1830's, at approximately 158, (85 males, 73 females) and the the lowest at 75 pupils (43 males, 32 females) through the 1850's.

From September 1844 to March 1845 there were 97 Males and 72 Females on the role.

From March to end of September 1845 there were 111 Males and 65 Females enrolled.

September 1845 to March 1946, 106 Males, 62 Females.

March to September 1846, 84 Males, 57 Females.

From the above figures (1844 to 1846) it can be determined that male enrolment exceeded female enrolment by approximately 35%. This is somewhat consistent with the average attendance figures where attendance by males exceeded attendance by females by approximately 25%. This pattern of boys attendance exceeding that of girls was consistent up to the mid 1800's. However from the 1860's (after the famine period) to the end of the century the girls attendance exceeded that of the boys.

From 1900 to 1965 the average numbers had dropped slightly to 109, with a high of 116 pupils occurring in the first decade of the 1900's, and the lowest at 100, during 1930's.

No figures are available for the decade 1910 to 1919.

From 1920 through to 1965 the average attendance never exceeded 120 in total (boys and girls).

APPENDIX 2

Attendance at Examination during the 'Pay by Results' period

Following the Royal Commission of Inquiry into Primary Education in Ireland (Powis Commission) which found that 'the progress of the children in the national schools of Ireland is very much less than it ought to be', the Board of Education introduced a 'pay by results' scheme, whereby a portion of a teachers salary was dependent on pupils performance at examinations conducted annually by the inspectorate. The pay by results scheme was abolished in 1900.

During the period of pay by results the visiting inspector recorded the number of pupils presenting for examination on the particular day. This serves to give us an accurate figure of attendance on that day and to compare these figures for the average attendance for the whole year. The inspector recorded not only the total attendance on the day, he also recorded the number of pupils in each grade, and this serves to give us valuable data that is not available for earlier or later years.

The charts show the figures for pupil attendance on the day of examination.

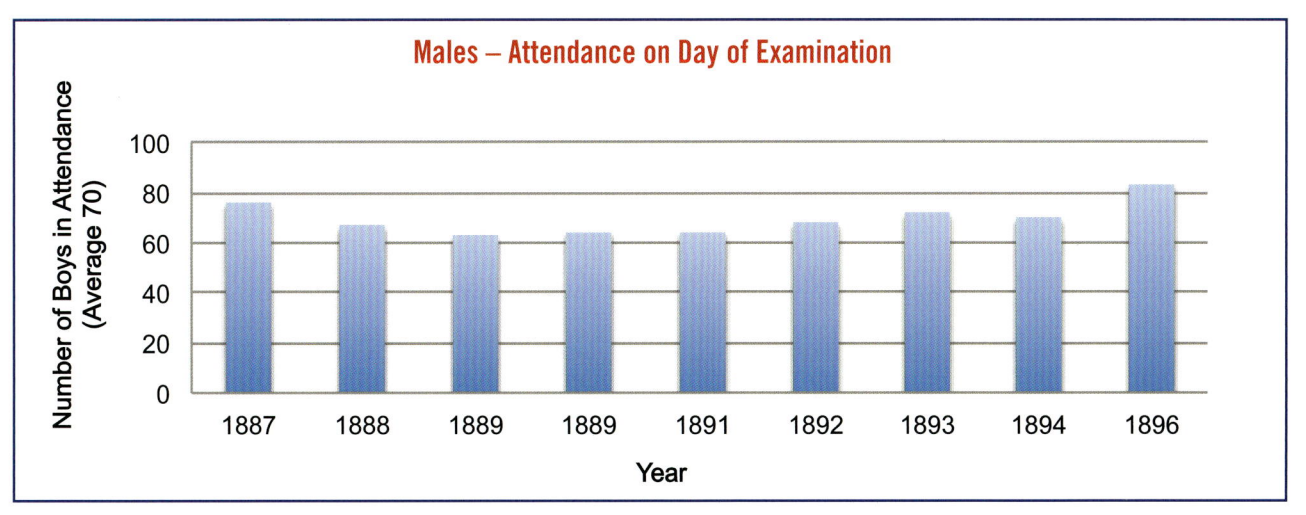

Chart 5

Males – Attendance on Day of Examination (Number of Boys in Attendance, Average 70) by Year: 1887, 1888, 1889, 1889, 1891, 1892, 1893, 1894, 1896

Examinations were held mostly in the month of October. Where the charts below show figures twice in the same year this is where examinations were held in January and October.

Note: Figures for some of the years are not available in the records, so there are some gaps.

Chart 6

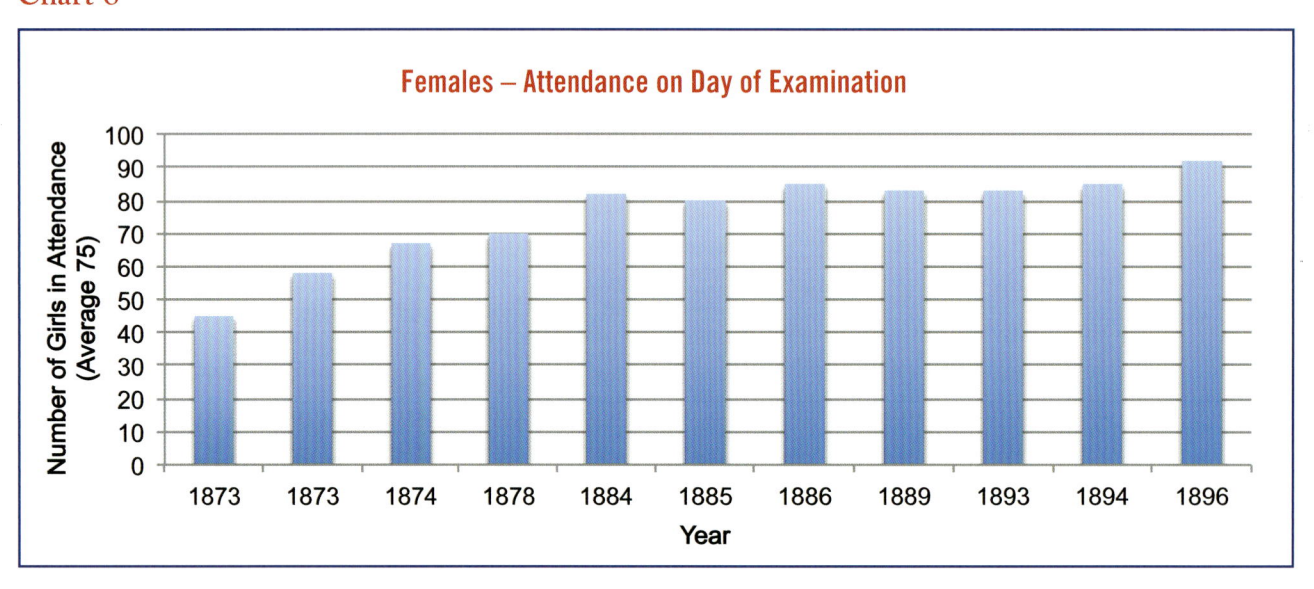

Females – Attendance on Day of Examination

Year	Number of Girls in Attendance (Average 75)
1873	45
1873	58
1874	67
1878	70
1884	82
1885	80
1886	85
1889	83
1893	83
1894	85
1896	92

Based on the figures in Charts 5 and 6 and making a comparison with the average annual attendance for the same period, it can be concluded that attendance on days of examinations exceeded the average annual attendance by approximately 16% for boys and 21% for girls.

Appendices

Chart 7

Number of Boys attending for Examinations during the 'pay by results' years

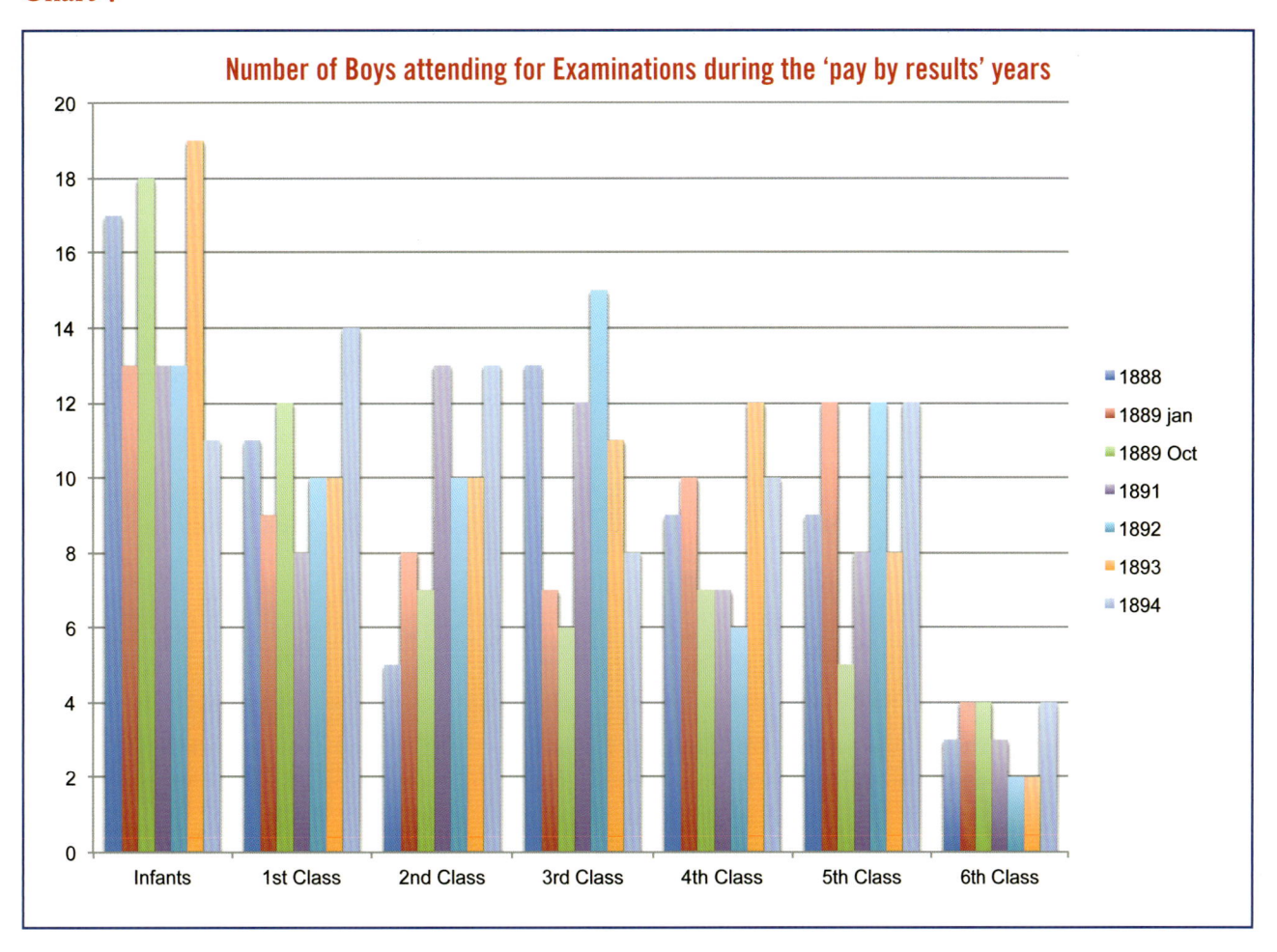

Charts 7 and 8 indicate a marked gradual decline in the number of pupils presenting for examination (and presumably in attendance generally) from the infant classes through to the senior classes. This clearly indicates that a considerable number of pupils were not completing the full cycle of primary education during this period. For example (referring to Chart 8) twenty-two Infant pupils presented for examination in 1889, this same group of pupils would be expected to be in 4th class in 1894 (allowing for two years in infant class), however in the 4th class of 1894 only seven pupils presented for examination, a drop of over 30%.

Chart 8

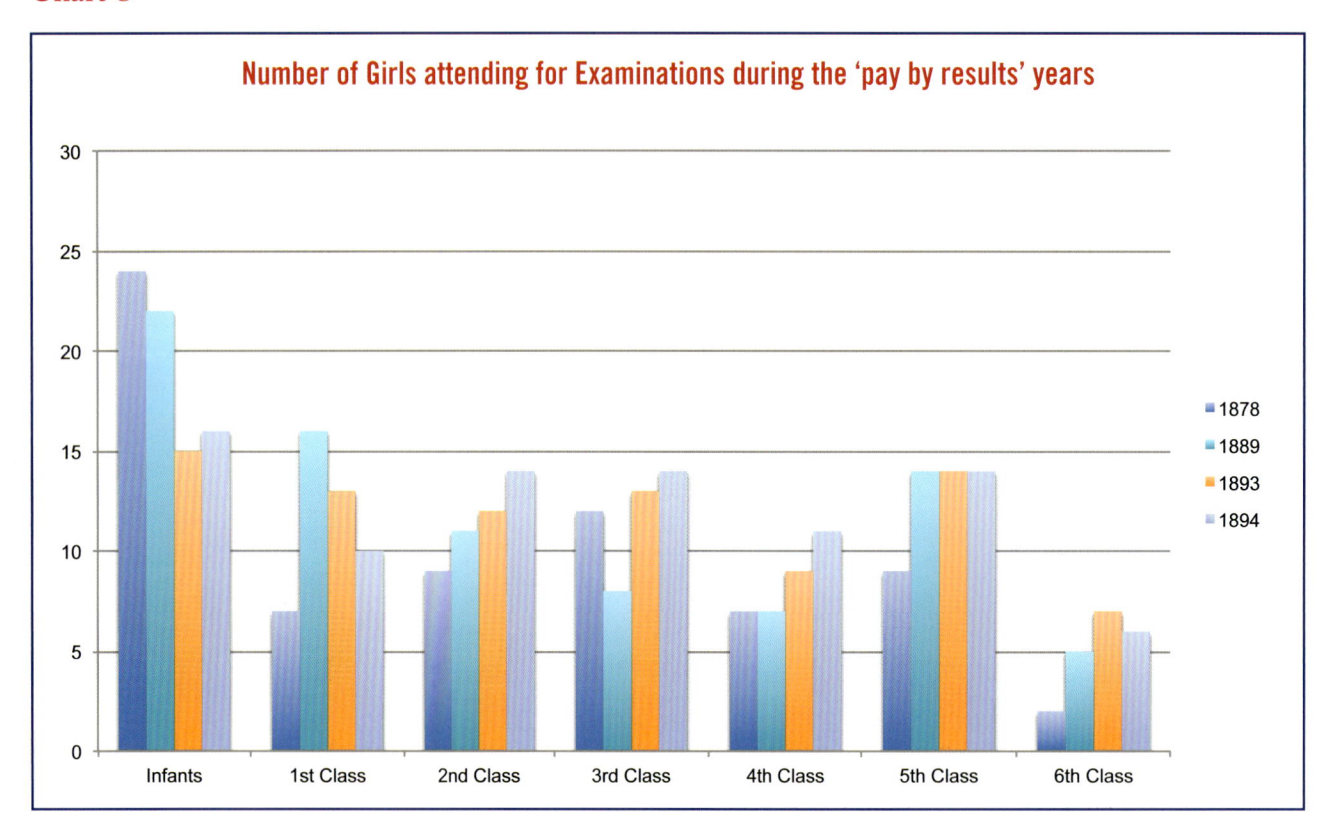

Number of Girls attending for Examinations during the 'pay by results' years

Class	1878	1889	1893	1894
Infants	24	22	15	16
1st Class	7	16	13	10
2nd Class	9	11	12	14
3rd Class	12	8	13	14
4th Class	7	7	9	11
5th Class	9	14	14	14
6th Class	2	5	7	6

In 1926 the School Attendance Act was introduced in Ireland. This had the effect of increasing the percentage of children attending school. The most important educational effect of the Act was considered to be the increase in the percentage of children in the higher standards, i.e. more pupils completing the full primary cycle than in earlier years.[171]

---

[171] Department of education 1929-30, report (www.education.ie/en/Publications/statistics/stats_statistical_report_1929_30.pdf) (21st Jan 2015).

APPENDIX 3

Teacher Salaries

Chart 9

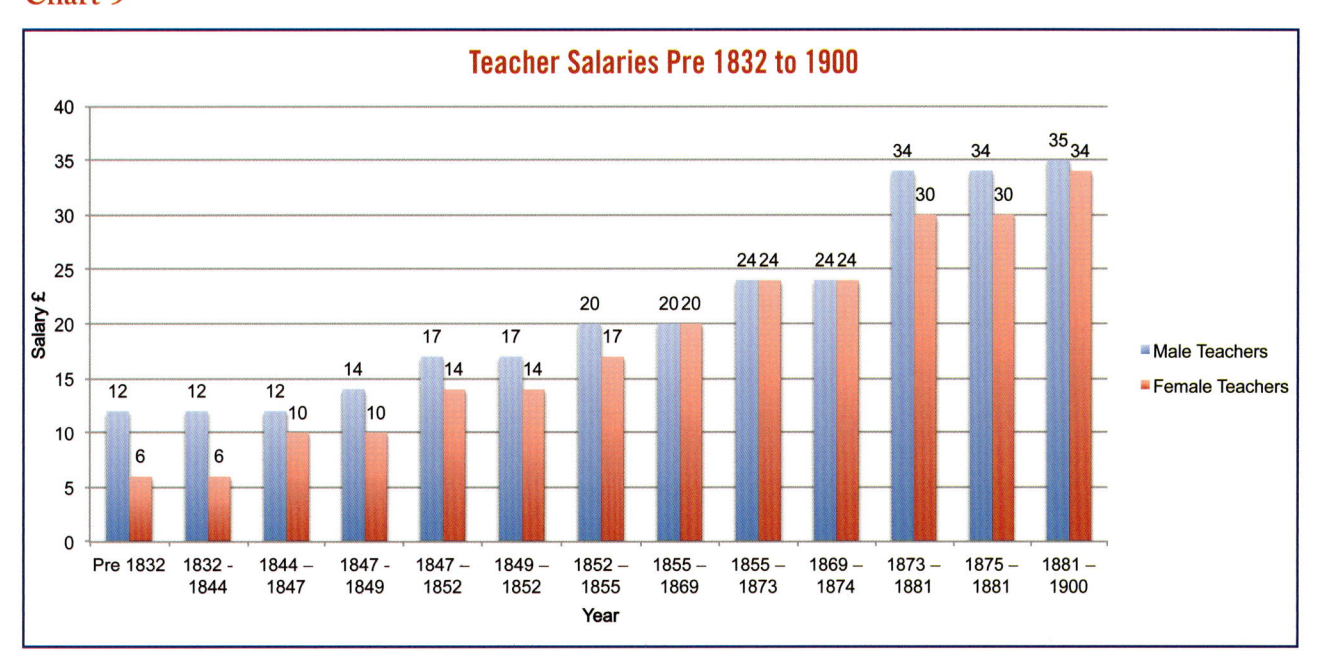

Teacher Salaries Pre 1832 to 1900

Year	Male Teachers	Female Teachers
Pre 1832	12	6
1832 – 1844	12	6
1844 – 1847	12	10
1847 – 1849	14	10
1847 – 1852	17	14
1849 – 1852	17	14
1852 – 1855	20	17
1855 – 1869	20	20
1855 – 1873	24	24
1869 – 1874	24	24
1873 – 1881	34	30
1875 – 1881	34	30
1881 – 1900	35	34

Salary £

Chart 10

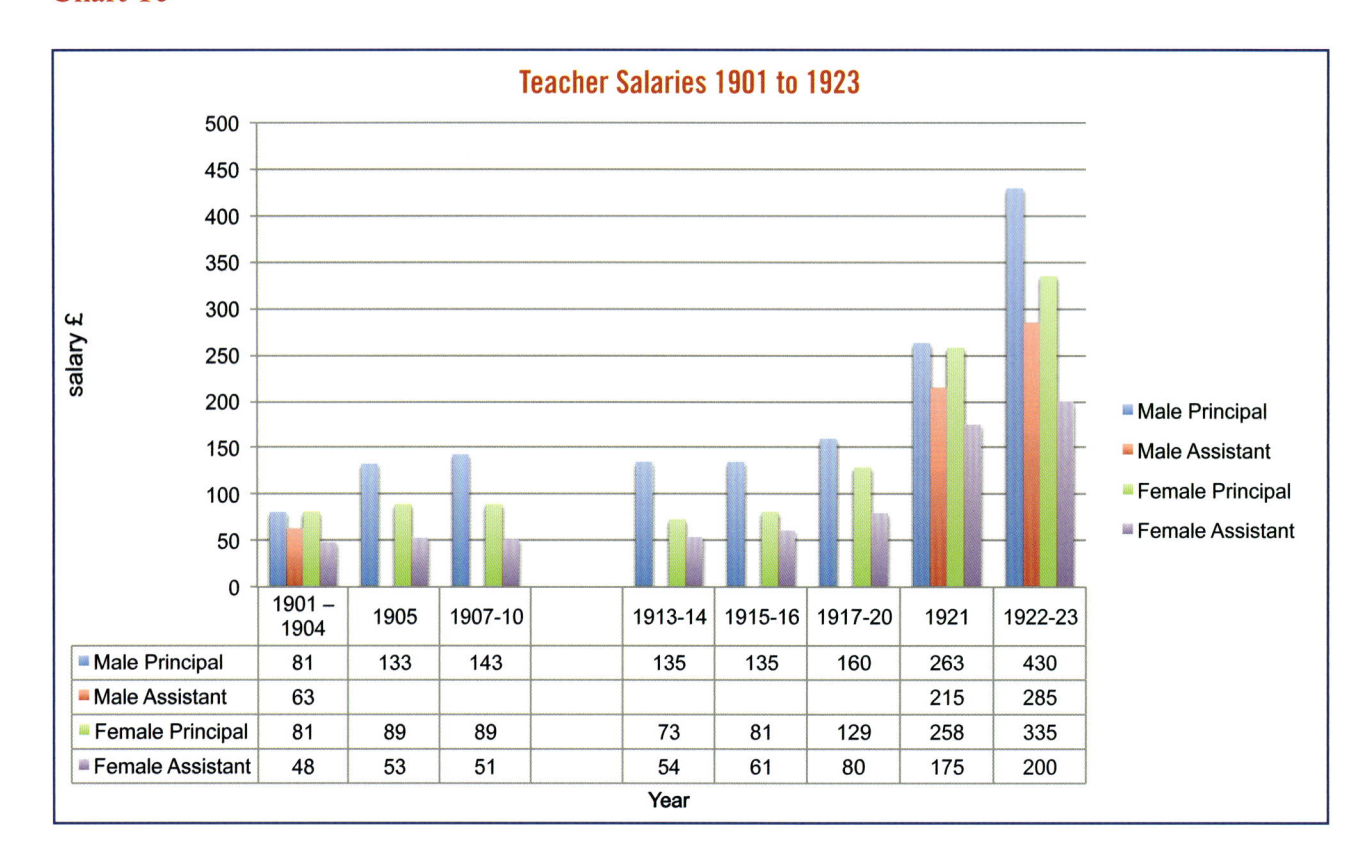

Teacher Salaries 1901 to 1923

Year	1901–1904	1905	1907-10	1913-14	1915-16	1917-20	1921	1922-23
Male Principal	81	133	143	135	135	160	263	430
Male Assistant	63						215	285
Female Principal	81	89	89	73	81	129	258	335
Female Assistant	48	53	51	54	61	80	175	200

Appendices

Chart 11

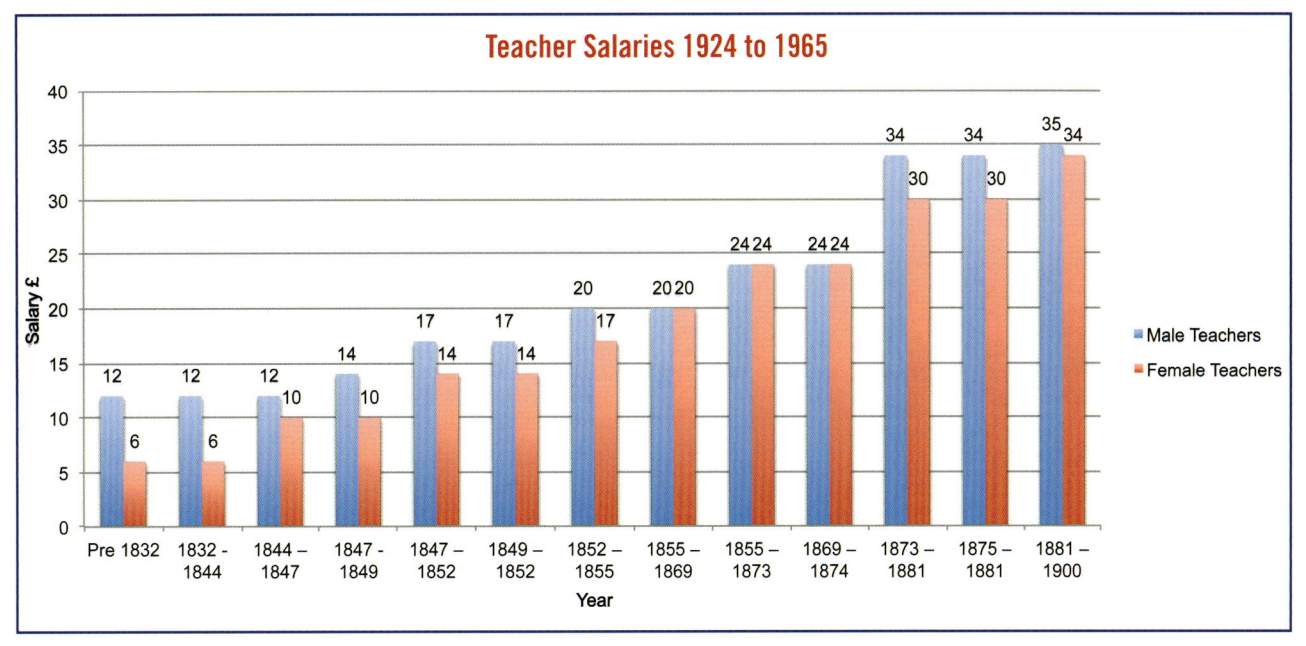

Teacher Salaries 1924 to 1965

Year	Male Teachers	Female Teachers
Pre 1832	12	6
1832 – 1844	12	6
1844 – 1847	12	10
1847 – 1849	14	10
1847 – 1852	17	14
1849 – 1852	17	14
1852 – 1855	20	17
1855 – 1869	20	20
1855 – 1873	24	24
1869 – 1874	24	24
1873 – 1881	34	30
1875 – 1881	34	30
1881 – 1900	35	34

Note: The actual year when salary increases occurred is approximate.

In the earlier years salaries were paid half-yearly and in later years were paid every quarter.

Towards the end of the 1800's and into the early 1900's payments were made more frequently and increments were applied.

Also, depending on experience and qualifications, teachers were classified as class 1, class 2 and class 3 teachers, depending on their qualifications, and salaries were determined accordingly.

In the early 1920's increments were in the region of £10 per annum.

A bonus of £20 was paid for holders of a BA Degree.[172]

---

[172] National archives of Ireland, *ED/4*.

APPENDIX 4

Chronology of Teachers

Lusk Primary School

Teachers Name		Period of service		Approximate period of service
Boys School	Girls School	From	To	
James Carey		From 1823 (pre establishment of the formal education system).		Precise period of service (for these 4 teachers) is uncertain but its likely that at least some of them were teaching in the school from 1823 to 1833 approximately
Christopher Gilmore				
Patrick McDonagh				
	Mary Hoey			
		From the establishment of formal education system in 1832		
Thomas Evlin		1834	1837	3 years
	Anne Evlin	1834	1837	3 years
Michael McCormick		1837	1840	3 years
	Anne McCormick	1837	1840	3 years
Patrick J O'Brien		1839	1841	2 years
	Jane Murphy	1838	1840	2 years
James Jordan		1841	1844	3 years
	Anne Jordan	1841	1846	5 years
John O'Brien		1844	1848	4 years
	Anne O'Brien	1844	1848	4 years
	Maria Thomson	1847	1848	1 year
Thomas Keogh		1848	1852	4 years
	Anne Keogh	1848	1852	4 years
Laurence Philips		1852	1853	1 year
	Susan Philips	1852	1853	1 year
James Wall		1852	1855	5 years
	Sarah Wall	1852	1855	3 years
	Mary Gaynor	1855	1894	39 years
Jeremiah Long		1856	1857	1 year
Joseph McSweeney		1857	1858	1 year
Laurence Early (Eardly)		1858	1873	15 years
John Donnelly		1874	1902	28 years. Had been a monitor in this school 1869 - 70

Appendices

Teachers Name		Period of service		
Boys School	Girls School	From	To	Approximate period of service
	Bridget Connor	1874	1903	29 years Had been a monitor from 1869 to 1874, a total of 34 years continuous service.
Francis Flanagan		1873 (June)	1873 (Dec)	
Joseph Donnelly		1880	?	A monitor for a short period
James Cowley		1885 (Oct)	1888	3 Years As a monitor
James Atley		1885 (Oct)	1888	3 Years As a monitor
Michael Roche		1896	1903	7 years Became principal in Feb. 1901
John Sweeney		1903 (August)	1903 (Sept)	Both John Sweeney and William Cotter were substitutes for Michael Roche who had taken ill in August 2003.
William Cotter		1903 (Sept)	1903 (Nov)	
	Margaret Coleman	1894	1909	15 years
Daniel Murphy		1902 (April)	1902 (Sept)	6 months
Patrick O'Shea		1902 (Sept)	1903	1 year
Richard Hegarty		1903	1906	3 years
John Dowling		1904 (Jan)	1904 (Mar)	3 months (Locum)
James Fenton		1904	1907	3 years. Appointed Principal of Lusk Boys school May 1st 1904 Appointed Inspector of national school system in February 1907
	Alice Reilly	1903	1909	3 years
Bridget Fenton		1906	1907	1.5 years Had been principal in Corduff school up to May 14th 1906.
	Mary Murtagh	1909	1909	2 months
	Mary Keenan	1909	1909	3 months (Locum)
James Kelly		1907 (Mar)	1907 (July)	4 months (Locum principal)
Thomas O'Connell		1907	1912	5 years
Edward Monks		1907	1910	3 years
Emily Leonard		1907	1909	2 Years Had previously been a monitor in Rush school
Thomas Devine		1912	1928	16 years
Peter Leonard		1909	1912	3 years Had been in Rush school as a monitor from 1907
Sara Mulligan		1912	1915	3 years
James Monks		1914	1917	3 years Monitor

Teachers Name		Period of service		
Boys School	Girls School	From	To	Approximate period of service
Ellen Long		1915	1925	10 years
	Hannah M O'Sullivan	1909	1941	32 years
	Elizabeth McCaffrey	1910	1918	8 years
	Katie Kavanagh	1918	1919	1 year
	Annie Doran	1919	1921	2 years
	Mrs. Mary Seaver (nee Doran)	1921	1929	8 years
Mary Elizabeth (Maureen) Maguire (Mrs. Mansfield)		1925	1930	5 years Transferred to Hedgestown school in 1930.
Laurence Dunne		1928	1966	37 Years
	Miss Mary Kelly	1929	1930	1 Year
Mrs. Mary Dunne		1930	1938	8 Years
	Kathleen Moloney	1931	1960	29 Years
	Mrs. Mary Dunne	1941	1965	24 years Plus an earlier period of 8 years as assistant in the boys school. Appointed principal of girls school on 1st August 1941.
Mrs. Annie Dunne		1939	1965	26 years in the Boys school
	Mrs. Annie Dunne	1966	c.1972	33 years in total In the boys school from 1939, see above
	Ms. S. Garvey	1960 (Sept.)	1962 (Jan)	1 year 4 months
	Mrs. M. McGee	1962	?	
Colman Dunne		1965	1966	1 year
Mr. D. Doherty		1966	1974	8 years
Mrs. Doherty		1966	1974	8 years
It was c.1966/67 when the boys and girls schools were combined into a mixed school.				
Mr. D. O'Leary (Principal)		1975	2007	33 years

Other Teachers not in any particular order: (up to 1992)			
Ms. Mary Hannon	Mr. John Prendergast,	Ms. Maura McKiernan	Ms. Kathleen Ferry
Ms. Geraldine O'Rourke	Ms. Bernadine Gainey	Ms. Maria Mullane	Ms. Orla Farrell
Ms. Roisin Madden	Mr. Paddy Fay	Ms. Anne Treanor	Ms. Aine Lawlor O'Cathasaigh
Mrs Mary Durkan	Ms. Frances Murtagh	Ms. Laura Bouzzah	Ms. Joan O'Donoghue
Ms. Olive Durkin	Ms. Deirdre Darcy	Ms. Mary Phelan	Ms. Siobhan Burke
Mr. Liam Murphy	Ms. Peggy O'Connor	Mr. John Curran	Mr. Joe O'Reilly
Mr. Cronin	Ms. Sheila Curran	Mr. John Lyons	Ms. Colette Ward
Mr. Sean O'Reilly,	Ms. Maire O'Dwyer	Ms. Catriona Casey	Ms. Anne Marie Gillespie

APPENDIX 5

List of pupils registered in Lusk School from c.1862-1992 for Girls, and from 1892-1992 for Boys.
In the earlier years registers were either not maintained, or not preserved. It was not compulsory to maintain registers and attendance until the pay by results (for teachers) was introduced in 1870's. There are no records of boys who attended Lusk school before 1891.

Note: In most instances where pupils' date-of-birth is shown these are considered to be correct and reliable. However, it has been noted by the author that a very small number of dates-of-births were incorrectly entered in the registers and the author has not adjusted the dates from the original entries unless absolutely certain that the original entry is incorrect. For anyone doing family research this should be borne in mind.

The spellings of a pupils' name, both first names and surnames, are a direct transcription from the original records and no attempt has been made to alter any spellings, even where they might appear to be incorrect. Such judgment can be left to the reader to make if they consider they have a connection to the person. It should also be remembered that very often a first name (Christian name) used in the school register may be the original name given to the child but may not be the name that the person was commonly referred to in later years. Typical examples of this for girls are Catherine, becoming Kate or Katie, Margaret as Maggie or even Peg, Peggy. John of course was most often called Jack, Francis was Frank, and so on. These are the more obvious ones but there may be other less obvious, such as Margaret being known as Greta or Rita, coming from Margarita, also when a child was given a first and second name, such as William-Christopher, he may have been registered as William but be more commonly known later on as Christy or Kit. For the most part however it should be said that it will be relatively easy to find the person being sought.

With regard to place names (pupils address) the author has also directly transcribed the spellings as they appear in the original records. In some instances there are many variations of the place name. A good example of this is for the townland of Rahenny. This has many variations of spellings, Raheny, Rahenny, Ratheny, Ratheney, etc.

Boys

List of Boys 1892 to 1899

Note: For the period 1892 to 1899 the dates shown in column 1 and 2 are for the most part the date the pupil started in infant class. However for some of the pupils the date shown in said columns was their entry into 'first class' having been transferred from infant class, so in fact they had started school a couple of years earlier than the date shown. Where the difference between the 'birth date' (column 6) and the year shown in column 2 is approximately 7 years, then this is most likely the explanation.

Month registered in the school	Year	Pupils Register No.	Pupils Surname	First Name	DOB	Place of Residence	Occupation of Parent/ Guardian	Previous School, if any
Jan	1892	360	Connolly	Richard		Collinstown	Farmer	
May	1892	373	Carton	Joseph	15-10-1887	Lusk	Grocer	
July	1892	375	Kelly	Richard		Lusk	Farmer	
Oct	1892	378	Jenkinson	James	16-10-1887	Newhaggard	Stewart	
Dec	1889	364	Sweetman	Thomas	24-2-1888	Lusk	Labourer	
Nov	1895	385	Jenkinson	Michael		Newhaggard	Stewart	
Apr	1891	351	Hoey	William		Figures	Farmer	
Oct	1901	523	Masterson	Peter		Corduff	Labourer	Corduff
Dec	1895	390	Kiernan	Austin		Lusk	Farmer	
Dec	1895	392	Meehan	Nicholas	30-3-1890	Lusk	Farmer	
Dec	1895	395	Lambe	John		Lusk	Herd	
Dec	1895	413	Mathews	John		Lusk	Farmer	
Sept	1896	417	Flanagan	James	10-6-1890	Lusk	Deaceased	
Oct	1900	515	Carton	Joseph		Corduff	Labourer	Corduff
Feb	1898	416	Teeling	Peter		Corduff	Labourer	Corduff
Feb	1897	431	Cox	Harold		Ballough	Farmer	Hedgestown
Sept	1896	397	Clarke	Joseph	9-2-1890	Lusk	Farmer	
Sept	1897	409	Moore	Patrick	12-3-1890	Lusk	Labourer	
Oct	1897	412	Lamb	Richard	31-1-1889	Ballaly	Herd	
Mar	1894	414	Jenkinson	Thomas	13-10-1890	Newhaggard	Stewart	
Sept	1895	423	Hynes	Richard	26-3-1889	Commons	Deaceased	America
May	1897	440	Brogan	Patrick	24-9-1889	Commons	Farmer	

Appendices

Month registered in the school	Year	Pupils Register No.	Pupils Surname	First Name	DOB	Place of Residence	Occupation of Parent/Guardian	Previous School, if any
Nov	1895	358	Donnelly	Thomas	26-3-1888	Lusk	Tailor	
Mar	1900	494	Lamb	John		Balcunnin	Farmer	Balcunnin
Apr	1901	519	Griffin	Mathew		Corduff	Farmer	Corduff
Nov	1895	381	Seaver	Richard		Commons	Farmer	
Oct	1897	422	Devine	Hugh		Lusk	Labourer	
Dec	1895	382	Maypother	John		Lusk	Labourer	
Mar	1900	495	Hurley	Charles	7-5-1888	Man O War	Porter	Balcunnin
Oct	1897	407	McGuire	Patrick		Rathmooney	Farmer	
June	1899	488	Murphy	Patrick		Corduff	Herd	Hedgestown
May	1895	420	Connolly	Michael		Lusk	Labourer	
June	1897	421	Cruise	Joseph	??-3-1888	Lusk	Farmer	
June	1896	443	Fay	James		Kingstown	Labourer	
Sept	1896	446	Sweetman	Thomas		Lusk	Farmer	
Oct	1897	410	Williams	James	25-4-1889	Lusk	Labourer	
Sept	1896	404	Seaver	Thomas	25-3-1889	Commons	Farmer	
Aug	1894	408	Whelan	John	??-2-1891	Lusk	Labourer	
Feb	1895	433	Mathews	Edward		Commons	Farmer	
Feb	1896	435	Sweetman	John	28-3-1892	Lusk	Labourer	
May	1896	439	Devine	John	18-7-1892	Lusk	Labourer	
June	1899	487	Murphy	Francis		Corduff	Herd	Hedgestown
Oct	1897	383	McCann	Thomas	1-11-1889	Lusk	Labourer	
Feb	1896	434	Rafferty	John	10-7-1891	Lusk	Labourer	
Nov	1896	449	Monks	Edward	10-6-1892	Rush+Lusk Station	Railway Porter	
Aug	1898	473	Boyle	Charles	10-11-1891	Oberstown	Deaceased	
Feb	1896	436	Maypother	Patrick	2-3-1892	Lusk	Labourer	
Nov	1896	441	Seaver	Michael	19-3-1891	Commons	Farmer	
Nov	1896	448	Dennis	Michael	23-10-1892	Lusk	Farmer	
Apr	1897	456	McCluskey	Patrick		Jordanstown	Farmer	
May	1897	457	Lamb	Joseph	14-6-1891	Ballaly	Herd	
Mar	1901	517	Sweetman	Joseph	13-5-1894	Balcunnin	Farmer	Balcunnin
May	1896	438	Clarke	Thomas		Lusk	Farmer	

Month registered in the school	Year	Pupils Register No.	Pupils Surname	First Name	DOB	Place of Residence	Occupation of Parent/Guardian	Previous School, if any
Mar	1897	453	Doyle	Patrick	15-8-1893	Lusk	Labourer	
Jan	1899	437	Masterson	James	18-9-1892	Lusk	Labourer	
		455	Rafferty	Thomas	6-10-1893	Lusk	Labourer	
		458	Flanagan	James	4-10-1894	Lusk	Servant	
		460	Sweetman	William		Lusk	Farmer	
		468	Peppard	Thomas	8-2-1894	Lusk	Labourer	
		473	Dennis	Thomas	18-9-1894	Lusk	Farmer	
		503	Brogan	John	27-8-1891	Nth Common	Farmer	
		419	Kelly	Michael	19-1-1892	Lusk	Labourer	
		447	Clarke	James	29-1-1893	Lusk	Farmer	
		480	Halpin	William	28-8-1893	Nth Common	Carpenter	
		481	Hynes	John	21-10-1893	Nth Common	Deaceased	

Appendices

List of Boys 1909 to 1970

Note: Date of pupils' birth is shown in most but not all cases. Where the date of birth is shown and the date of starting school in column 1 and 2, it can be determined the age that the pupil started school.

Month registered in the school	Year	Pupils Register No.	Pupils Surname	First Name	DOB	Residence	Occupation of Parent/ Guardian	Previous School, if applicable
July	1900	509	Sweetman	Thomas	28-6-1894	Nth Common	Relieving Officer	
Mar	1901	469	Sweetman	Joseph	13-5-1893	Lusk	Labourer	
Mar	1902	530	Fay	Joseph	6-5-1890	Lusk	Labourer	Ballyboghill
Apr	1902	531	Murtagh	Vincent	12-4-1891	Lusk	Police Constable	Balbriggan
Sept	1902	543	Seaver	Thomas		Nth Common	Farmer	
Jan	1902	544	Sheridan	Owen	25-4-1890	Corduff	Gardener	Hedgestown
Jan	1902	545	Sheridan	Michael	27-5-1893	Corduff	Gardener	Hedgestown
May	1898	470	Seaver	John	14-6-1892	Nth Common	Farmer	
Nov	1898	477	Bambrick	William	14-2-1894	Lusk	Police Constable	
Apr	1899	483	Devine	Joseph		Lusk	Labourer	
July	1899	485	McCann	James		Lusk	Labourer	
Aug	1900	511	Clarke	George	12-9-1893	Kingstown	Farmer (Guardian)	
Dec	1899	493	McGee	Patrick	24-10-1893	Lusk	Drayman	
Apr	1900	497	Clarke	John		Lusk	Farmer	
July	1899	486	McCann	Joseph		Lusk	Labourer	
June	1900	503	McNally	Thomas	15-8-1897	Lusk	Farmer	
Nov	1900	514	Kiernan	James	4-10-1896	Lusk	Farmer	
Apr	1902	532	Murtagh	Bernard	6-2-1896	Lusk	Police Constable	
Feb	1903	546	Peters	Patrick		Lusk	Labourer	Balrothery
Mar	1903	548	Halpin	Patrick	??-3-1892	Lusk	Carpenter	Balcunnin
May	1903	549	Martin	Samuel	5-9-1895	Railway Station	Station Master	Rush
July	1903	554	Daly	John		Lusk	Labourer	Rush
Sept	1903	555	McCann	Peter		Lusk	Labourer	Rush
Sept	1903	556	Daly	Thomas		Lusk	Labourer	
Sept	1903	557	O'Kelly	James		Lusk	Labourer	
Sept	1903	558	Peters	James		Lusk	Labourer	

National Primary Education in the Village of Lusk

Month registered in the school	Year	Pupils Register No.	Pupils Surname	First Name	DOB	Residence	Occupation of Parent/Guardian	Previous School, if applicable
Sept	1903	559	Clarke	Francis		Lusk	Mason	
Nov	1903	560	Masterson	Thomas		Lusk	Labourer	
Jan	1904	561	Murtagh	Patrick			Policeman	
Mar	1904	562	Johnson	Arthur			Labourer	
June	1904	563	Doyle	William			Labourer	
June	1904	564	Sweetman	Richard			Relieving Officer	
Dec	1903	565	Weston	Thomas			Labourer	
Aug	1904	566	Peters	William	??-3-1901	Lusk	Labourer	
Aug	1904	549	Hurley	Thomas	??-10-1892	Lusk	Labourer	Balcunnin
Aug	1904	560	Clinton	George	??-3-1894	Lusk	Engineer	Kingsland
Aug	1904	565	Martin	Thomas John	??-3-1900	Lusk	Station Master	
Sept	1904	567	Quinn	John	??-5-1902	Dalystown, Co. W'Meath	Car Man	Dalystown Co. W'Meath
Oct	1904	568	Daly	Andrew	?/-9-1901	Lusk	Farmer	
Oct	1904	569	Seaver	Chris	??-1-1900	Commons	Farmer	
Oct	1904	570	Sweetman	John	??-1-1901	Lusk	Farmer	
Nov	1904	571	Kiernan	Joseph	??-4-1901	Lusk	Farmer	
Dec	1904	572	Hughes	Thomas	??-12-1898	Railway Station	Signalman	
Jan	1905	573	Bird	Reginald T	??-7-1899	Lusk	Soldier	
Feb	1905	574	Hogan	Edward	??-8-1900	Lusk	Labourer	
May	1905	575	Hanratty	Edward	??-3-1895	Lusk	Labourer	Darver, Co. Louth
May	1905	576	Groves	Henry	??-3-1899	Lusk	Labourer	
May	1905	577	Groves	Robert	??-3-1890	Lusk	Labourer	
June	1905	578	Martin	Laurence	??-6-1890	Lusk	Farmer	
Aug	1905	579	Norton	John	??-8-1896	Lusk	Army Pensioner	Richmond Bks.
Sept	1905	580	McCann	James	??-8-1896	Railway Station	Porter	
Oct	1905	581	Fitzsimons	John	??-5-1894	Nth Common	Labourer	Baldoyle NS
Jan	1906		Connolly	Laur.	??-1-1902	Lusk	Labourer	
Jan	1906	582	Connolly	Joseph	??-1-1902	Lusk	Labourer	
Jan	1906	583	Daly	Patrick	??-2-1901	Lusk	Labourer	
Jan	1906	584	Foster	Harry T	??-2-1901	Lusk	Soldier	

Appendices

Month registered in the school	Year	Pupils Register No.	Pupils Surname	First Name	DOB	Residence	Occupation of Parent/Guardian	Previous School, if applicable
Feb	1906	585	Foster	Arthur L	??-2-1902	Lusk	Soldier	
Mar	1905	586	Maguire	Ed.	??-3-1896	Rogerstown	Labourer	Corduff
Mar	1906	587	McNally	George	??-3-1902	Lusk	Farmer	
Mar	1906	588	Masterson	Patrick	??-3-1903	Lusk	Labourer	
Apr	1906	589	Thacher	Lionel	??-4-1900	Lusk	Soldier	
Apr	1906	510	Reilly	John	??-11-1902	Lusk	Labourer	
Apr	1906	511	Rooney	James J	??-4-1904	Lusk	Farmer	
Apr	1906	512	Barror	Patrick	??-4-1894	Lusk	Labourer	Kilworth, Waterford
May	1906	513	Barror	Edward	??-4-1903	Lusk	Labourer	
June	1906	514	Peppard	John J	??-6-1901	Corduff	Labourer	
July	1906	515	Morgan	John	??-7-1902	Lusk	Farmer	
Aug	1906	516	Grimes	William	??-8-1902	Lusk	Labourer	
Oct	1906	517	Connor	Thomas	??-9-1903	Lusk	Labourer	
Dec	1906	518	Harrison	James	??12-1899	Lusk	Labourer	
Dec	1906	519	Harrison	Louis	??-12-1900	Lusk	Labourer	
Jan	1907	520	Griffin	Philip	??-4-1895	Corduff	Labourer	
Jan	1907	521	Kelly	Richard	??-3-1895	Corduff	Labourer	
Apr	1907	522	Hughes	Patrick J	??-2-1902	Railway Station	Signalman	
Apr	1907	523	Haslam	John Philip	??-3-1903	Lusk	Engineer	
Apr	1907	524	Seaver	James	??-7-1901	Commons	Farmer	
June	1907	525	Devine	Francis	??-7-1903	Lusk	Labour	
Aug	1907	526	McNally	Thomas		Lusk	Farmer	
Aug	1907	527	Hogan	Thomas	??-1-1903	Lusk	Labourer	
Nov	1907	528	McMahon	Christopher	??-12-1902	Lusk	Labourer	
Jan	1908	529	Mescal	John	??-4-1904	Lusk	Constable RIC	
Feb	1908	530	Donnelly	Laurence	28/05/1903	Lusk	Postman and Shopkeeper	
Feb	1908	531	Healy	Christopher	??-8-1903	Rogerstown	Farmer	
Apr	1908	532	Davis	James		Lusk	Labourer	
June	1908	533	Davis	Kevin		Lusk	Labourer	
June	1908	534	McMahon	James	??-7-1904	Lusk	Labourer	

Month registered in the school	Year	Pupils Register No.	Pupils Surname	First Name	DOB	Residence	Occupation of Parent/Guardian	Previous School, if applicable
June	1902	538	Doyle	John	??-6-1898	Lusk	Labourer	
May	1903	551	Gough	Patrick	??-3-1900	Commons	Labourer	
June	1903	552	Masterson	Michael	??-4-1899	Lusk	Labourer	
Apr	1902	533	Doyle	Thomas	??-5-1897	Lusk	Labourer	
Apr	1901	525	Peters	Richard	??-6-1897	Lusk	Labourer	
Aug	1902	540	Clarke	Joseph	??-6-1899	Lusk	Labourer	
Sept	1903	556	Daly	Thomas	??-3-1900	Lusk	Labourer	
May	1902	537	Fulham	Thomas	??-4-1898	Lusk	Labourer	
June	1903	553	Seaver	Michael	??-6-1898	Commons	Farmer	
Aug	1900	512	McCann	Patrick	??-4-1897	Lusk	Farmer	
Apr	1901	523	Gough	James	??-6-1897	Commons	Labourer	
Sept	1901	528	Murphy	Francis	??-1-1898	Lusk	Nurse	
Apr	1900	498	Sweetman	Christopher	??-6-1896	Lusk	Farmer	
Apr	1900	497	Clarke	John	??-7-1896	Lusk	Farmer	
Apr	1900	518	McNally	John	??-10-1896	Lusk	Farmer	
Sept	1901	527	Clarke	Richard	??-4-1897	Lusk	Farmer	
Apr	1902	535	Morgan	Francis	??-5-1896	Bride Tree	Farmer	
Aug	1902	541	Thomson	Thomas	??-6-1897	Commons	Farmer	
Aug	1902	542	Monks	James	??-7-1897	Railway Station	Signalman	
Aug	1908	35	Kelly	James		Lusk	Labourer	
Aug	1908	36	Browne	John		Lusk	Labourer	Phibsborough
Nov	1908	37	MacArthur	Louis		Military Farm	In charge of military canteen	
Nov	1908	38	McGavin	Luke	1-6-1898	Lusk	Labourer	Kilcoole Co. Wicklow
May	1909	39	Haslam	Charles	20/01/1906	Lusk	Engineer	
May	1909	40	Carton	James	??-81905	Lusk	Labourer	
June	1909	41	Lenehan	Patrick	16-6-1899	Lusk	Cattle Dealer	Swords
June	1909	42	Lenehan	William	22/03/1901	Lusk	Cattle Dealer	Swords
June	1909	43	O'Dea	Joseph	??-4-1903	The Commons	Ironmonger (Dubliin)	Domnick St. Convent
June	1909	44	McNally	Peter	??-3-1905	Lusk	Farmer	
June	1909	45	McNally	John	??-3-1905	Lusk	Farmer	

Appendices

Month registered in the school	Year	Pupils Register No.	Pupils Surname	First Name	DOB	Residence	Occupation of Parent/Guardian	Previous School, if applicable
June	1909	46	Dennis	Thomas	??-6-1906	Lusk	Labourer	
June	1909	47	Donovan	Daniel		Rogerstown	Tinsmith	
June	1909	48	Donovan	James		Rogerstown	Tinsmith	
June	1909	49	Donovan	Martin		Rogerstown	Tinsmith	
July	1909	50	Day	Thomas		Lusk	Labourer	
Mar	1909	51	Gormley	Francis	??-7-1903	Railway Station	GNR Porter (Railway)	
Aug	1909	52	Hand	Thomas	02/06/1906	Lusk	Farmer	
Aug	1909	53	Daly	John		Lusk	Labourer	
Aug	1909	54	Hoare	Joseph Kevin	??-1-1905	Commons	Farmer	
Oct	1909	55	Clarke	Christy	??-11-1905	Lusk	Labourer	
Jan	1910	56	Hogan	Patrick	??-6-1906	Lusk	Labourer	
Apr	1910	57	Hoare	Thomas		Commons	Farmer	
May	1910	58	Doyle	Nicholas	08/12/1905	Commons	Labourer	
May	1910	59	Brown	Charles	03/11/1906	Commons	Labourer	
May	1910	60	Clarke	John	??-7-1906	Lusk	Labourer	
May	1910	61	Austin	William	15/02/1905	Gov. Farm	Soldier	
June	1910	62	Miles	William Christopher	??-12-1904	Gov. Farm	Soldier	
June	1910	63	Miles	Joseph	??-4-1906	Gov. Farm	Soldier	
June	1910	64	Courtney	Luke		Lusk	Stud Groom	Donabate
Aug	1910	65	Smeed	George	??-11-1904	Gov. Farm	Soldier	
Aug	1910	66	Daly	John	??-4-1907	Lusk	Labourer	
Nov	1910	67	Dennis	Francis		Lusk	Labourer	
Feb	1911	68	Cowley	Robert	??-2-1908	Lusk	Harness Maker	
Apr	1911	69	McNally	William	??-3-1907	Lusk	Farmer	
May	1911	70	Hoare	John	23/08/1906	The Commons	Farmer	
May	1911	71	Russell	James	21/01/1907	Railway Rd.	Labourer	
May	1911	72	Dennis	John	15/11/1907	Lusk	Labourer	
May	1911	73	Barrett	John William	12/02/1906	Ballaly	Labourer	
June	1911	74	Morgan	Brendan	??-5-1906	Bride Tree	Farmer	
Aug	1911	75	Grimes	Alphonsus	??-4-1907	Lusk	Labourer	

Month registered in the school	Year	Pupils Register No.	Pupils Surname	First Name	DOB	Residence	Occupation of Parent/Guardian	Previous School, if applicable
Nov	1911	76	Carton	Matthew	04/02/1908	Lusk	Labourer	
Mar	1912	77	Browne	Alphonsus	??-12-1907	Lusk	Labourer	
Apr	1912	78	Owens	Patrick Joseph	??-8-1908	Lusk	Harness Maker	
May	1912	79	Gosson	John Joseph	??-3-1907	The Commons	Labourer	
June	1912	80	Grimes	Thomas	15/05/1909	Lusk	Labourer	
Aug	1912	81	Donnelly	James	13/05/1908	Lusk	Post Office Clerk	
Aug	1912	82	Clifford	Charles	20/05/1905	Bride Tree	Soldier	
Sept	1912	83	Sherry	Daniel	??-10-1908	Lusk	Labourer	
Sept	1912	84	Monks	James	??-9-1908	Lusk	Van Driver	
Sept	1912	85	Peters	Michael	??-3-1909	Lusk	Labourer	
Feb	1913	87	Smeed	George J		Lusk	Soldier	
Feb	1913	86	Maguire	Peter	??-6-1893	Lusk	PL Quarters	Balrothery Union
Feb	1913	88	Maguire	Thomas	??-6-1899	Lusk	PL Quarters	Balrothery Union
Feb	1913	89	Maguire	Peter	??-1-1897	Lusk	PL Quarters	Balrothery Union
Aug	1912	81	Donnelly	James	??-2-1908	Lusk	Labourer	
Aug	1912	555	McCann	Peter	??-1-1901	Lusk	Farmer	
Aug	1912	59	Browne	Charles	??-6-1907	Lusk	Labourer	
Aug	1912	55	Clarke	Christy	??-10-1906	Lusk	Labourer	
Aug	1912	60	Clarke	John	??-3-1908	Lusk	Labourer	
Apr	1913	567	Donnelly	Bernard	??-12-1908	Lusk	Labourer	
Apr	1913	568	Magee	Joseph	??-10-1908	Lusk	Farmer	
May	1913	569	Fay	John	??3-1909	Lusk	Labourer	
June	1913	570	Gosson	Peter	??-4-1909	Lusk	Farmer	
June	1913	571	Monks	Brendan	??-5-1909	Lusk	Van Driver	
Nov	1913	572	Hand	Robert	23/02/1910	Lusk	Farmer	
Nov	1913	573	Hurley	Charles	??-2-1909	Lusk	Farmer	
Nov	1913	574	Sherwin	Nicholas	??-2-1910	Lusk	Farmer	
Nov	1913	575	Hogan	Francis	??-81909	Lusk	Labourer	
Oct	1913	576	Magee	Christopher	10/07/1910	Lusk	Releiving Officer	
Mar	1914	577	Miles	Horace	??4-1909	Gov. Farm	Soldier	

Appendices

Month registered in the school	Year	Pupils Register No.	Pupils Surname	First Name	DOB	Residence	Occupation of Parent/Guardian	Previous School, if applicable
Apr	1914	578	Doyle	Joseph	??-3-1910	Raheny	Labourer	
Apr	1914	579	Sherwin	Nicholas	??-1-1909	Station Rd.	Labourer	
May	1914	580	Hogan	George	??-2-1909	Lusk	Labourer	
July	1914	581	Peacock	Sydney	??-7-1907	Gov. Farm	Soldier	
July	1914	582	Murphy	Seamus	??-7-1910	Lusk	Carpenter	
Aug	1914	583	Fulham	Joseph	??-7-1907	Lusk	Farmer	
Aug	1914	584	Mills	Reginald	01/07/1908	Farm, Lusk	Soldier	
Aug	1914	585	Hall	Robert	06/07/1909	Farm, Lusk	Soldier	
Aug	1914	586	O'Brien	Thomas	02/10/1908	Station Rd.	Labourer	
Sept	1914	587	O'Brien	John	01/07/1909	Station Rd.	Railway Porter	
Sept	1914	106	Davis	Arthur	06/01/1910	Lusk	Soldier	
Apr	1914	565	Doyle	Joseph	06/03/1910	Great Common	Labourer	
Mar	1915	107	Cowley	Seamus	10/11/1911	Lusk	Harness Maker	
Mar	1915	108	Bentley	William	10/12/1908	Lusk	Carrier	
Apr	1915	109	Monks	Eamon	09/03/1912	Lusk	Van Driver	
Apr	1915	110	Russell	William	07/01/1911	Lusk	Labourer	
May	1915	111	Fay	Thomas	07/01/1911	Lusk	Labourer	
May	1915	112	Hurley	Charles	06/03/1909	Lusk	Labourer	
May	1915	113	Magee	Christopher	10/03/1909	Lusk	Releiving Officer	Originally registered in 1913
June	1915	114	Daly	James	09/10/1909	Lusk	Labourer	Originally registered in 1913
June	1915	115	Magee	William	01/09/1909	Great Common	Postman	
June	1915	116	Bentley	Owen	22/02/1911	Lusk	Carrier	
June	1915		Jolly	Albert	07/01/1904	Gov. Farm	Soldier	
Aug	1915	118	McNally	Richard	15/08/1910	Lusk	Farmer	
Aug	1915	119	Groves	Thomas	06/01/1908	Lusk	Labourer	
Aug	1915	120	Gallagher	James	29/07/1911	Station Rd.	Labourer	
Sept	1915	121	Williams	William	11/10/1912	Lusk	Soldier	
May	1916	122	Connolly	Michael	05/12/1910	Lusk	Soldier	
Aug	1916	125	Wade	John	08/03/1907	Lusk	Labourer	Rush
Aug	1916	124	Sherwin	Eugene	07/04/1912	Lusk	Labourer	
June	1913	102	Williams	John	06/07/1911	Lusk	Labourer	

Month registered in the school	Year	Pupils Register No.	Pupils Surname	First Name	DOB	Residence	Occupation of Parent/Guardian	Previous School, if applicable
Jan	1917	127	Morgan	Joseph P Myles	15/03/1911	Bride Tree	Farmer	
Apr	1917	128	Gosson	Michael	11/12/1912	Nth Common	Labourer	
Apr	1917	129	Wade	Richard	14/04/1912	Rogerstown	Labourer	
May	1917	130	Hogan	James	10/01/1913	Lusk	Labourer	
May	1917	131	Sherwin	Joseph	06/09/1913	Lusk	Labourer	
June	1917	132	Bentley	James	12/07/1913	Lusk	Carrier	
June	1917	133	Deane	John	22/08/1905	Gov. Farm	Blacksmith	
June	1917	134	Deane	Christopher	07/01/1907	Gov. Farm	Blacksmith	
June	1917	132	O'Sullivan	Bartholomew	22/03/1907	Lusk	Farmer	
Aug	1917	138	McNally	Christopher	07/03/1913	Lusk	Farmer	
Aug	1917	139	Skelly	Thomas	17/06/1913	Lusk	Dealer	
Sept	1917	140	McCann	Patrick	12/05/1909	Lusk	Shopkeeper	
Sept	1917	141	Nicholas	John	13/01/1908	Lusk	Farmer	
Sept	1917	142	Nicholas	George	15/09/1911	Lusk	Farmer	
Oct	1917	143	Browne	David	??-1-1913	Lusk	Soldier	
Jan	1918	144	Derham	Richard	??-10-1911	Great Common	Farmer	
Apr	1918	145	Russell	Patrick	??-1-1914	Lusk	Labourer	
June	1918	146	Sweetman	Joseph	15/03/1914	Lusk	Farmer	
June	1918	147	Dennis	John V.	??-2-1914	Rogerstown	Labourer	
June	1918	148	Deane	Richard	??-2-1915	Rogerstown	Blacksmith	
June	1918	149	Daly	Nicholas	??-??-1914	Lusk	Labourer	
June	1918	150	Daly	Robert	??-5-1914	Lusk	Labourer	
Mar	19??	126	Butler	Maurice	??-1-1908	Lusk	Widow	
Oct	1912	86	Browne	Jem	??-8-1909	Lusk	Carpenter	
Apr	1916	122	Keane	Robert	??-6-1910	Lusk	clerk	
Oct	1910	123	Browne	Michael	??-7-1915	Lusk	Soldier	
Aug	1918	151	Ryan	Thomas	??-11-1911	Lusk	Labourer	
Aug	1918	152	Bentley	Richard	??-8-1915	Lusk	Labourer	
Aug	1918	153	Gosson	Thomas	??-5-1918	Nth Common	Labourer	
Apr	1919	154	Malone	Joseph	13/12/1912	Lusk	Labourer	

Appendices

Month registered in the school	Year	Pupils Register No.	Pupils Surname	First Name	DOB	Residence	Occupation of Parent/Guardian	Previous School, if applicable
Apr	1919	155	Malone	Seamus	06/12/1914	Lusk	Labourer	
Apr	1919	156	Russell	Christy	01/09/1915	Lusk	Labourer	
May	1919	157	McCann	Michael	06/02/1913	Dromin	Herd	
May	1919	158 ?	Carton	Joseph	03/11/1915	Lusk	Labourer	
Apr	1919	158	Malone	Peter	22/03/1911	Lusk	Labourer	
Sept	1919	159	Malone	Michael	07/09/1916	Lusk	Labourer	
Sept	1919	160	Gallagher	Patrick	16/07/1915	Rogerstown	Labourer	
Sept	1919	165	Skelly	Michael	20/04/1916	Lusk	Dealer	
June	1920	161	Cowley	William (Liam)	05/02/1917	Lusk	Harness Maker	
June	1920	172	O'Brien	Peter	10/02/1915	Railway Station	Signalman	
Aug	1920	166	Hampton	Louis	19/09/1907	Lusk	Labourer	
Aug	1920	167	Lennon	John	13/05/1916	Lusk	Chauffeur	
Nov	1920	168	Bentley	Michael	27/09/1917	Lusk	Labourer	
Feb	1921	169	Langan	Thomas	13/05/1914	Lusk	Soldier	
Mar	1921	170	Dorney	Thomas	16/02/1912	Lusk	Shopkeeper	
Apr	1921	171	Wade	William	03/12/1914	Rogerstown	Labourer	
May	1921	172	Russell	James	23/12/1917	Lusk	Labourer	
May	1921	173	Cruise	Patrick	17/05/1916	Lusk	Tailor	
May	1921	175	Hogan	Seamus	13/04/1914	Lusk	Labourer	
May	1921	182	Donnelly	Frank	14/08/1909	Lusk	Labourer	Swords
Jan	1922	175 ?	Byrne	James	12/07/1913	Lusk	Labourer	Whitefriar St.
Apr	1922	176	Dennis	Joseph	17/01/1919	Lusk	Labourer	
May	1922	177	Jenkinson	Thomas	13/07/1917	Lusk	Poor Law Clerk	
May	1922	178	Seaver	Michael	12/09/1916	Nth Common	Farmer	
May	1922	179	O'Brien	Frank	27/02/1916	Railway Station	Signalman	
May	1922	180	Deane	Joseph	13/02/1918	Rogerstown	Blacksmith	
May	1922	181	Fay	Frank	10/04/1916	Rogerstown	Labourer	
Oct	1922	182	Fay	Patrick	09/05/1918	Rogerstown	Labourer	
Jan	1923	183	Browne	Jack	08/11/1918	Lusk	Carpenter	
Mar	1923	184	Magee	John V.	20/01/1919	Nth Common	Engineer	
Apr	1923	185	Magee	Patrick	16/04/1918	Nth Common	Postman	

Month registered in the school	Year	Pupils Register No.	Pupils Surname	First Name	DOB	Residence	Occupation of Parent/Guardian	Previous School, if applicable
Apr	1923	186	Seaver	Patrick	16/05/1919	Nth Common	Farmer	
Sept	1923	187	Bentley	John	28/02/1920	Lusk	Labourer	
Sept	1923	188	O'Brien	Eugene	12/03/1918	Railway Station	Railway Porter	
Sept	1923	189	Hanratty	Patrick	14/10/1919	Lusk	Soldier	
Sept	1923	190	Scally	Patrick	12/02/1919	Lusk	Carter	
May	1921	174	McGee	Michael	16/12/1917	Nth Common	Postman	
Oct	1922	165	Egan	John	16/10/1912	Lusk	Widow	
May	1924	191	McCann	Matthew	07/07/1919	Lusk	Labourer	
May	1924	192	Carton	John	10/06/1920	Lusk	Labourer	
June	1924	193	Clarke	Patrick	02/06/1919	Nth Common	Labourer	
Sept	1924	194	Magee	Matthew	07/04/1921	Lusk	Farmer	
Sept	1924	195	Connolly	Michael	09/07/1920		Mental Hosp. Attendant	
Sept	1924	196	Boylan	Thomas	16/08/1920	Lusk	Blacksmith	
Sept	1924	197	Langan	Seamus	13/08/1919	Lusk	Shopkeeper	
Apr	1925	198	Jenkinson	Christy	12/04/1920	Lusk	Clerk	
June	1925	199	Kavanagh	John	13/07/1921	Lusk	Labourer	
June	1925	200	Boylan	Michael	06/04/1922	Lusk	Blacksmith	
Sept	1925	201	Skelly	Seamus	05/08/1922	Lusk	Labourer	
Sept	1925	202	Carton	Nicholas	17/07/1922	Lusk	Labourer	
Sept	1925	203	Monks	Enda	05/07/1921	Lusk	Van Driver	
Sept	1925	204	O'Ceallaig	Padraig	18/03/1922	Lusk	Cycle Agent	
Nov	1925	205	McNally	Seamus	16/10/1922	Lusk	Farmer	
Nov	1925	206	Devine	Richard M	15/04/1921	Lusk	Labourer	
Nov	1925	207	Devine	Richard J	13/12/1920	Lusk	Labourer	
Nov	1925	208	Bentley	Oliver	17/10/1922	Lusk	Labourer	
Nov	1925	209	Hoey	William	13/04/1920	Rathmooney	Farmer	
May	1926	211	O'Brien	Art	11/10/1921	Rogerstown	Railway Porter	
Mar	1926	210	Kavanagh	Thomas	23/05/1923	Lusk	Labourer	
Mar	1927	212	Conlon	Michael	02/09/1920	Bride Tree	Labourer	Loretto, Dublin
Mar	1927	213	Conlon	Charles	18/11/1921	Bride Tree	Labourer	
Apr	1927	214	Jenkinson	William	24/06/1923	Lusk	Clerk	

Appendices

Month registered in the school	Year	Pupils Register No.	Pupils Surname	First Name	DOB	Residence	Occupation of Parent/Guardian	Previous School, if applicable
Apr	1927	215	Boylan	Laurence	20/05/1923	Lusk	Blacksmith	
May	1927	216	Ferguson	John	24/03/1922	Lusk	Asylum Attd.	
June	1927	217	Owens	David	14/03/1922	Rogerstown	Saddler	
Apr	1928	218	Wright	Nicholas E	13/11/1921	Rogerstown	Labourer	
Apr	1928	219	Carton	Peter	01/05/1924	Lusk	Labourer	
Feb	1928	220	Hoey	Michael	04/06/1923	Rathmooney	Farmer	
May	1928	221	Magee	Gerard	01/04/1923	Lusk	Postman	
May	1928	222	Devine	Aidan	03/02/1923	Ratheny	Labourer	
May	1928	223	Purcell	Thomas	04/05/1916	No official Res.	Tinker	
June	1928	224	Fay	Oliver	08/06/1922	Rogerstown	Labourer	
Sept	1928	225	Davis	George	22/09/1923	Lusk	Labourer	
Sept	1928	226	Dennis	Michael	03/08/1924	Ballaly	Labourer	
Oct	1928	227	Whelan	Edward	??-1-1916	Balrothery Union	Deaceased	Rush
Oct	1928	228	Whelan	Raymond	??-11-1919	Balrothery Union	Deaceased	Rush
Dec	1928	229	O'Brien	John	11/01/1917	Balrothery Union	Stewart	Ashbourne
Dec	1928	230	O'Brien	Martin	10/07/1918	Balrothery Union	Stewart	Ashbourne
Jan	1929	231	Neary	Michael	??-3-1922	Rogerstown Lane	Ex-Soldier	Wharf Rd. NS Dublin
Mar	1929	232	O'Brien	Patrick	06/07/1915	Balrothery Union	Stewart	Ashbourne
Apr	1929	233	O'Ceallaig	Sean	12/11/1924	Lusk	Cycle Mechanic	
Apr	1929	234	Maypother	James	26/02/1924	Commons	Labourer	
Sept	1929	235	Nulty	Joseph	09/09/1923	Station Cottages	Signalman	
Sept	1929	236	McGirl	Patrick J	17/01/1924	Gov. Farm	Labourer	
Sept	1929	237	Groves	Patrick	??-1-1922	Ballymaguire	Herd	Donnycarney Co. Meath
Nov	1929	238	McKenna	Stephen	15/03/1929	Lusk	Asylum Attd.	Portrane NS
Nov	1929	239	McKenna	Thomas	14/06/1924	Lusk	Asylum Attd.	Portrane NS
Sept	1929	240	Savage	John	04/10/1918	Balrothery Union	Labourer	Swords NS
Feb	1930	241	Boylan	Patrick	09/05/1925	Lusk	Blacksmith	

Month registered in the school	Year	Pupils Register No.	Pupils Surname	First Name	DOB	Residence	Occupation of Parent/Guardian	Previous School, if applicable
Apr	1930	242	McKenna	John	04/05/1925	Lusk	Asylum Attd.	Portrane NS
Apr	1930	243	Brogan	John	13/08/1925	Lusk	Labourer	
Apr	1930	244	Connolly	Joseph	11/03/1922	Lusk	Orphan	East Wall Dublin
Apr	1930	245	Edwards	Henry	05/10/1921	Lusk	Orphan	Kings Inn St Dublin
June	1930	246	Whelan	Patrick	14/10/1924	Balrothery Union	Orphan	
Sept	1930	247	Connor	Nicholas	28/04/1923	Station Rd.	Labourer	Hedgestown
Sept	1930	248	Connolly	Laurence	06/01/1926	Lusk		
Sept	1930	249	Brogan	Thomas	02/02/1927	Lusk	Labourer	
Nov	1930	250	Connor	Brendan	??-9-1924	Station Rd.	Labourer	Hedgestown
Nov	1930	251	Redmond	Thomas	22/08/1918	Balrothery	Labourer	Rush
Nov	1930	252	Redmond	Patrick	11/03/1920	Balrothery	Labourer	Rush
Nov	1930	253	Woods	Patrick	??-5-1923	Railway Station	Porter	Ardee
Apr	1931	254	Dennis	Thomas	11-9-192?	Ballaly	Labourer	
Apr	1931	255	Skelly	Sean	11/03/1928	Lusk	Labourer	
May	1931	256	Hanratty	James	14/02/1928	Balrothery Union	Labourer	
May	1931	257	Maypother	Christopher	14/09/1926	Ratheny	Labourer	
May	1931	258	Murray	Jeremiah	23/12/1925	Lusk	Publican	
May	1931	259	Kelly	Kevin	19/11/1927	Lusk	Cycle Mechanic	
July	1932	265	Doyle	John	24/07/1926	Balrothery Union	Labourer	
July	1932	266	Walsh	Thomas	02/09/1927	Balrothery Union	Labourer	
Sept	1932	267	Spencer	Patrick	14/08/1927	Lusk	Asylum Attd.	
Oct	1932	268	Delaney	Alexander Joseph	??-2-1928	Commons	Orphan	
Mar	1933	269	Hussey	Eamon	??-12-1928	The Green	Orphan	
May	1933	270	Maypother	Nicholas	05/02/1928	Ratheney Cottages	Labourer	
May	1933	271	Casey	Laurence	22/11/1927	Rogerstown Lane	Orphan	
May	1933	272	Tracey	Alexander	25/01/1926	Shanterlands	Farmer	Clondalkin Convent
May	1933	273	Tracey	Sean	26/02/1928	Shanterlands	Farmer	Clondalkin Convent

Appendices

Month registered in the school	Year	Pupils Register No.	Pupils Surname	First Name	DOB	Residence	Occupation of Parent/Guardian	Previous School, if applicable
May	1933	274	McGirl	Desmond	25/05/1927	Gov. Farm	Labourer	
June	1933	275	O'Connor	Patrick	??-6-1928	Oberstown	Labourer	
Sept	1933	276	Sweetman	Thomas	10/08/1927	Lusk	Car Man	
Sept	1933	277	Sweetman	John	20/09/1928	Lusk	Car Man	
Sept	1933	278	Walsh	Nicholas	26/10/1929	Oberstown	Labourer	
Apr	1934	279	Oglesby	Christopher	??-12-1927	Lusk	Groom	
May	1934	280	Murray	Martin	11/05/1929	Lusk	Publican	
June	1934	281	Sweetman	Nicholas	15/04/1930	Lusk	Labourer	
Aug	1934	282	Jenkinson	Michael	15/06/1930	Lusk	Clerk	
Jan	1935	283	Sweetman	Tomas	23/12/1928	Lusk	Farmer	
Jan	1935	284	Sweetman	Sean	29/01/1930	Lusk	Farmer	
Jan	1935	285	Walsh	Sean	29/12/1930	Oberstown	Labourer	
Mar	1935	286	Donnelly	Thomas	13/09/1930	Rogerstown	Labourer	
Apr	1935	287	Aungier	John	23/12/1929	Lusk	Carpenter	
May	1935	288	Dennis	Desmond	04/04/1931	Ballaly	Labourer	
May	1935	289	Browne	John	06/04/1930	Lusk	Labourer	
Sept	1935	290	Brogan	Patrick	06/10/1930	Collinstown	Labourer	
Sept	1935	291	Gaffney	Cornelius	20/12/1930	Lusk	Labourer	
Sept	1935	292	McLeod	Richard	29/06/1931	Lusk		
Sept	1935	293	McCann	Joseph	21/12/1930	Lusk	Labourer	
Apr	1936	294	Carroll	Joseph	12/04/1929	Baldrummond	Labourer	Ballyboghill
Apr	1936	295	Kelly	Dermot	16/04/1931	Lusk	Cycle Mechanic	
Apr	1936	296	Dennigan	Samuel	23/05/1930	Irishtown	Farmer	
June	1936	297	Hogan	Noel	24/12/1930	Lusk	Labourer	
June	1936	298	Carroll	Thomas	08/06/1931	Johnstown	Labourer	
Aug	1936	299	Smith	William	24/01/1931	Commons	Labourer	
Aug	1936	300	Whelan	Thomas	05/09/1930	Lusk	Labourer	
Sept	1936	301	Devine	Matthew	29/05/1931	Ratheny	Labourer	
Oct	1936	302	Brophy	John	29/09/1930	Lusk	Ex-Army Officer	Ahascragh, Co. Galway
Oct	1936	303	Brophy	Daniel	02/09/1925	Lusk	Ex-Army Officer	Synge St. Dublin

Month registered in the school	Year	Pupils Register No.	Pupils Surname	First Name	DOB	Residence	Occupation of Parent/Guardian	Previous School, if applicable
Oct	1936	304	Cluskey	Patrick	23/06/1932	Lusk	Labourer	
Nov	1936	305	Kavanagh	Michael	05/11/1930	Lusk	Labourer	
Apr	1937	306	Dowling	Dermot	21/04/1931	Lusk	Garda Sgt.	
May	1937	307	Garrigan	John	09/06/1931	Lusk	Asylum Attd.	Portrane NS
May	1937	308	Garrigan	Paschal	19/06/1932	Lusk	Asylum Attd.	Portrane NS
May	1937	309	MacDonnell	Sean	05/04/1932	Lusk	Garda	
Sept	1937	310	Little	Joseph	15/08/1932	Station Rd.	Labourer	
Nov	1937	311	Carroll	John	05/03/1930	Johnstown	Labourer	Ballyboghill
Nov	1937	312	Carroll	Francis	18/05/1932	Johnstown	Labourer	Ballyboghill
Mar	1938	313	Brennan	Michael	05/03/1933	Lusk	Orphan	
Apr	1938	314	Hoey	James	03/10/1932	Rathmooney	Farmer	
May	1938	315	Hogan	Francis	18/05/1933	Newhaggard	Labourer	
May	1938	316	O'Connor	Bernard	04/08/1933	Newhaggard	Labourer	
May	1938	317	Hogan	George	01/05/1934	Newhaggard	Labourer	
June	1938	318	Fulham	Thomas	17/07/1932	Newhaggard	Dairy man	
Sept	1938	319	Brogan	Christopher	14/03/1933	Nth Commons	Labourer	
Jan	1939	320	McGuigan	Sean	??-12-1933	The Green	Sailor	
Jan	1939	321	O'Sullivan	Sean	??-12-1933	Lusk	Labourer	
Jan	1939	322	Thomson	John	??-7-1934	Lusk	Carpenter	
Apr	1939	323	Jenkinson	Noel	01/01/1932	Lusk	Clerk	
May	1939	324	Martin	Bartholonew	25/03/1934	Lusk	Labourer	
May	1939	325	Clogherty	Paul	18/02/1935	Lusk	Labourer	
May	1939	326	Collins	Patrick Noel	15/12/1933	Rathmooney	Labourer	
May	1939	327	Fay	James Joseph	11/12/1934	Station Cottages	Labourer	
May	1939	328	Hogan	Liam	16/01/1934	Lusk	Labourer	
May	1939	329	Fay	Laurence	03/02/1934	Railway Station	Railway Porter	
May	1939	330	Madden	Eric	09/07/1934	Lusk	Orphan	
Sept	1939	331	Hanratty	Thomas	14/08/1934	Rogerstown	Labourer	
Sept	1939	332	Donnelly	Bernard	28/07/1934	Rogerstown	Labourer	
Sept	1939	333	Boylan	Joseph	01/09/1934	Rogerstown	Blacksmith	

Appendices

Month registered in the school	Year	Pupils Register No.	Pupils Surname	First Name	DOB	Residence	Occupation of Parent/Guardian	Previous School, if applicable
Sept	1939	334	Grimes	William	21/05/1934	Lusk	Labourer	
Jan	1940	335	Oglesby	Matthew	08/11/1933	Newhaggard	Groom	
Jan	1940	336	Haslam	John	02/12/1933	Lusk	Carpet Layer	
Apr	1940	337	Murray	Liam	11/12/1933	Lusk	Publican	
Apr	1940	338	Brogan	Eamon	20/02/1935	Commons	Labourer	
Apr	1940	339	Kelly	John	19/07/1934	Newhaggard	Motor Driver	
Apr	1940	340	Hogan	Leo	06/12/1934	Newhaggard	Labourer	
Apr	1940	341	Dunne	Eamon	25/09/1934	Corduff	Teacher	Corduff
June	1940	342	Clarke	Patrick	12/02/1935	Lusk	Labourer	
June	1940	343	Clarke	Sean	17/05/1936	Lusk	Labourer	
Sept	1940	344	Sweetman	Noel	18/08/1935	Lusk	Farmer	
Sept	1940	345	Groves	Patrick Pierce	01/05/1934	Newhaggard	Labourer	Swords
Sept	1940	346	Groves	Thomas Paul	29/06/1935	Newhaggard	Labourer	Swords
Sept	1940	347	Peters	Richard	19/08/1934	Newhaggard	Labourer	
Sept	1940	348	Peters	George	03/10/1935	Newhaggard	Labourer	
Sept	1940	349	Micheau	Patrick	13/02/1935	Rogerstown	Cabinet Maker	
Nov	1940	350	Collins	James	16/11/1930	Man-O-War	Labourer	Hedgestown
Jan	1941	351	Sweetman	Charles	??-12-1934	Newhaggard	Labourer	
Apr	1941	352	Fitzgerald	Garrett Edward	06/02/1936	Lusk	Merchant	
Apr	1941	353	Kelly	Gabriel	22/04/1935	Rogerstown	Labourer	
May	1941	354	Taylor	John	22/12/1931	Commons	Moulder	St Charles, Glasgow
May	1941	355	Taylor	James	18/03/1934	Commons	Moulder	St Charles, Glasgow
May	1941	356	Taylor	Thomas	19/05/1935	Commons	Moulder	St Charles, Glasgow
Sept	1941	357	Sweetman	William J.	10/08/1936	Lusk		
Sept	1941	358	Sweetman	Christopher T.	25/01/1934	Lusk		
Sept	1941	359	O'Rourke	Conn	26/12/1932	Lusk	Contractor	Belturbet, Co. Cavan
Sept	1941	360	Patterson	John Francis	16/11/1936	Lusk	Retired, Circus	
Mar	1942	361	Byrne	Robert	05/07/1937	Lusk	Labourer	

Month registered in the school	Year	Pupils Register No.	Pupils Surname	First Name	DOB	Residence	Occupation of Parent/Guardian	Previous School, if applicable
Mar	1942	362	Bentley	Sean	27/12/1937	Lusk	Labourer	
Mar	1942	363	Garrigan	Fintan	17/02/1938	Lusk	Carrier	
Mar	1942	364	Nolan	James	29/10/1936	Lusk	Asylum Attd.	
Apr	1942	365	Nolan	Eric	29/10/1936	Lusk	Spinster	
Apr	1942	366	Thornton	Edward	06/06/1936	Lusk	Spinster	
Apr	1942	367	Clarke	Thomas	10/08/1936	Rogerstown	Labourer	
May	1942	368	McNally	Peter	11/04/1937	Lusk	Carrier	
May	1942	369	Dempsey	Desmond	??-10-1937	Lusk	Carpenter (foster parent)	
June	1942	370	Mansfield	Basil	09/06/1937	Lusk	Teacher	Hedgestown
June	1942	371	Mansfield	Leo	07/07/1934	Lusk	Teacher	Hedgestown
Aug	1942	372	Carey	Martin	26/11/1936	Lusk	Widow	
Aug	1942	373	Sherwin	Sean	28/07/1937	Lusk	Carpenter	
Sept	1942	374	Bentley	Patrick	28/10/1937	Lusk	Labourer	
Sept	1942	375	Gaffney	Peter	30/10/1937	Lusk	Labourer	
Sept	1942	376	Wright	Michael	20/02/1936	Lusk	Labourer	
Sept	1942	377	Knott	Thomas	29/05/1936	Rogerstown	Labourer	
Apr	1943	378	Hynes	Seamus	17/05/1937	Rallykaystown	Farmer	
May	1943	379	Bentley (W)	John	12/06/1935	Commons	Labourer	
May	1943	380	Brogan	Matthew	30/09/1937	Commons	Labourer	
June	1943	381	Micheau	John	13/10/1937	Lusk	Cabinet Maker	Weaver Sq. Dublin
Sept	1943	382	Donnelly	James	03/08/1937	Rogerstown	Labourer	
Sept	1943	383	McCann	James	29/07/1937	Lusk	Labourer	
Sept	1943	384	Bentley	Anthony	05/09/1939	Lusk	Carrier	
Sept	1943	385	Peters	William	03/09/1936	Newhaggard	Labourer	
Nov	1943	386	Grimes	Peter	21/02/1938	Lusk	Bread Van Driver	
Apr	1944	387	Browne	Dermot	09/05/1938	Lusk	Labourer	
Apr	1944	388	Neary	Leo Patrick	29/05/1939	Lusk	Labourer	
Apr	1944	389	Dennis	Francis	30/03/1938	Lusk	Labourer	
June	1944	390	Collier	Thomas	19/06/1936	Lusk	Hairdresser	Crumlin, Dublin
June	1944	391	Collier	Stephen	07/05/1932	Lusk	Hairdresser	Crumlin, Dublin

Appendices

Month registered in the school	Year	Pupils Register No.	Pupils Surname	First Name	DOB	Residence	Occupation of Parent/Guardian	Previous School, if applicable
Sept	1944	392	Garrigan	Brendan	27/07/1940	Lusk	Asylum Attd.	
Sept	1944	393	Bentley	Eugene	05/04/1940	Lusk	Labourer	
Sept	1944	394	Kelly	Charles	19/05/1938	Newhaggard	Labourer	
Jan	1945	395	Dennis	Richard	01/04/1940	Lusk	Labourer	
Feb	1945	396	Peters	Raymond	01/06/1939	Newhaggard	Labourer	
Mar	1945	397	Gough	Anthony	25/04/1939	Lusk	Labourer	
Apr	1945	398	Sherry	William	05/11/1939	Lusk	Asylum Attd.	
Apr	1945	399	Monks	Brian	02/04/1940	Lusk	Plasterer	
Apr	1945	400	Markey	John	13/11/1939	Railway Station	Railway Linesman	
Apr	1945	401	McNally	George	23/11/1939	Lusk	Carrier	
June	1945	402	Hogan	Thomas	31/12/1939	The Green	Labourer	
Aug	1945	403	Grimes	Thomas	23/08/1939	Dublin Rd.	Vanman	
Aug	1945	404	Fulham	Richard	06/01/1939	Lusk	Vanman	
Aug	1945	405	Fulham	Patrick	11/04/1940	Lusk	Vanman	
Sept	1945	406	Clarke	Patrick	31/03/1939	Rogerstown	Labourer	
Sept	1945	407	Rogan	Seamus	26/07/1940	Lusk	Carrier	
May	1945	408	Peters	Gerard	23/07/1940	Newhaggard	Labourer	
May	1946	409	Clare	Liam	20/01/1941	Lusk	Carpenter	
May	1946	410	Clare	Patrick	02/02/1942	Lusk	Carpenter	
May	1946	411	Daly	Patrick	06/05/1941	Lusk	Market Gardener	
May	1946	412	Carton	Anthony	05/01/1942	Lusk	Mason	
July	1946	413	Dennis	Anthony	24/06/1941	Lusk	Labourer	
Sept	1946	414	Scally	Richard	01/01/1941	Lusk	Labourer	
Sept	1946	415	Kelly	Martin	01/04/1940	Newhaggard	Mechanic	
Nov	1946	416	Markey	Noel	25/12/1940	Railway Station	Railway Linesman	
Apr	1947	417	Clarke	John	26/07/1941	Rogerstown	Labourer	
May	1947	418	Daly	Thomas	12/04/1943	Lusk	Labourer	
May	1947	419	Sherwin	Enda	08/07/1941	Ballaly	Labourer	
May	1947	420	Peters	Vincent	28/04/1941	Newhaggard	Labourer	
June	1947	421	Gaffney	Macculin	06/01/1943	Lusk	Labourer	
June	1947	422	Oglesby	Noel	06/01/1941	Newhaggard	Labourer	

Month registered in the school	Year	Pupils Register No.	Pupils Surname	First Name	DOB	Residence	Occupation of Parent/Guardian	Previous School, if applicable
June	1947	423	Shortt	Dominick	03/01/1942	Rush Rd.	Railway Clerk	
Sept	1947	424	Grimes	Bernard	27/03/1942	Dublin Rd.	Vanman	
Sept	1947	425	Cruise	Michael	23/04/1943	Lusk	Carpenter	
Sept	1947	426	Knott	Noel	28/11/1940	Rogerstown Lane	Labourer	
Oct	1947	427	Bentley	George	29/09/1943	Lusk	Labourer	
Nov	1947	428	Kelly	Thomas Clement	23/09/1943	Lusk	Aer Lingus Emp.	
Feb	1948	429	Clare	Richard	04/07/1943	Lusk	Carpenter	
Apr	1948	430	Monks	Brendan	03/07/1943	Lusk	Plasterer	
May	1948	431	Neary	Denis	02/05/1944	Lusk	Labourer	
May	1948	432	Gough	Breffni	19/02/1943	Lusk	Labourer	
May	1948	433	Wall	Sean	16/05/1944	Lusk	Civil Servant	
May	1948	434	Fitzgerald	Martin	27/02/1943	Lusk	Garda	
June	1948	435	McCann	Christopher	08/09/1943	Lusk	Labourer	
Sept	1948	436	Lyons	Anthony Francis	28/11/1937	Lusk	Showman	Ballyboghill
Sept	1948	437	Lyons	Keith David	08/09/1939	Lusk	Showman	Ballyboghill
Sept	1948	438	Lyons	Derek Christopher	16/06/1941	Lusk	Showman	Ballyboghill
Sept	1948	439	Carton	Seamus	28/07/1943	Lusk	Labourer	
Sept	1948	440	Rogan	Seamus	21/02/1943	The Square	Farmer	
Sept	1948	441	Cruise	Patrick	29/04/1944	Lusk	Carpenter	
Sept	1948	442	Connor	Patrick	23/05/1943	Newhaggard	Labourer	
Jan	1949	443	Rogan	Christopher	25/01/1945	Lusk	Carrier	
Feb	1949	444	Mullen	Leo Declan	27/02/1943	Dublin Rd.	Aer Lingus Emp.	St. Patricks Drogheda
Apr	1949	445	Dennis	Sean (Johnny)	03/10/1944	Lusk	Labourer	
Apr	1949	446	Hurley	Patrick	25/04/1944	Lusk	Contractor	
June	1949	447	Cruise	Sean	07/06/1945	Lusk	Carpenter	
June	1949	448	Clarke	Phelim	12/02/1942	Ratheney	Labourer	Grettallen, Baileboro, Co Cavan
June	1949	449	Clarke	Oliver	03/08/1940	Ratheney	Labourer	Grettallen, Baileboro, Co Cavan

Appendices

Month registered in the school	Year	Pupils Register No.	Pupils Surname	First Name	DOB	Residence	Occupation of Parent/Guardian	Previous School, if applicable
Sept	1949	450	Carton	John		Lusk		
Sept	1949	451	Russell	Michael		Lusk		
Oct	1949	452	Clare	Sean		Lusk		
Mar	1950	453	Russell	James (Seamus)		Lusk		
May	1950	454	Daly	Kevin		Lusk		
Sept	1950	455	Neary	Canice		Lusk		
Sept	1950	456	McGee	Patrick		Lusk		
Sept	1950	457	Dennis	Thomas Edward		Lusk		
Oct	1950	458	Kinsella	John Baptist		Lusk		Rathoe, Co. Carlow
Oct	1950	459	Peters	Brian		Newhaggard		
Nov	1950	460	Clarke	Gerard		Lusk		
Jan	1951	461	Sherry	Gerard		Knockdromin		Convent School Newbridge
Jan	1951	462	Sherry	William		Knockdromin		Christian Bros. Newbridge
Mar	1951	463	Grimes	Ernest		Lusk		
Mar	1951	464	Bentley	Brendan		Lusk		
Mar	1951	465	Dennis	Gerard		Lusk		Donabate
Mar	1951	466	Dennis	Noel		Lusk		Donabate
Apr	1951	467	Dennis	John Joseph		Lusk		
Apr	1951	468	Dunne	Colman		Corduff		
June	1951	469	Dennis	Edward		Lusk		
June	1951	470	Garrigan	Noel		Lusk		
June	1951	471	Magee	John		Lusk		
June	1951	472	Clarke	Eugene		Ratheney		
Sept	1951	473	Sherry	Sean		Lusk		
Sept	1951	474	Wall	Seamus		Lusk		
Mar	1952	475	Cruise	Albert		The Green		
Mar	1952	476	Connor	Noel		Newhaggard		
Mar	1952	477	Cowley	Sean		Skerries Rd.		
May	1952	478	Hanberry	Michael		Colecot		Balrothery

Month registered in the school	Year	Pupils Register No.	Pupils Surname	First Name	DOB	Residence	Occupation of Parent/Guardian	Previous School, if applicable
June	1952	479	Clare	Eamon		The Green		
Sept	1952	480	Skelly	Michael Patk.		Lusk		
Sept	1952	481	Dennis	Dermot		Lusk		
Sept	1952	482	Sherry	Donal		Lusk		
Jan	1953	483	Boland	Patrick		Rogerstown		
Apr	1953	484	Hand	Robert		Lusk		
Apr	1953	485	Clare	Ciaran		Lusk		
Apr	1953	486	Cowley	Seamus		Lusk		
Apr	1953	487	Jenkinson	Philip		Lusk		
Apr	1953	488	Wynne	Dermot		The Commons		
May	1953	489	O'Brien	Brian		Lusk		
Aug	1953	490	Knott	James		Lusk		
Sept	1953	491	Cowley	Robert		Lusk		
Sept	1953	492	Wynne	Bernard		The Commons		
Sept	1953	493	Magee	Brendan		Lusk		
Sept	1953	494	Dennis	Thomas		Lusk		
Sept	1953	495	Daly	Dominick		Lusk		
Nov	1953	496	Dennis	Seamus		Lusk		
Apr	1954	497	McDonnell	Michael		Lusk		
May	1954	498	Wall	Conor		Lusk		
June	1954	499	Rooney	Patrick		Quickpenny		
July	1954	500	McGee	Stephen		Commons		
July	1954	501	McGee	Richard		Commons		
Sept	1954	502	Rooney	Richard		Quickpenny		
Sept	1954	503	Monks	Colm		Lusk		
Sept	1954	504	Morgan	Patrick		Commons		
Sept	1954	505	Russell	Dermot		Lusk		
Sept	1954	506	McDonald	David		Ministers Rd.		
Sept	1954	507	Ryan	Donal		The Green		
Nov	1954	508	Burke	John		Ballaly (C/o Boylans)		

Appendices

Month registered in the school	Year	Pupils Register No.	Pupils Surname	First Name	DOB	Residence	Occupation of Parent/Guardian	Previous School, if applicable
Apr	1955	509	O'Brien	Martin		Lusk		
Sept	1955	510	Monks	Gerard		Lusk		
Sept	1955	511	Hand	Joseph		Lusk		
Jan	1956	512	Daly	John		Lusk		
Jan	1956	513	Seaver	Michael		Lusk		
Apr	1956	514	Magee	Gabriel		Lusk		
Apr	1956	515	Dennis	Liam		Ballaly		
Apr	1956	516	Cruise	Kevin		The Green		
Apr	1956	517	Cowley	Seamus (Jimmy)		Skerries Rd.		
May	1956	518	Ryan	Martin		The Green		
Sept	1956	519	Hand	Kevin		The Green		
Oct	1956	520	Hickey	Joseph		Ministers Rd.		
Jan	1957	521	Harford	Denis		Rush Rd.		
Jan	1957	522	Skelly	Patrick		P.O. Road		Rush
May	1957	523	Dennis	Michael		Ballaly		
May	1957	524	Seaver	Patrick		Lusk		
May	1957	525	Hughes	Thomas		Newhaggard		
June	1957	526	Russell	Patrick		Dublin Rd. Cotts		
Sept	1957	527	Cruise	Bernard		The Green		
Sept	1957	528	Clarke	Eugene		Dublin Rd. Cotts		
Sept	1957	529	Magee	Fintan		Skerries Rd.		
Sept	1957	530	Ryan	John		The Green		Loreto Coll. Dublin
Oct	1957	531	Rooney	Nicholas J		Quickpenny		
Jan	1958	532	Rogan	Anthony		Dublin Rd.		
May	1958	533	Cowley	Brian		Skerries Rd.		
May	1958	534	Browne	James		The Brewery		
Sept	1958	535	Skelly	Martin		Lusk		
Sept	1958	536	Skelly	Sean		Lusk		
Sept	1958	537	Donnelly	Martin		Railway Rd.		

Month registered in the school	Year	Pupils Register No.	Pupils Surname	First Name	DOB	Residence	Occupation of Parent/Guardian	Previous School, if applicable
Apr	1959	538	Sherry	Fintan		Lusk		
Apr	1959	539	Cruise	Joseph		The Green		
Apr	1959	540	Boylan	Christopher		Station Rd.		
June	1959	541	Russell	Anthony		Station Rd.		
July	1959	542	Connor	Maurice		Newhaggard		
Sept	1959	543	Harford	Gerard		Rush Rd.		
Sept	1959	544	Magee	Declan		Skerries Rd.		
Sept	1959	545	Knott	Kenneth		Chapel Green		
Oct	1959	546	Russell	Gerard		Dublin Rd. Cotts		
May	1960	547	Clarke	Martin		Chapel Rd.		
May	1960	548	Hanberry	Vincent		Colecot Cotts		
Sept	1960	549	Jenkinson	Thomas		Iona House		
Oct	1960	550	Gallagher	Patrick		Skerries Rd. C/o Gaffneys		Balscadden, Co. Meath
Apr	1961	551	Hurley	Catal		Regles, Lusk		
Apr	1961	552	Skelly	John Jo		Rush Rd.		
Apr	1961	553	Hughes	John		Newhaggard		
May	1961	554	Neary	Thomas		Lusk		
May	1961	555	Browne	Michael		Lusk		
June	1961	556	Casey	Gerard		The Green		
June	1961	557	Russell	Christopher		Dublin Rd. Cotts		
June	1961	558	Cowley	Gerard		Skerries Rd.		
Sept	1961	559	Hogan	Michael		Newhaggard		
Sept	1961	560	Hogan	Seamus		Newhaggard		
Sept	1961	561	Sheridan	Leo		Quickpenny Rd.		
Feb	1962	562	Boylan	William		Station Rd.		
Feb	1962	563	Daly	Joseph		Skerries Rd.		
May	1962	564	Hanberry	Joseph		coldcot		
May	1962	565	Russell	Thomas		Dublin Rd.		
May	1962	566	Neary	Anthony		P.O. Road		
May	1962	567	Sheridan	Damien		Quickpenny Rd.		

Appendices

Month registered in the school	Year	Pupils Register No.	Pupils Surname	First Name	DOB	Residence	Occupation of Parent/Guardian	Previous School, if applicable
May	1962	568	Skelly	Leo		Skerries Rd.		
May	1962	569	Bentley	Leo		Ballealy		
May	1962	570	Russell	Joseph		Dublin Rd.		
Sept	1962	571	McCann	John		Back Lane		
Sept	1962	572	Seaver	Andrew		Commons		
Sept	1962	573	Gerrard	Niall		Dublin Rd.		
Sept	1962	574	Rooney	James		Quickpenny		
Sept	1962	575	Cowley	Noel		Skerries Rd.		
Oct	1962	576	Skelly	Myles		Skerries Rd.		
Apr	1963	577	Bennett	George		P.O. Lusk		Coolock
Apr	1963	578	Dennis	Martin		Rush Rd.		
May	1963	579	O'Rourke	Declan		Back Lane		
May	1963	580	Bennett	Eugene, Oliver		P.O. Lusk		
May	1963	581	Cruise	Andrew		The Green		
May	1963	582	Jenkinson	William		Ministers Rd.		
May	1963	583	Doyle	Patrick		The Commons		
July	1963	584	Boylan	Martin		Rush Rd.		
July	1963	585	Hogan	Brian		The Green		
July	1963	586	Casey	Sean		The Green		
July	1964	587	Devine	Joseph		The Square		
July	1964	588	Devine	Martin		The Commons		
July	1964	589	Boylan	Michael		Rush Rd.		
July	1964	590	Hanberry	Thomas		Colecot		
July	1964	591	Bentley	Ronan		Ballealy		
July	1964	592	Hughes	Joseph		Newhaggard		
Sept	1964	593	Murphy	Oliver		Knockdromin		
Sept	1964	594	Stone	Andrew		Knockdromin		
Sept	1964	595	Neary	Gerard		Lusk		
Sept	1964	596	Kelly	Denis		Ministers Rd.		
July	1965	597	Sheridan	Patrick		Quickpenny Rd.		
July	1965	598	Austin	Gabriel		Ratheney		

Month registered in the school	Year	Pupils Register No.	Pupils Surname	First Name	DOB	Residence	Occupation of Parent/ Guardian	Previous School, if applicable
July	1965	599	Doyle	John		Bridestree		
July	1965	600	Russell	Gabriel		Dublin Rd.		
July	1965	601	Doyle	Edward		Commons		
July	1965	602	Magee	James		Commons		
July	1965	603	Gerrard	Donal		Dublin Rd.		
July	1965	604	Lambe	Martin		Ballaly		
July	1965	605	Magee	Gerard		Lusk		
July	1965	606	Dennis	Anthony		Station Rd.		
July	1965	607	McGuinness	Lorcan		Lusk		
July	1965	608	Seaver	John		Commons		
Feb	1966	609	O'Dochartiagh	Padraig		Skerries		St Marys, Donegal
June	1966	610	Sheridan	Eamon		Quickpenny Rd.		
June	1966	611	Fay	James		Lusk		
July	1966	612	Sweetman	Noel		Lusk		
July	1966	613	Bentley	Gerard		Ballaly		
July	1966	614	Browne	Martin		The Green		
July	1966	615	McGuinness	Robert		Lusk		
May	1967	616	Sweetman	Alan		Lusk		Rush
June	1967	617	O'Dochartiagh	Sean		Baile Atha Cliath		
July	1967	618	Devine	Michael		The Square		
July	1967	619	Devine	Dermot		The Commons		
July	1967	620	O'Rourke	Kevin		Newhaggard		
July	1967	621	O'Sullivan	Martin		Treen Hill		
July	1967	622	Sweetman	Brendan		P.O. Road		
July	1967	623	Scally	Thomas		Skerries Rd.		
July	1967	624	Doyle	Thomas		The Commons		
Aug	1967	625	Bentley	Mark		The Green		
Aug	1967	626	Bennett	Noel		P.O. Road		
May	1967	627	Ryan	Brendan		Lusk		Rush
July	1968	628	Hoey	Michael		Rathmooney		

Appendices

Month registered in the school	Year	Pupils Register No.	Pupils Surname	First Name	DOB	Residence	Occupation of Parent/Guardian	Previous School, if applicable
July	1968	629	Dennis	Garry		Station Rd.		
July	1968	630	Dennis	Eamon		Ballay		
July	1968	631	Gerrard	Ciaran		Lusk		
July	1968	632	Butterly	Gerard				
July	1968	633	Hogan	Leo		Lusk		
July	1968	634	Devine	Ciaran		Lusk		
July	1968	635	Peters	Paul		St Maccullins Close		
July	1968	636	Sweetman			Main St.		
July	1968	637	Sweetman	Gerard		P.O. Road		
July	1968	638	Harford	Lorcan		Hill Home Stn. Rd.		Skerries
July	1968	639	Hughes	Leo		Newhaggard		
Jan	1969	640A	Fay	Thomas		Lusk		??
Jan	1969	640	Fay	Joseph		Lusk		??
July	1969	641	McGuinness	Sean		Lusk		
July	1969	642	Lambe	Joseph		Ballay		
July	1969	643	O'Hara	Paul		The Green		
July	1969	644	Neary	Dathai		Lusk		
July	1969	645	Skelly	Philip		Lusk		
July	1969	646	Skelly	Gerard		Lusk		
July	1969	647	McNally	James		The Green		
Sept	1969	648	Foster	Liam		Skerries Rd.		
Sept	1969	649	Peters	Derek		Ballay Lane		
Jan	1970	650	White	Lorcan		Ballay		
May	1970	651	Doyle	Aidan		Kelly pK.		
July	1970	652	Knott	Francis		Lusk		
July	1970	653	Butterly	Noel		Newhaggard		
July	1970	654	Doyle	Sean		Commons		
July	1970	655	Hughes	Patrick		Newhaggard		
July	1970	656	Dennis	Robert		Station Rd.		
July	1970	657	Browne	Peter		Lusk		

Month registered in the school	Year	Pupils Register No.	Pupils Surname	First Name	DOB	Residence	Occupation of Parent/Guardian	Previous School, if applicable
July	1970	658	Hoey	Gabriel		Rathmooney		
July	1970	659	Ryan	Declan		Main St.		
July	1970	660	Sweetman	Eric		P.O. Road		
July	1970	661	Devine	Richard		The Square		
July	1970	662	Peters	David		Back Lane		
July	1970	663	Brogan	Philip		Collinstown		
July	1970	664	Sherwin	John		Remount Farm		
July	1970	665	Skelly	Derek		Lusk		
July	1970	666	Cruise	Patrick		Lusk		
July	1970	667	McPhilips	Brian		Lusk		
Nov	1970	668	McBride	Patrick		Lusk		Corduff
Nov	1970	669	McBride	David		Lusk		Corduff
Nov	1970	670	Sheridan	James		Ministers Rd.		Donabate
Nov	1970	671	Sheridan	John		Ministers Rd.		Donabate
Nov	1970	672	Sheridan	Vincent		Ministers Rd.		Donabate

Appendices

List of Boys 1971 to 1992

Month Registered in the School	Year	Pupils Register No.	Pupils Surname	First Name	Place of Residence
June	1971	673	Leonard	Thomas	Oberstown House
June	1971	674	Leonard	William	Oberstown House
July	1971	675	Skelly	Gerard	The Square
July	1971	676	Peters	William	Lusk
July	1971	677	O'Toole	Christopher	The Square
July	1971	678	Grimes	Patrick	Ash Grove
July	1971	679	Hogan	Mark	Ash Grove
July	1971	680	Butterly	Adrian	Ballay
July	1971	681	Bentley	David	Treen Hill
July	1971	682	Watson	John	Newhaggard
July	1971	683	Green	Patrick	Collinstown
July	1971	684	O'Neill	Brendan	Bridestree
July	1971	685	Dennis	Stephen	Station Rd.
July	1971	686	Sweetman	William	Skerries Rd.
July	1971	687	Peters	Garrett	Ballay
July	1971	688	McNally	Gerard	The Green
July	1971	689	Durkin	Garrett	Dublin Rd.
July	1971	690	Seaver	Richard	Commons
July	1971	691	O'Connor	Gerard	Kelly Pk
July	1971	692	McDonald	Edward	Skerries Rd.
Sept	1971	693	Hogan	Paul	Ash Grove
Sept	1971	694	Lumsden	John	St Maccullins Close
Sept	1971	695	Peters	Leslie	Lusk
Dec	1971	696	Weston	Charles	The Green
July	1972	697	Hogan	Mark	The Green
July	1972	698	Bentley	David	Lusk
July	1972	699	Sweetman	Liam	Lusk
July	1972	700	Watson	Sean	The Green
Sept	1971	701	Hogan	Paul	The Green
July	1972	702	O'Herlihy	Brendan	Station Rd.

Month Registered in the School	Year	Pupils Register No.	Pupils Surname	First Name	Place of Residence
July	1972	703	Finnegan	James	Main St.
July	1972	704	Clare	Raymond	Dublin Rd.
July	1972	705	Butterly	Fergus	Ballaly
July	1972	706	Clare	John	The Green
July	1972	707	Skelly	William	The Green
July	1972	708	McNally	Colm	P.O. Road
July	1972	709	White	Robert	Racecourse Commons
July	1972	710	O'Reilly	John	St Maccullins Close
July	1972	711	O'Neill	Paul	Rathmooney
July	1972	712	Gilmartin	Paul	Newhaggard
July	1972	713	Taylor	Mark	Chapel Farm
July	1972	714	Neary	Leo	Station Rd.
July	1972	715	Grimes	Bernard	Ash Grove
July	1972	716	Cruise	Martin	St Maccullins Close
July	1972	717	Watson	Vincent	Racecourse Commons
July	1972	718	Connors	Michael J.	Bridestree
Aug	1972	719	Hughes	Martin	Newhaggard
Aug	1972	720	Bentley	Colin	Dublin Rd.
Aug	1972	721	Brogan	Paul	Collinstown
Aug	1972	722	Grimes	Adrian	Ash Grove
Sept	1972	723	Peters	Gregory	St Maccullins Close
Sept	1972	724	Donnelly	Donal	Lusk
Sept	1972	725	Donnelly	Karlton	Lusk
May	1974	728	Monks	John	Kelly Pk
May	1974	729	Green	Gerard	Kelly Pk
July	1973	730	Boylan	Joseph	Station Rd.
July	1973	731	Boylan	Patrick	Station Rd.
July	1973	732	Russell	Paul	Kelly Pk
July	1973	733	Sweetman	Anthony	Main St.
July	1973	734	Thornton	Eamonn	Ash Grove
July	1973	735	Gordon	George	Commons
July	1973	736	Grimes	Mark	The Square

Appendices

Month Registered in the School	Year	Pupils Register No.	Pupils Surname	First Name	Place of Residence
July	1973	737	Cruise	Michael	Ash Grove
July	1973	738	Brogan	Mark	Commons
July	1973	739	Neary	Adrian	Station Rd.
July	1973	740	McNally	Paul	P.O. Road
July	1973	741	Smith	Mark	Commons
July	1973	742	Browne	Desmond	Treen Hill
July	1973	743	McCann	Michael	Back Lane
July	1973	744	Sherwin	Brendan	Station Rd.
July	1973	745	McKittrick	Kevin	Kelly Pk
July	1973	746	Leonard	Andrew	Oberstown
July	1973	747	Peters	Ian	Ballaly
July	1973	748	Hogan	Thomas	Dublin Rd.
July	1973	749	Clare	Patrick	Ash Grove
July	1973	750	Grimes	Paul	Ash Grove
Sept	1973	751	Cardiff	Myles	Skerries Rd.
Sept	1973	752	O'Leary	John	Kelly Pk
July	1974	753	Boylan	Noel	Ash Grove
July	1974	754	Finnegan	Paul	Main St.
July	1974	755	Cruise	Albert	St Maccullins Close
July	1974	756	Cardiff	Barry	Skerries Rd.
July	1974	757	Daly	Patrick	Kelly Pk
July	1974	758	Plunkett	Bartholomew	Dublin Rd.
July	1974	759	Skelly	Leo	The Green
July	1974	760	Weldon	Alan	Ash Grove
July	1974	761	Boardman	Derek	Commons
July	1974	762	O'Brien	Brendan	Skerries Rd.
July	1974	763	Durkan	Mark	Dublin Rd.
July	1974	764	Bentley	Justin	Ballaly
July	1974	765	Jones	Peter	
Sept	1974	766	Sherry	Donal	Back Lane
Sept	1974	767	Delaney	Declan	Kelly Pk
Sept	1974	768	Watson	John	Kelly Pk

Month Registered in the School	Year	Pupils Register No.	Pupils Surname	First Name	Place of Residence
May	1974	769	Monks	Thomas	Kelly Pk
Sept	1974	770	McArdle	Seamus	Dublin Rd.
Sept	1974	771	Flynn	Paul	Dublin Rd.
Sept	1974	772	Lawlor	Colm	Kelly Pk
Sept	1974	773	Dennis	Joseph	Kelly Pk
Sept	1974	774	Carthy	Gerard	Skerries Rd.
Sept	1974	775	Healy	Padraig	Kelly Pk
Oct	1974	776	Fletcher	Stephen	Chapel Lane
Oct	1974	777	Fletcher	Michael	Chapel Lane
Sept	1974	778	Watson	Vincent	Kelly Pk
Oct	1974	779	McKenna	Kieran	Kelly Pk
July	1975	780	Sullivan	Garry	Kelly Pk
July	1975	781	Lowndes	Nigel	Kelly Pk
July	1975	782	Kelly	John	Dublin Rd.
July	1975	783	Hogan	Patrick	Dublin Rd.
July	1975	784	Durkan	Michael	Dublin Rd.
July	1975	785	Clare	Richard	P.O. Road
July	1975	786	Peters	Philip	Ballaly Lane
July	1975	787	Gaffney	Peter	Commons
July	1975	788	De Jong	Gilbert	Church Rd.
July	1975	789	Bentley	Sean	Treen Hill
July	1975	790	Daly	Philip	Main St.
July	1975	791	Skelly	Richard	The Green
July	1975	792	Skelly	Patrick	P.O. Road
July	1975	793	Neary	Denis	Dublin Rd.
July	1975	794	McGee	Robert	Kelly Pk
July	1975	795	Gaffney	Brendan	Commons
July	1975	796	Weston	Richard	The Green
July	1975	797	Cruise	Declan	The Green
Sept	1975	798	Austin	Leslie	Station Rd.
July	1976	799	Bentley	Dermot	Treen Hill
July	1976	800	Sweetman	Ciaran	Commons

Appendices

Month Registered in the School	Year	Pupils Register No.	Pupils Surname	First Name	Place of Residence
July	1976	801	Cahill	Lingard	Raheny Rd.
July	1976	802	McKenna	Eamonn	Kelly Pk
July	1976	803	Rafferty	Desmond	Kelly Pk
July	1976	804	McDonnell	David	Dublin Rd.
July	1976	805	Boylan	Thomas	Rogerstown Lane
July	1976	806	Christie	Aidan	Kelly Pk
July	1976	807	Farrell	Noel	Kelly Pk
July	1976	808	Peters	Stephen	Ballaly Lane
July	1976	809	Dennis	Paul	St Josephs Ave.
July	1976	810	Sandford	Derek	Kelly Pk
July	1976	811	Monks	Laurence	Kelly Pk
July	1976	812	Delaney	Alan	Kelly Pk
July	1976	813	Butterly	Darren	Ballaly
July	1976	814	Donnelly	Gary	Kelly Pk
July	1976	815	Healy	Seamus	Kelly Pk
July	1976	816	Doyle	Bernard	Kelly Pk
July	1976	817	Crudden	Robert	Kelly Pk
July	1976	818	Neary	Ciaran	Station Rd.
July	1976	819	Carthy	Stephen	Kelly Pk
July	1976	820	Clare	Anthony	Ash Grove
July	1976	821	De Jong	Andrew	Church Rd.
July	1976	822	Moore	Simon	Commons
July	1976	823	McNally	George	P.O. Road
July	1976	824	Bentley	Darren	Church Rd.
July	1976	825	Peters	Jason	Ministers Rd.
July	1976	826	Gaffney	Cornelius	Skerries Rd.
Aug	1976	827	Russell	Martin	Kelly Pk
Sept	1976	828	Hogan	Liam	Dublin Rd.
Sept	1976	829	Sandford	Graham	Kelly Pk
Sept	1976	830	Sullivan	Joseph	Kelly Pk
Sept	1976	831	Carton	John	Rogerstown Lane
Oct	1976	832	Daly	Thomas	Ministers Rd.

Month Registered in the School	Year	Pupils Register No.	Pupils Surname	First Name	Place of Residence
Oct	1976	833	Daly	John	Ministers Rd.
Oct	1976	834	Mannering	Richard	Racecourse Commons
Dec	1976	835	McGee	Stephen	The Green
Dec	1976	836	Morgan	Ian	Woodlawn, Commons
Dec	1976	837	Lowrey	John	Chapel Green
Dec	1976	838	Finnegan	Sean	Main St.
Dec	1976	839	Greene	Mark	Kelly Pk
July	1977	840	McGee	Damien	Kelly Pk
July	1977	841	McGee	William	Kelly Pk
July	1977	842	Rafferty	David	Kelly Pk
July	1977	843	Weldon	James	Ash Grove
July	1977	844	Lord	Barry	Skerries Rd.
July	1977	845	Sherry	Adrian	Barrack Rd.
July	1977	846	Bentley	Ralph	Tree View, Lusk
July	1977	847	Grimes	David	Ash Grove
July	1977	848	Cruise	Kevin	The Green
July	1977	849	Boardman	Patrick	The Commons
July	1977	850	Lowndes	Jason	Kelly Pk
July	1977	851	Hughes	Neil	Kelly Pk
July	1977	852	Rogan	Raymond	Kelly Pk
July	1977	853	Hand	Thomas	The Green
July	1977	854	Doran	Jeremiah	Dublin Rd.
July	1977	855	Mannering	David	
July	1977	856	O'Herlihy	Gearoid	Station Rd.
July	1977	857	Carton	Philip	Corduff
July	1977	858	O'Reilly	Karl	St Maccullins Close
Oct	1977	859	Leane	Thomas	Commons
Oct	1977	860	McQuillan	Darren	Kelly Pk
Oct	1977	861	McNally	Sean	Main St.
July	1977	862	Peters	Alan	St Maccullins Close
Oct	1977	863	Cowley	Barry	Kelly Pk
Oct	1977	864	Neary	Barry	Rush Rd.

Appendices

Month Registered in the School	Year	Pupils Register No.	Pupils Surname	First Name	Place of Residence
Feb	1978	865	Hall	David	Skerries Rd.
Mar	1978	866	Moylan	Paul	Kelly Pk
Apr	1978	867	O'Rourke	David	Orlynn Pk.
Sept	1978	868	McNally	Kevin	P.O. Road
Sept	1978	869	Walsh	Anthony	
Sept	1978	870	Blessing	James	Ash Grove
Sept	1978	871	Thornton	Brendan	Ash Grove
Sept	1978	872	Skelly	Alan	The Green
Sept	1978	873	Dennis	James	St Josephs Ave.
Sept	1978	874	Stafford	Paul	Kelly Pk
Sept	1978	875	Lawlor	Raymond	Kelly Pk
Sept	1978	876	Morgan	Alan	Kelly Pk
Sept	1978	877	Campbell	Graham	Kelly Pk
Sept	1978	878	Brogan	Martin	The Commons
Sept	1978	879	Gaffney	Kevin	Skerries Rd.
Sept	1978	880	Dennis	Aidan	P.O. Road
Sept	1978	881	Boylan	Damien	Ash Grove
Sept	1978	882	Daly	Joseph	Ministers Rd.
Oct	1978	883	Connors	Joseph	Kelly Pk
Sept	1978	884	Kearns	Martin	Orlynn Pk.
Sept	1978	885	Walsh	William	
Oct	1978	886	Sugrue	Gerard	
Sept	1978	887	Walsh	Brian	
Jan	1979	888	Hussey	Christopher	Orlynn Pk.
Mar	1979	889	O'Cathain	Labhras	P.O. Rd.
Dec	1978	890	Maguire	Adrian	Orlynn Pk.
Apr	1979	891	Milligan	Andrew	Orlynn Pk.
June	1979	892	O'Broin	Marcus	Orlynn Pk.
Jan	1979	893	Ryan	Damien	Dublin Rd.
Sept	1979	894	Crowley	Mark	Orlynn Pk.
Sept	1979	895	Cronin	Daniel	Orlynn Pk.
Sept	1979	896	Cronin	Tony	Orlynn Pk.

Month Registered in the School	Year	Pupils Register No.	Pupils Surname	First Name	Place of Residence
Sept	1979	897	O'Sullivan	Michael	Orlynn Pk.
Sept	1979	898	Fox	Michael	Orlynn Pk.
Oct	1979	899	Byrne	Mark	Rogerstown
Sept	1979	900	Bentley	Eric	Ministers Rd.
Sept	1979	901	De Burca	Wayne	Ministers Rd.
Sept	1979	902	O'h-Iomhair	Fintan	Kelly Pk.
Sept	1979	903	MacUilin	Fergus	Kelly Pk.
Sept	1979	904	MacDonnacha	Padraig	Chapel Green
Sept	1979	905	Pleimeamn	Daithi	Commons
Sept	1979	906	Christie	Stuart	Kelly Pk.
Sept	1979	907	McGowan	Ian	Orlynn Pk.
Oct	1979	908	Lowrey	Fintan	P.O. Rd.
Oct	1979	909	O'Byrne	David	
Sept	1979	910	Carthy	Keith	Kelly Pk.
Sept	1979	911	O'Herlihy	Sean	Station Rd.
Sept	1979	912	Taylor	Alan	Dublin Rd.
Sept	1979	913	Peters	Barry	Ministers Rd.
Sept	1979	914	Keelan	Julian	Kelly Pk.
Sept	1979	915	Doran	Morgan	Dublin Rd.
Sept	1979	916	Blessing	Dermot	Ash Grove
Sept	1979	917	Kearns	Stephen	Orlynn Pk.
Sept	1979	918	Cruise	Bernard	Ministers Rd.
Sept	1979	919	Christie	Ian	Kelly Pk.
Sept	1979	920	Dennis	David	P.O. Rd.
Jan	1980	921	Culleton	Mark	Orlynn Pk.
Nov	1979	922	Hegarty	Owen	Orlynn Pk.
Sept	1980	923	O'Leary	Michael	Orlynn Pk.
Jan	1979	924	Curran	Garrett	Rush
Sept	1980	925	Leane	Oliver	Commons
Sept	1980	926	Boylan	David	Rogerstown
Sept	1980	927	Campbell	Darren	Kelly Pk.
Sept	1980	928	Daly	Paul	Ministers Rd.

Appendices

Month Registered in the School	Year	Pupils Register No.	Pupils Surname	First Name	Place of Residence
Sept	1980	929	Conerey	Colin	Orlynn Pk.
Sept	1980	930	Christie	Jason	Kelly Pk.
Sept	1980	931	Burke	Paul	Ministers Rd.
Sept	1980	932	Monks	Jason	Ministers Rd.
Sept	1980	933	Boylan	Patrick	Rogerstown
Sept	1980	934	Cruise	Stephen	The Green
Sept	1980	935	Derham	Mark	Collinstown
Sept	1980	936	Dennis	Alan	Ballealy
Sept	1980	937	Lynch	Brendan	Ministers Rd.
Sept	1980	938	Barry	Trevor	Ministers Rd.
Sept	1980	939	Blessing	Graham	Ash Grove
Sept	1981	940	Doolin	Mark	Orlynn Pk.
Sept	1981	941	Collins	Terence	Kelly Pk.
Dec	1981	943	Rosney	Stephen	Orlynn Pk.
Sept	1981	944	Cruise	Brendan	St. Macullins Close
Sept	1981	945	Doolin	David	Orlynn Pk.
Sept	1981	946	Pullen	Shane	Kelly Pk.
Sept	1981	947	Murphy	Thomas	Ministers Rd.
Sept	1981	948	Teeling	Derek	Kelly Pk.
Sept	1981	949	Howard	David	Kelly Pk.
Jan	1982	950	O'Gorman	Patrick	Ministers Rd.
Sept	1981	951	Buckley	Jeremy	
Nov	1981	952	Corbally	Fabian	Orlynn Pk.
Feb	1982	953	O'Gorman	William	Ministers Rd.
Jan	1982	954	O'Gorman	Noel	Ministers Rd.
Sept	1981	955	Gaffney	Shane	Man 'o War
Sept	1981	956	Sherry	Conor	Church Rd.
Sept	1981	957	Sherry	Michael	Church Rd.
Sept	1981	958	Finnegan	Patrick	Commons
Sept	1981	959	Burke	Paul	Ministers Rd.
Sept	1981	960	Finnegan	Peter	Main St.
Sept	1981	961	Sugrue	Darren	Dublin Rd.

Month Registered in the School	Year	Pupils Register No.	Pupils Surname	First Name	Place of Residence
Sept	1981	962	Doran	Myles	Dublin Rd.
Sept	1981	963	Kearns	David	Orlynn Pk.
Sept	1981	964	Cowley	Robert	Kelly Pk.
Sept	1981	965	Bird	Niul	Orlynn Pk.
Sept	1981	966	O'Sullivan	Shane	Orlynn Pk.
Sept	1981	967	Dennis	John	Chapel Green
Sept	1981	968	Sandford	Brian	Kelly Pk.
Sept	1981	969	Dennis	Mark	Commons
Sept	1981	970	Peters	Jason	Ballealy
Sept	1981	971	Russell	Stuart	Rogerstown Lane
Sept	1981	972	McGratten	Eamonn	Orlynn Pk.
Sept	1981	973	O'Gorman	Gearoid	Ministers Rd.
Sept	1981	974	McGowan	Colm	Orlynn Pk.
Sept	1982	975	McKenna	Damien	Kelly Pk.
Sept	1982	976	O'Reilly	Stephen	Orlynn Pk.
Sept	1982	977	Russell	David	Ministers Rd.
Sept	1982	978	Neary	Raymond	Station Rd.
Sept	1982	979	Clarke	Edward	Ministers Rd.
Sept	1982	980	Murphy	Noel	Kelly Pk.
Sept	1982	981	Farrell	Joseph	Kelly Pk.
Sept	1982	982	Daly	Mark	Ministers Rd.
Sept	1982	983	Blessing	Gerard	Ash Grove
Sept	1982	984	Fleming	Kevin	Ministers Rd.
Sept	1982	985	Turner	John	Kelly Pk.
Sept	1982	986	English	Paul	Kelly Pk.
Sept	1982	987	Burke	David	Orlynn Pk.
Sept	1982	988	Lowndes	Wesley	Kelly Pk.
Sept	1982	989	Hogan	Stephen	Ministers Rd.
Sept	1982	990	Leetch	John	Orlynn Pk.
Sept	1982	991	Creegan	David	Orlynn Pk.
Sept	1982	992	Moore	Richard	Commons
Sept	1982	993	Teeling	L	Newhagard

Appendices

Month Registered in the School	Year	Pupils Register No.	Pupils Surname	First Name	Place of Residence
Sept	1982	994	Farrell	Glenn	Orlynn Pk.
Sept	1982	995	Roseinhare	Damien	Grace Dieu
Sept	1982	996	Dunne	Kevin	P.O. Rd.
Sept	1982	997	Dunne	Stephen	P.O. Rd.
Oct	1982	998	Carr	John	Chapel Lane
Sept	1982	999	Mulligan	Noel	Skerries Rd.
Jan	1982	1000	Rogers	Peter	Orlynn Pk.
Oct	1982	1001	Carr	Nigel	Chapel Lane
June	1983	1002	O'Neill	Philip	Orlynn Pk.
May	1983	1003	Cronin	Kenneth	Ministers Rd.
May	1983	1004	Hamilton	Gerard	Orlynn Pk.
Mar	1983	1005	Ridgeway	Mark	Orlynn Pk.
May	1983	1006	Hamilton	Mark	Orlynn Pk.
May	1983	1007	Quinn	Stephen	Orlynn Pk.
Mar	1983	1008	Ridgeway	Colin	Orlynn Pk.
Sept	1983	1009	Walsh	Richard	Ash Grove
Sept	1983	1010	Teeling	L	Ministers Rd.
Sept	1983	1011	Weldon	Thomas	Kelly Pk.
Sept	1983	1012	Boylan	Paul	Ministers Rd.
Sept	1983	1013	McGee	Jason	P.O. Rd.
Sept	1983	1014	Skelly	Edward	P.O. Rd.
Sept	1983	1015	Darragh	Nathan	Orlynn Pk.
Sept	1983	1016	McGee	Stephen	Chapel Lane
Sept	1983	1017	McMahon	Daniel	Ministers Rd.
Sept	1983	1018	Teeling	Philip	Kelly Pk.
Sept	1983	1019	Morgan	Neil	Commons
Sept	1983	1020	Boylan	David	Kelly Pk.
Sept	1983	1021	Farrell	Dane	Kelly Pk.
Sept	1983	1022	McNally	Barry	Tower View
Sept	1983	1023	Rooney	James	Kelly Pk.
Sept	1983	1024	Ryan	Terry	Dublin Rd.
Sept	1983	1025	Cruise	Thomas	Ash Grove

Month Registered in the School	Year	Pupils Register No.	Pupils Surname	First Name	Place of Residence
Sept	1983	1026	English	David	Kelly Pk.
Sept	1983	1027	Stafford	Owen	Kelly Pk.
Sept	1983	1028	Weldon	Kevin	Ash Grove
Sept	1983	1029	Jones	Christopher	The Green
Sept	1983	1030	O'Donovan	Brian	Orlynn Pk.
May	1984	1031	Crowe	Clive	Rathmooney
Sept	1984	1032	Finnegan	Martin	Main St.
Sept	1984	1033	Burke	Eoin	Orlynn Pk.
Sept	1984	1034	Brogan	Kevin	Commons
Sept	1984	1035	Blessing	Mark	Ash Grove
Sept	1984	1036	Lawlor	Adrian	Kelly Pk.
Sept	1984	1037	Hogan	John Paul	Dublin Rd.
Sept	1984	1038	Weldon	Brendan	Ash Grove
Sept	1984	1039	Butterly	Mark	Orlynn Pk.
Sept	1984	1040	Winters	Peter	Orlynn Pk.
Sept	1984	1041	Dennis	Thomas	Chapel Green
Sept	1984	1042	Conway	Richard	Orlynn Pk.
Sept	1984	1043	O'Neill	Sean	Kelly Pk.
Sept	1984	1044	Harford	Eoin	Station Rd.
Sept	1984	1045	Cowley	Sean	Kelly Pk.
Sept	1984	1046	Leane	Declan	Commons
Sept	1984	1047	Ryan	Paul	Regeens
Sept	1984	1048	Skelly	Michael	Ministers Rd.
Sept	1984	1049	Christie	Clifford	Kelly Pk.
Sept	1984	1050	Clare	Brendan	The Green
Sept	1984	1051	Barry	Mark	Ministers Rd.
Sept	1984	1052	Daly	Kevin	Ministers Rd.
Nov	1985	1053	O'Crinigan	Andrew	Lusk House
Sept	1984	1054	Boylan	Michael	Ministers Rd.
Sept	1984	1055	Farrell	Stephen	Orlynn Pk.
Sept	1984	1056	Ryan	Colin	Regeens
Sept	1984	1057	Teeling	Simon	Ministers Rd.

Appendices

Month Registered in the School	Year	Pupils Register No.	Pupils Surname	First Name	Place of Residence
Sept	1984	1058	Sherry	Sean	Main St.
Sept	1984	1059	Russell	Trevor	Ministers Rd.
Sept	1984	1060	Donnelly	Ciaran	Orlynn Pk.
Sept	1984	1061	Skelly	Michael	Ministers Pk.
Sept	1984	1062	Cartwright	Eoin	Orlynn Pk.
Sept	1984	1063	Byrne	Edward	Orlynn Pk.
Sept	1984	1064	Turner	Gerard	Kelly Pk.
Jan	1985	1065	McWaney	Ian	Orlynn Close
Oct	1984	1066	Minihane	Rory	Ministers Rd.
Oct	1985	1067	Carroll	John	Orlynn Pk.
Oct	1985	1068	O'Donoghue	Damien	Main St.
Sept	1985	1069	Deeb	Knel	Collinstown
Apr	1985	1070	Holmes	George	Orlynn Pk.
Jan	1985	1071	Russell	Stuart	Ministers Rd.
Nov	1985	1072	Crinigan	Andrew	Lusk House
Sept	1985	1073	Teeling	Alan	Kelly Pk.
Sept	1985	1074	Burns	Paul	Kelly Pk.
Sept	1985	1075	Daly	David	Ministers Rd.
Sept	1985	1076	Moore	Oliver	Commons
Sept	1985	1077	Maguire	Ciaran	Orlynn Pk.
Sept	1985	1078	O'Neill	Neasan	Orlynn Pk.
Sept	1985	1079	O'Laoghaire	Desmond	Malahide
Sept	1985	1080	Walsh	Stephen	Ministers Pk.
Sept	1985	1081	Vinters	Keith	Orlynn Pk.
Sept	1985	1082	Kane	Mark	P.O. Rd.
Sept	1985	1083	Monks	Colm	Ministers Rd.
Sept	1985	1084	Rooney	John	Orlynn Pk.
Sept	1985	1085	Cruise	Danny	Ash Grove
Sept	1985	1086	Colgan	Brian	Commons
Sept	1985	1087	Delaney	James	Ministers Pk.
Sept	1985	1088	Skelly	Francis	Ministers Pk.
Sept	1985	1089	Campbell	Thomas	Orlynn Pk.

Month Registered in the School	Year	Pupils Register No.	Pupils Surname	First Name	Place of Residence
Sept	1985	1090	Russell	Gerard	Ministers Pk.
Sept	1985	1091	McCarthy	Colm	Orlynn Pk.
Sept	1985	1092	Tracy	Jonathan	Orlynn Pk.
Sept	1985	1093	Farrell	Kevin	Kelly Pk.
Sept	1985	1094	Harding	John	Orlynn Pk.
Sept	1985	1095	O'Toole	Darren	Ministers Pk.
Sept	1985	1096	Charlton	Thomas	
Sept	1985	1097	Pullen	John	Kelly Pk.
Sept	1985	1098	Harding	Liam	Orlynn Pk.
Sept	1985	1099	Skelly	David	Ministers Pk.
Sept	1986	1100	Neville	Cathal	Orlynn Pk.
Sept	1986	1101	Hurley	Rossa	Orlynn Pk.
Sept	1986	1102	Cartwright	Darren	Orlynn Pk.
Sept	1986	1103	Marry	Shane	Ministers Rd.
Sept	1986	1104	Hayes	Anthony	P.O. Rd.
Sept	1986	1105	Callen	Damien	Ministers Rd.
Sept	1986	1106	Sheehan	Robert	Orlynn Pk.
Sept	1986	1107	Ryan	Rory	Orlynn Pk.
Sept	1986	1108	Byrnes	Mark	Kelly Pk.
Sept	1986	1109	Murphy	David	Kelly Pk.
Sept	1986	1110	Hoare	Gerard	Orlynn Pk.
Sept	1986	1111	Cruise	Joseph	Ministers Rd.
Sept	1986	1112	Crinigan	Simon	Station Rd.
Sept	1986	1113	Skelly	Francis	Ministers Rd.
Sept	1986	1114	Daly	David	Ministers Rd.
Sept	1986	1115	Cruise	Daniel	Ash Grove
Sept	1986	1116	Darcy	Keith	Orlynn Close
Sept	1986	1117	Darcy	Oran	Orlynn Pk.
June	1986	1118	Beatty	Daragh	Commons
Dec	1987	1119	Geraghty	Mark	P.O. Rd.
Sept	1987	1120	Dunne	Keith	Orlynn Close
Sept	1987	1121	Lynch	Michael	Orlynn Pk.

Appendices

Month Registered in the School	Year	Pupils Register No.	Pupils Surname	First Name	Place of Residence
Sept	1987	1122	McNamara	Daniel	Orlynn Pk.
Sept	1987	1123	Lynch	Darren	Orlynn Pk.
Sept	1987	1124	O'Neill	Turlough	Orlynn Pk.
Sept	1987	1125	McGuire	Ronan	Orlynn Pk.
Sept	1987	1126	Murtagh	Donail	Orlynn Pk.
Sept	1987	1127	Fraher	Ian	Orlynn Pk.
Sept	1987	1128	Stears	Donal	Orlynn Pk.
Sept	1987	1129	Weir	David	Commons
Sept	1987	1130	Barry	Keith	Ministers Rd.
Sept	1987	1131	Farrell	Tomas	Kelly Pk.
Sept	1987	1132	Quinn	Eoin	The Green
Sept	1987	1133	Murphy	Damien	Ministers Pk.
Sept	1987	1134	Dennis	Eric	P.O. Rd.
Sept	1987	1135	Keelan	Glenn	Kelly Pk.
Sept	1987	1136	Savage	Michael	Ministers Pk.
Sept	1987	1137	Dennis	Austin	Racecourse Common
Sept	1987	1138	Hayes	Anthony	Orlynn Pk.
Sept	1987	1139	Darcy	Keith	Orlynn Close
Sept	1987	1140	Burns	Mark	Kelly Pk.
Sept	1987	1141	Cruise	Joseph	Ministers Rd.
Sept	1987	1142	Ryan	Brian	Regeens
Sept	1987	1143	Caffrey	Scott	Ballyboughal
Sept	1987	1144	Dennis	Stephen	Racecourse Common
Sept	1987	1145	Dunne	Paul	The Close, Orlynn Pk.
Sept	1988	1146	Carroll	Aaron	Orlynn Pk.
Sept	1988	1147	Brick	Ronan	Orlynn Pk.
Sept	1988	1148	Bailey	Graham	Orlynn Pk.
Sept	1988	1149	Howlin	Stephen	Ministers Pk.
Sept	1988	1150	Doyle	Dwyane	Ministers Pk.
Sept	1988	1151	Boardman	Robert	Rathmooney
Sept	1988	1152	Kavanagh	Sean	Kelly Pk.
Sept	1988	1153	Hoare	Mark	Orlynn Pk.

Month Registered in the School	Year	Pupils Register No.	Pupils Surname	First Name	Place of Residence
Sept	1988	1154	Rogan	Neil	Dublin Rd.
Sept	1988	1155	Nolan	Aidan	Orlynn Pk.
Sept	1988	1156	Smith	Brian	Orlynn Pk.
Sept	1988	1157	Delaney	David	Ministers Pk.
Sept	1988	1158	Hickey	Sean	Orlynn Pk.
Sept	1987	1159	Danagher	Brian	Malahide
Dec	1982	1160	Vaughan	Patrick	Orlynn Pk.
Jan	1989	1161	Dayman	Anthony	Orlynn Pk.
Jan	1989	1162	Dayman	Matthew	Orlynn Pk.
Sept	1989	1163	Gosson	Kevin	Commons
Sept	1989	1164	Gilsenan	Keith	Ministers Pk.
Sept	1987	1165	Stapleton	Michael	Orlynn Pk.
Sept	1987	1166	Conway	Stephen	Orlynn Pk.
Sept	1987	1167	Butterly	Morgan	Orlynn Pk.
Sept	1987	1168	Hughes	Thomas	Ministers Pk.
Sept	1987	1169	Farrell	Paul	Ministers Pk.
Sept	1987	1170	Harford	Conor	Station Rd.
Sept	1987	1171	Horgan	Oisin	Church View, B'rk. Rd.
Sept	1987	1172	Kee	David	Ministers Rd.
Sept	1987	1173	Teeling	Darren	Ministers Pk.
Sept	1987	1174	Roberts	Gareth	Orlynn Close
Sept	1987	1175	Cruise	Barry	The Green
Sept	1987	1176	McCarthy	Brian	Orlynn Pk.
Sept	1988	1177	Duignan	Colin	Orlynn Pk.
Sept	1988	1178	Murphy	Mark	Orlynn Pk.
Sept	1988	1179	Bonner	Cormac	Orlynn Pk.
Sept	1988	1180	Bonner	Neil	Orlynn Pk.
Sept	1988	1181	Daly	Gerard	Orlynn Pk.
Sept	1988	1182	Neville	Christopher	Orlynn Pk.
Sept	1988	1183	Hughes	Denis	Ministers Pk.
Sept	1988	1184	Walsh	Anthony	Ash Grove
Sept	1988	1185	Colgan	Anthony	The Commons

Appendices

Month Registered in the School	Year	Pupils Register No.	Pupils Surname	First Name	Place of Residence
Sept	1988	1186	Hogan	Declan	Ministers Pk.
Sept	1988	1187	McGrath	Christopher	Ministers Pk.
Sept	1988	1188	Hussey	Keith	Orlynn Pk.
Sept	1988	1189	Nicholas	Mark	The Drive Orlynn Pk.
Sept	1988	1190	Russell	Mark	The Drive Orlynn Pk.
Sept	1988	1191	Teeling	Barry	Kelly Pk.
Sept	1988	1192	Savage	Shane	Ministers Pk.
Sept	1988	1193	Callan	Patrick	Ministers Rd.
Sept	1988	1194	Lynch	Raymond	Orlynn Pk.
Sept	1988	1195	Lynch	Bryan	
Sept	1989	1196	Kenny	Shane	
Sept	1989	1197	O'Toole	Joseph	Ministers Pk.
Sept	1989	1198	McGrath	Jason	Ministers Pk.
Sept	1989	1199	Hogan	Warren	Ministers Pk.
Sept	1989	1200	Harford	Ross	Hiill House, Lusk
Sept	1989	1201	O'Hara	John	Orlynn Pk.
Sept	1989	1202	O'Connor	Eoin	Orlynn Pk.
Sept	1989	1203	Ridgeway	David	The Close, Orlynn Pk.
Sept	1989	1204	Harold	James	Balleally Lane
Sept	1989	1205	Hickey	Derek	Orlynn Pk.
Sept	1989	1206	Farrell	Mark	Ministers Pk.
Sept	1989	1207	Quinn	Neil	The Green
Sept	1989	1208	Walsh	John	Ministers Pk.
Sept	1989	1209	Weston	Patrick	Orlynn Pk.
Sept	1989	1210	Horgan	Ciaran	Barrack Rd.
Sept	1989	1211	Ball	Gareth	Orlynn Pk.
Sept	1989	1212	Cruise	Andrew	Ministers Pk.
Sept	1989	1213	Daly	Michael	Chael Rd.
Sept	1989	1214	McGarry	Ross	Orlynn Pk.
Sept	1989	1215	Doyle	Daniel	Ministers Pk.
Sept	1989	1216	Haughton	Harry	Orlynn Pk.
Sept	1989	1217	Hussey	Mark	Orlynn Pk.

Month Registered in the School	Year	Pupils Register No.	Pupils Surname	First Name	Place of Residence
Sept	1989	1218	Kealey	Graham	The Close, Orlynn Pk.
Sept	1989	1219	O'Reilly	Kevin	Orlynn Pk.
Sept	1989	1220	O'Reilly	Derek	St. Macullins Close
Sept	1989	1221	O'Rouurke	Paul	Remount Farm
Sept	1989	1222	Shortall	Robert	Orlynn Pk.
Sept	1989	1223	Blessing	Paul	Ash Grove
Mar	1990	1224	Godkin	Ronan	Orlynn Pk.
Sept	1989	1225	Morley	David	Orlynn Pk.
Sept	1989	1226	Aupy	Brendan	Orlynn Pk.
Sept	1989	1227	Martin	Colin	Main St.
Sept	1989	1228	Halpin	Gerard	Orlynn Pk.
Sept	1989	1229	Martin	Alan	Main St.
Nov	1990	1230	Redmond	John	Orlynn Pk.
Sept	1990	1231	Courtney	Michael	Orlynn Pk.
Sept	1990	1232	Goulding	Thomas	Orlynn Pk.
Sept	1990	1233	Murphy	Brian	Orlynn Pk.
Sept	1990	1234	Goulding	Barry	Orlynn Pk.
Oct	1990	1235	Gregory	Karl	Orlynn Pk.
Sept	1990	1236	Gray	Caslan	Orlynn Pk.
Sept	1990	1237	Donoghue	Stephen	Orlynn Pk.
Sept	1990	1238	Madigan	Alan	Orlynn Pk.
Sept	1990	1239	Jones	Neil	Orlynn Pk.
Sept	1990	1240	Leech	Mark	Orlynn Pk.
Sept	1990	1241	McMahon	Colm	Orlynn Pk.
Sept	1990	1242	Murphy	Robert	Kelly Pk.
Sept	1990	1243	Boylan	Carl	Ministers Rd.
Sept	1990	1244	Byrnes	Noel	Kelly Pk.
Sept	1990	1245	Cruise	Peter	Ministers Rd.
Sept	1990	1246	Darby	Eoin	Orlynn Pk.
Sept	1990	1247	Devine	Robert	Orlynn Pk.
Sept	1990	1248	Gosson	Raymond	Commons
Sept	1990	1249	Hurley	Barry	Orlynn Pk.

Appendices

Month Registered in the School	Year	Pupils Register No.	Pupils Surname	First Name	Place of Residence
Sept	1990	1250	Hynes	Alan	Tower View
Sept	1990	1251	Teeling	Colin	Ministers Pk.
Sept	1990	1252	Teeling	Paul	Ministers Rise
Sept	1990	1253	Cruise	Andrew	Kelly Pk.
Sept	1990	1254	Daly	Brian	Church Rd.
Sept	1990	1255	Cruise	Alex	Ministers Pk.
Sept	1990	1256	Delaney	Martin	Ministers Pk.
Sept	1990	1257	Godkin	Ronan	Orlynn Pk.
Sept	1990	1258	McGealy	Martin	Kelly Pk.
Sept	1990	1259	McGee	Christopher	P.O. Rd.
Sept	1990	1260	Meaghar	Cathal	Orlynn Pk
Sept	1990	1261	Monks	Brendan	Station Rd.
Sept	1990	1262	Murphy	Neil	Ministers Rise
Sept	1990	1263	Murphy	Ian	Ministers Pk.
Sept	1990	1264	Murphy	Peter	Orlynn Pk
Sept	1990	1265	O'Connell	Joseph	Orlynn Pk
Sept	1990	1266	Phipps	Stephen	Orlynn Pk
Sept	1990	1267	Daly	Colin	Orlynn Pk
Oct	1991	1268	Cruise	Damien	Rush
Sept	1991	1269	Tonge	Brian	Orlynn Pk
Sept	1991	1270	Cruise	Daryl	Rush
Sept	1991	1271	Boardman	Luke	Rathmooney
Sept	1991	1272	Boylan	Gary	Kelly Pk.
Sept	1991	1273	Butterly	Kevin	Orlynn Pk
Sept	1991	1274	Courtney	Christopher	The Avenue
Sept	1991	1275	Daly	Domnic	Ministers Rd.
Sept	1991	1276	Dennis	Graham	Racecourse Commons
Sept	1991	1277	Morley	Alan	Orlynn Pk
Sept	1991	1278	McQuillan	Colm	Kelly Pk.
Sept	1991	1279	O'Connor	Rory	The Commons
Sept	1991	1280	Skelly	Christopher	P.O. Rd.
Sept	1991	1281	Skelly	Martin	P.O. Rd.

Month Registered in the School	Year	Pupils Register No.	Pupils Surname	First Name	Place of Residence
Sept	1991	1282	Reilly	Diarmuid	Orlynn Pk
Sept	1991	1283	Skelly	Sean	Ministers Pk.
Sept	1991	1284	Doyle	Michael	Tower View
Sept	1991	1285	Smith	Kevin	Orlynn Pk
Sept	1991	1286	Gilsenan	Jamie	Ministers Pk.
Sept	1991	1287	Hurley	Cathal	Regles
Sept	1991	1288	McNally	Adrian	Tower View
Sept	1991	1289	Christie	Sean	Kelly Pk.
Sept	1991	1290	O'Donoghue	Shane	Loughshinny
Sept	1991	1291	Thornton	Philip	Orlynn Pk
Sept	1991	1292	Doyle	Joseph	Bridetree
Sept	1991	1293	Brady	Jason	Orlynn Pk
Sept	1992	1294	Hennessy	Richard	Stoneview, Dublin Rd.
May	1992	1295	O'Hara	Richard	Orlynn Pk
Sept	1992	1296	Bracken	Ciaran	The Close, Orlynn Pk.
Sept	1992	1297	Daly	Stephen	
Sept	1992	1298	Hennessy	Ruari	Newhaggard
Sept	1992	1299	Phipps	Christopher	The Park, Orlynn Pk.
Sept	1992	1300	Foran	Sean	Orlynn Pk
Sept	1992	1301	Horgan	Ultan	Church View, B'rk. Rd.
Sept	1992	1302	Barry	Daniel	Orlynn Pk
Sept	1992	1303	Devine	Mark	Orlynn Pk
Sept	1992	1304	Daly	John	Kelly Pk.
Sept	1992	1305	Darby	Brendan	Orlynn Pk.
Sept	1992	1306	O'Donovan	Sean	Orlynn Pk.
Sept	1992	1307	Donoghue	Garry	Orlynn Pk.
Sept	1992	1308	Keatley	Ross	The Close, Orlynn Pk.
Sept	1992	1309	Hand	Robert	Orlynn Pk.
Sept	1992	1310	Leech	George	Orlynn Pk.
Sept	1992	1311	Mahon	Robert	Skerries
Sept	1992	1312	Rogan	Ciaran	Clay Cottage, Lusk
Sept	1992	1313	Russell	Ciaran	Ministers Rd.

Appendices

Month Registered in the School	Year	Pupils Register No.	Pupils Surname	First Name	Place of Residence
Sept	1992	1314	Shanahan	Sean	Orlynn Pk.
Sept	1992	1315	Teeling	Kit	Ministers Rise
Sept	1992	1316	McCullagh	Sean	Orlynn Pk.
Sept	1992	1317	McQuillan	Daniel	Kelly Pk.
Sept	1992	1318	Hennessy	Alan	Stoneview, Dublin Rd.
Sept	1992	1319	Toft	Emmett	Ministers Rd.
	1993	1320	Ward	Brian	No Permanent Address
		1321	Ward	Michael	No Permanent Address
	1992	1322	Meade	Mark	Ballealy East
	1993	1323	Ward	Daniel	No Permanent Address
		1324	Ward	John	No Permanent Address

Girls

List of Girls c.1862 to 1891

Note: In the earlier years, 1860's to c.1880, the records show date of last birthday of the pupils (column 6). In most cases this was their age when the pupil entered the advanced classes, 2nd, 3rd, 4th or 5th, not to be confused with the age the pupil started school.

The dates in column 1 and 2 are in most cases the date the pupil started school but in some cases this is the date the pupil started in the advanced class. Therefore for someone doing family research the information given in this table (1862 to 1891) should be treated with caution because of the different methods used to record the pupils details. The Table below (1892 to 1899) is somewhat more reliable, although there are still a few instances as described above.

Month Registered in the School	Year	Pupils Register No.	Pupils Surname	First Name	Age last birthday	Residence	Occupation Of Parent/ Guardian
Aug	1862	1	Dennis	Bridget	14	Lusk	Farmer
May	1863	82	sweet man	Margaret	14	Lusk	Grocer
May	1865	2	Andrews	Kate	10	Lusk	Grocer
May	1866	3	Dennis	Margaret	9	Nth Commons	Labourer
Jun	1867	5	Muztagh	Mary	8	Lusk	Farmer
Sept	1867	6	Connor	Ellen	8	Lusk	Mason
Feb	1868	7	Dennis	Kate	9	Lusk	Carpenter
Apr	1868	8	White	Margaret	11	Nth Commons	Farmer
Apr	1868	10	Connolly	Kate	8	Nth Commons	Farmer
Apr	1868	9	Muztagh	Alicia	7	Lusk	Farmer
May	1868	11	Kelly	Frances	9	Nth Commons	Widow
May	1868	12	Pepperd	Mary Jane	7	Lusk	Herd
June	1868	13	Donnelly	Anne	7	Lusk	Labourer
May	1869	15	McGee	Eliza	9	Nth Commons	Labourer
May	1869	14	McGuiness	Eliza	9	Nth Commons	Labourer
May	1869	4	Skelly	Mary Anne	9	Lusk	Farmer
May	1869	16	Andrews	Kate	10	Nth Commons	Farmer
Jun	1869	47	Kelly	Eliza	8	Nth Commons	Widow

Appendices

Month Registered in the School	Year	Pupils Register No.	Pupils Surname	First Name	Age last birthday	Residence	Occupation Of Parent/Guardian
June	1869	18	Lowry Mannion	Anne	7	Lusk	Constable
Sept	1869	17	Skelly	Eliza	7	Lusk	Farmer
Mar	1870	20	Andrews	Ellen	7	Lusk	Blacksmith
Mar	1870	20	Farrell	Mary Anne	7	Lusk	Dealer
May	1870	22	Murtagh	Mary	5	Lusk	Farmer
May	1870	23	Murtagh	Ellen	4	Lusk	Farmer
Mar	1870	24	Connolly	Mary Anne	6	Nth Commons	Farmer
May	1870	25	Clarke	Mary	5	Lusk	Widow
Aug	1870	26	Donnelly	Margaret	9	Lusk	Tailor
Aug	1870	27	McArdle	Kate	12	Lusk	Laborer
Apr	1871	28	Farrell	Frances	5	Lusk	Dead
Apr	1871	29	Hand	Margaret	5	Lusk	Farmer
May	1871	30	Toole	Jane	6	Nth Commons	Dealer
May	1871	21	Kiernan	Mary	8	Nth Commons	Labourer
May	1871	31	Russell	Margaret	8	Nth Commons	Labourer
May	1871	83	Kiernan	Ellen	5	Nth Commons	Labourer
May	1871	37	Russell	Eliza	4	Nth Commons	Labourer
Jun	1871	36	Kiernan	Bridget	6	Nth Commons	Labourer
June	1871	32	Kean	Teresa	6	Lusk	Farmer
June	1871	33	Whelan	Mary Anne	5	Lusk	Labourer
Jun	1871	32	Kean	Teresa	7	Lusk	Farmer
July	1871	34	Hughes	Mary Anne	5	Nth Commons	Labourer
Nov	1871	36	Kiernan	Bridget	5	Nth Commons	Labourer
Nov	1871	38	Kean	Mary	4	Lusk	Labourer
Nov	1871	35	Kiernan	Ellen	6	Nth Commons	Labourer
Feb	1872	39	Masterson	Bridget	6	Lusk	Labourer
Mar	1872	83	Kean	Margaret	11	Lusk	Labourer
Mar	1872	41	White	Mary	8	Lusk	Labourer
Mar	1872	42	White	Rose	6	Lusk	Labourer
May	1872	43	Kean	Ellen	12	Lusk	Farmer
May	1872	46	Kean	Alicia	6	Lusk	Farmer

Month Registered in the School	Year	Pupils Register No.	Pupils Surname	First Name	Age last birthday	Residence	Occupation Of Parent/Guardian
May	1872	47	White	Anna Maria	6	Nth Commons	Farmer
May	1872	49	Muztagh	Helena	4	Lusk	Farmer
May	1871	35	Kiernan	Ellen	5	Nth Commons	Laborer
May	1872	45	Gaynor	Ellen	4	Lusk	Station Master
May	1872	48	Kelly	Elly	6	Nth Commons	Lab
May	1872	44	Bray	Eliza	13	Nth Commons	Laborer
May	1872	47	White	Anna Maria	7	Nth Commons	Farmer
Sept	1872	90	Sweetman	Margaret	15	Lusk	Widow
Oct	1872	51	Carton	Ellen	7	Lusk	Blacksmith
Oct	1872	50	Carton	Kate	9	Lusk	Blacksmith
Oct	1872	52	Carton	Susan	6	Lusk	Blacksmith
Nov	1872	53	Connolly	Jane	12	Nth Commons	Farmer
Feb	1872	40	Masterson	Mary	8	Lusk	Labourer
Dec	1872	54	Bray	Rose	9	Nth Commons	Labourer
Dec	1872	55	Clarke	Kate	12	Tyrrelstown	Farmer
Jan	1873	56	Dennis	Margaret	10	Nth Commons	Laborer
Feb	1873	57	Daly	Eliza	12	Lusk	Teacher
Mar	1873	58	McCann	Mary Anne	9	Lusk	Labourer
Mar	1873	59	Masterson	Margaret	10	Lusk	Labourer
Apr	1873	60	Hoey	Mary	11	Figures	Farmer
Apr	1873	62	McNally	Bridget	8	Lusk	Labourer
Apr	1873	61	Boyle	Kate		Lusk	Labourer
Apr	1873		Matthews	Margaret	7	Commons	Labourer
Apr	1873	85	Seaver	?	4	Lusk	Labourer
May	1873	64	Marmion	Davidina	6	Lusk	Constable
May	1873	68	Kavanagh	Mary	7	Figures	Herd
May	1873	74	Daly	Mary	13	Lusk	Labourer
May	1873	63	Bentley	Mary	4	Lusk	
May	1873	65	Peppard	Margaret	5	Lusk	Labourer
May	1873	66	Peppard	Bridget	5	Lusk	Labourer
May	1873	67	Peppard	Christina	4	Lusk	Labourer

Appendices

Month Registered in the School	Year	Pupils Register No.	Pupils Surname	First Name	Age last birthday	Residence	Occupation Of Parent/ Guardian
May	1873	69	Reilly	Kate	6	Lusk	Grocer
May	1873	71	Donnelly	Jane	3	Lusk	Labourer
May	1873	72	Daly	Ellen	4	Lusk	Labourer
May	1873	73	McGee	Anne	4	Labourer	Labourer
May	1873	75	Smyth	Catherine	4	Lusk	Labourer
May	1873	70	Peppard	Mary Anne	13	Lusk	
May	1873	86	Davis	Ellen	8	Lusk	
Jun	1873	87	Kiernan	Sarah	10	Nth Commons	
Jun	1873	88	Fitzpatrick	Anne	10	Jordanstown	Farmer
Jun	1873	89	Fitzpatrick	Kate	12	Jordanstown	Farmer
June	1873	76	Connor	Teresa	3	Lusk	Mason
June	1873	77	McNally	Ellen	6	Lusk	Labourer
June	1873	78	Dennis	Hannah	3	Lusk	Carpenter
June	1873	79	Murray	Eliza	6	Tyrrelstown	Herd
June	1873	80	Dennis	Bridget	5	Nth Common	Labourer
June	1873	81	Doran	Ellen	5	Lusk	Labourer
June	1873	84	Taylor	Jane	3	Lusk	Farmer
June	1873		Seaver??	???	4	Lusk	Labourer
Mar	1874	69	Reilly	Kate	7	Lusk	Grocer
Apr	1874	95	Dennis	Bridget	12	Lusk	Farmer
June	1874	91	Sherry	Catherine	5	Lusk	Labourer
June	1874	92	sweet man	Catherine	5	Lusk	Labourer
June	1874	93	Byrne	Mary	4	Lusk	Porter
June	1874	94	Gray	Mary	4	Lusk	Labourer
June	1874	96	Cruise	Kate	3	Lusk	Farmer
May	1874	99	Murtagh	Eliza	3	Lusk	Farmer
May	1874	97	Teeling	Rose	9	Lusk	Labourer
May	1874	98	Teeling	Mary	11	Lusk	Labourer
June	1874	100	Kavanagh	Margaret	4	Lusk	Farmer
Aug	1874	66	Peppard	Bridget	7	Lusk	Labourer
Aug	1874	77	McNally	Ellen	7	Lusk	Labourer

Month Registered in the School	Year	Pupils Register No.	Pupils Surname	First Name	Age last birthday	Residence	Occupation Of Parent/Guardian
Sept	1874	101	Connolly	Bridget	4	Commons	Farmer
Sept	1874	102	Daly	Rose	5	Figures	Labourer
Feb	1875	104	Lennon	Mary	11	Man O War	Labourer
Feb	1875	105	Lennon	Anna E	9	Man O War	Labourer
Mar	1875	106	Brogan	Mary	5	Nth Commons	Labourer
Apr	1875	107	Peppard	Catherine	4	Lusk	Labourer
Apr	1875	108	Taylor	Sarah	4	Lusk	Farmer
Apr	1875	109	Lennon	Ellen	6	Man O War	Labourer
Apr	1875	113	Matthews	Margaret	6	Baldungan	Farmer
May	1875	115	Evans	Mary	4	Lusk	Farmer
May	1875	114	Andrews	Mary	4	Nth Common	Farmer
May	1875	116	Hughes	Frances	5	Nth Commons	Labourer
May	1875	71	Donnelly	Jane	7	Lusk	Labourer
June	1875	117	Powderly	Bridget		Lusk	Groom
June	1875	118	Doyle	Margaret		Lusk	Tailor
June	1875	119	Kiernan	Ellen	3	Lusk	Labourer
Jun	1875	118	Doyle	Margaret	7	Lusk	Tailor
July	1875	120	Skelly	Mary	3	Lusk	Labourer
Aug	1875	121	Murray	Margaret	4	Lusk	Herd
Aug	1875	122	Connor	Annie	5	Lusk	Warder
Aug	1875	123	Sweetman	Margaret	3	Lusk	Farmer
Oct	1875	103	Gannon	jane	12	Lusk	Labourer
?	1875	110	Hoey	Mary	6	Figures	Groom
?	1875	111	Carolan	Mary	9	Man O War	Labourer
?	1875	112	Thornton	Kate	12	Balcunnin	Farmer
?	1875	114	Farrell	Catherine	10	Lusk	Labourer
Mar	1876	124	Dennis	Mary J	4	Lusk	Carpenter
Apr	1876	125	Gaynor	Mary J	5	Lusk	
Mar	1876	126	Everard	Margaret	4	Commons	Farmer
Apr	1876	127	Devine	Mary J	6	Commons	Blacksmith
May	1876	128	Andrews	Mary	3	Lusk	Deceased

Appendices

Month Registered in the School	Year	Pupils Register No.	Pupils Surname	First Name	Age last birthday	Residence	Occupation Of Parent/Guardian
May	1876	129	Smyth	Bridget	3	Lusk	Labourer
May	1876	130	Murtagh	Catherine	3	Lusk	Farmer
May	1876	131	Carolan	Anne	8	Lusk	Labourer
May	1876	132	Donnelly	Mary	4	Lusk	Tailor
May	1876	133	Sweet man	Ellen	3	Lusk	Farmer
May	1876	134	Cruise	Christina	4	Lusk	Farmer
May	1876	135	Matthews	Sarah	5	Commons	Farmer
May	1876	136	Daly	Mary	4	Lusk	Labourer
May	1876	137	Carton	Mary A	3	Lusk	Blacksmith
May	1876	138	Hopkins	Mary	4	Lusk	Deceased
May	1876	139	Sweet man	Catherine	4	Lusk	Farmer
May	1876	140	Duffy	Margaret	5	Commons	Warder
June	1876	141	Meehan	Jane	3	Lusk	Labourer
July	1876	142	Bates	Mary J	8	Lusk	Deceased
July	1876	143	Davis	Kate	12	Lusk	Deceased
Sept	1876	144	Savage	Bridget	4	Lusk	Laborer
Oct	1876	145	Hoey	Charlotte	6	Lusk	Sailor
Jan	1877	146	Monaghan	Mary A	11	Lusk	Labourer
feb	1877	147	Dennis	Kate	4	Lusk	Labourer
Mar	1877	124	Dennis	Mary J	5	Lusk	Carpenter
Mar	1877	148	Cornwall	Susan	11	Lusk	Carpenter
Mar	1877	149	Cornwall	Maria	10	Lusk	Carpenter
Apr	1877	150	Daly	Kate	3	Lusk	Labourer
Apr	1877	151	Caddall	Catherine	4	Commons	Farmer
Apr	1877	152	Walsh	Margaret	4	Commons	Labourer
Apr	1877	153	Connor	Catherine	4	Lusk	Labourer
May	1877	154	Connor	Eliza	4	Nth Commons	Warder
May	1877	156	Clarke	Louisa	6	Tyrrelstown	Farmer
May	1877	157	Clarke	Mary	5	Tyrrelstown	Farmer
May	1877	159	Collins	Mary	5	Lusk	Sailor
May	1877	155	Carolan	Anne	7	Man O' War	Labourer

Month Registered in the School	Year	Pupils Register No.	Pupils Surname	First Name	Age last birthday	Residence	Occupation Of Parent/Guardian
May	1877	158	Carrick	Mary A	8	Man O' War	Labourer
June	1877	160	Bates	Jane	4	Lusk	Labourer
July	1877	161	Dennis	Anne	5	Nth Commons	Labourer
July	1877	163	Gill	Jane	6	Nth Commons	Labourer
July	1877	162	Monaghan	Kate	9	Lusk	Labourer
sept	1877	164	Hartford	Mary J	4	Nth Commons	Labourer
Sept	1877	165	Hughes	Sarah J	10	Lusk	Farmer
Nov	1877	166	Shiels	Margaret	5	Lusk	Labourer
Nov	1877	167	Gosson	Mary	9	Nth Commons	Labourer
Jan	1878	168	Hanratty	Mary	5	Lusk	Constable
Jan	1878	169	Carolan	Bridget	3	Lusk	Blacksmith
Feb	1878	170	Donnelly	Mary	4	Lusk	Labourer
Feb	1878	171	Owens	Margaret	5	Knightstown	Farmer
Mar	1878	172	Gaynor	Mary	11	Lusk	Warder
Apr	1878	173	Cowley	Mary A	4	Knockdrummin	Herd
Apr	1878	174	Kenny	Emily	5	Lusk	Butler
Apr	1878	175	Dennis	Mary	3	Lusk	Labourer
May	1878	176	Connolly	Josephine	4	Nth Commons	Farmer
May	1878	177	Clarke	Anne	4	Tyrrelstown	Farmer
May	1878	178	Kelly	Josephine	4	Quickpenny	Farmer
June	1878	179	Devine	Alicia	4	Rahenny	Labourer
June	1878	180	Meehan	Catherine	4	Lusk	Labourer
Jun	1878	184	Dunne	Mary	4	Lusk	Deceased
July	1878	181	Doyle	Mary A	5	Lusk	Labourer
July	1878	182	Maypother	Catherine	4	Lusk	Labourer
Oct	1878	183	Clarke	Mary	4	Lusk	Labourer
Oct	1878		Skelly	Margaret	12	Lusk	Dealer
Nov	1878	186	Bray	Mary	5	Commons	Labourer
Nov	1878	185	Jordan	Mary A	9	Lusk	Deceased
Mar	1879	188	Farrell	Christina	4	Lusk	Labourer
Apr	1879	189	Sweetman	Anna M	4	Lusk	Farmer

Appendices

Month Registered in the School	Year	Pupils Register No.	Pupils Surname	First Name	Age last birthday	Residence	Occupation Of Parent/Guardian
Apr	1879	190	Daly	Ellen	4	Lusk	Labourer
Apr	1879	191	Whyte	Catherine	5	Commons	Farmer
Apr	1879	192	Gray	Annie	3	Lusk	Mason
Apr	1879	193	Gaynor	Bridget	5	Lusk	Warder
Apr	1879	194	Dowdall	Mary	6	Commons	Labourer
May	1879	195	Devine	Catherine	4	Raheny	Labourer
June	1879	196	Hurley	Alice M	4	Commons	Labourer
Jun	1879	197	Branagan	Margaret	9	Commons	Labourer
Sept	1879	187	Maypother	Bridget	7	Lusk	Labourer
Sept	1879	198	Lawlor	Eliza	11	Lusk	Ploughman
Nov	1879	199	Sherry	Mary A	3	Lusk	Labourer
Nov	1879	200	Dennis	Christina	3	Lusk	Carpenter
Jan	1880	201	Peppard	Eliza	4	Lusk	
Feb	1880	202	Daly	Bridget	5	Lusk	Labourer
Apr	1880	204	Gill	Mary	7	Commons	Labourer
May	1880	203	Andrews	Eliza	5	Lusk	Labourer
May	1880	205	Cowley	Jane	4	Knockdrummin	Herd
May	1880	206	Andrews	Bridget	5	Lusk	Butcher
May	1880	208	Watson	Mary J	4	Lusk	Labourer
May	1880	207	Andrews	Mary C	7	Lusk	Butcher
June	1880	209	Donnelly	Ellen	5	Lusk	Labourer
July	1880	210	Matthews	Mary A	5	Lusk	Labourer
Aug	1880	211	Farrell	Mary A	5	Lusk	Labourer
Aug	1880	212	Carolan	Margaret	4	Lusk	Labourer
Aug	1880	213	Farrell	Margaret	3	Lusk	Labourer
Aug	1880	215	Cruise	Margaret	4	Lusk	Farmer
Aug	1880	214	Davis	Margaret	5	Lusk	Blacksmith
Aug	1880	120	Skelly	Mary A	8	Lusk	Labourer
Sept	1880	216	Early	Mary A	10	Ballystrane	Farmer
Sept	1880	153	Walsh	Margaret	7	Lusk	Labourer
Mar	1881	217	Sweet man	Alice	4	Lusk	Farmer

Month Registered in the School	Year	Pupils Register No.	Pupils Surname	First Name	Age last birthday	Residence	Occupation Of Parent/Guardian
Mar	1881	219	Clarke	Margaret	7	Tyrrelstown	Farmer
Apr	1881	220	Connolly	Margaret	4	Nth Commons	Farmer
May	1881	221	Dennis	Anna	3	Lusk	Labourer
May	1881	222	Keegan ??	Catherine	5	Lusk	Labourer
May	1881	223	Harris	Mary	3	Lusk	Labourer
May	1881	224	Gray	Jane	5	Lusk	Labourer
May	1881	225	Murphy	Julia	6	Lusk	Widow
July	1881	226	McArdle	Mary J	4	Commons	Labourer
July	1881	227	Dowdall	Eliza	6	Commons	Labourer
Oct	1881	228	Marmion	Mary J	6	Lusk	Labourer
Oct	1881	229	McMahon	Jane	4	Lusk	Deceased
Oct	1881	230	Kelly	Mary	6	Quickpenny	Farmer
Nov	1881	231	Donnelly	Bridget	4	Lusk	Painter
Nov	1881	232	Donnelly	Margaret	5	Lusk	Painter
Mar	1882	233	Gill	Margaret	7	Commons	Labourer
Apr	1882	234	Clarke	Eliza	6	Tyrrelstown	Farmer
May	1882	236	Daly	Margaret	3	Lusk	Labourer
Jun	1882	237	Daly	Bridget	4	Lusk	Labourer
May	1882	238	Clarke	Alice	5	Tyrrelstown	Farmer
June	1882	239	Meagher	Anne	6	Lusk	Deceased
July	1882	240	Cowley	Eliza	4	Knockdrummin	Herd
Oct	1882	242	Moore	MaryEe	3	Lusk	Servant
Oct	1882	243	Andrews	Margaret	4	Lusk	Butcher
Dec	1882	244	Gallagher	Anne	3	Lusk	Labourer
Apr	1883	246	Connelly	Jane M	5	Commons	Farmer
Apr	1883	249	Fay	Catherine	3	Lusk	Labourer
Apr	1883	248	Collins	Celia	7	Baldungan	Farmer
Apr	1883	249	McArdle	Catherine	4	Nth Commons	Labourer
Apr	1883	250	Duffy	Mary J	5	Nth Commons	Warder
May	1883	251	Horgan	Annie	3	Lusk	Labourer
May	1883	252	Brogan	Mary	4	Nth Commons	Labourer

Appendices

Month Registered in the School	Year	Pupils Register No.	Pupils Surname	First Name	Age last birthday	Residence	Occupation Of Parent/Guardian
July	1883	253	Carolan	Mary J	4	Lusk	Carpenter
Sept	1883	254	Farrell	Eliza	4	Lusk	Dealer
Oct	1883	255	Cruise	Eliza	4		Farmer
Oct	1883	256	Carolan	Teresa	4		Blacksmith
Mar	1884	260	Matthews	Eliza	8	Nth Commons	Labourer
Apr	1884	262	Cowley	Bridget	3	Knockdrummin	Herd
Apr	1884	262	Meehan	Mary A	4	Lusk	Laborer
Apr	1884	263	Skelly	Esther	4	Lusk	Labourer
May	1884	262	Clarke	Teresa	5	Tyrrelstown	Farmer
May	1884	265	Hand	Eliza	4	Lusk	Porter
June	1884	266	Kelly	Agnes	5	Quickpenny	Farmer
June	1884	267	Connolly	Mary	4	Nth Commons	Farmer
June	1884	268	Sweetman	Mary A	5	Lusk	Laborer
Sept	1884	269	Donnelly	Rose	4	Lusk	Painter
Sept	1884	270	Andrews	Christina	4	Lusk	Butcher
Sept	1884	272	Collins	Helena	5	Baldungan	Farmer
Nov	1884	276	Owens	Mary Agnes	6	Kingstown	Farmer
Nov	1884	277	Cruise	Mary Ellen	3	Lusk	Farmer
Dec	1884	278	Whelan	Mary	4	Lusk	Labourer
Jan	1885	279	Rafferty	Annie	4	Lusk	Labourer
Feb	1885	280	sweet man	Teresa	5	Lusk	Farmer
Feb	1885	281	Moore	Bridget	4	Lusk	Servant
Mar	1885	282	Kilbride	Eliza	3	Lusk	Labourer
Apr	1885	283	McCann	Mary	3	Lusk	Labourer
Nov	1885	284	Maypother	Eliza	6	Lusk	Labourer
May	1885	285	Reilly ??	Mary	6	Nth Commons	Deceased
May	1885	286	Bentley	Catherine	8	Lusk	Shoemaker
May	1885	287	Rickard	Eliza	5	Lusk	Deceased
May	1885	288	Gosson	Bridget	6	Nth Commons	Labourer
June	1885	290	Andrews	Mary	5	Tyrrelstown	Labourer
Jan	1886	292	Smyth	Agnes	3	Lusk	Farmer

Month Registered in the School	Year	Pupils Register No.	Pupils Surname	First Name	Age last birthday	Residence	Occupation Of Parent/Guardian
Mar	1886	293	Matthews	Bridget	7	Nth Commons	Farmer
Mar	1886	294	Connolly	alice	3	Nth Commons	Farmer
Mar	1886	295	Farrell	Frances	3	Lusk	Labourer
May	1886	300	Donnelly	Roseanne	3	Lusk	Labourer
May	1886	302	Connelly	Margaret	4	Lusk	Labourer
May	1886	303	McArdle	Alicia	3	Lusk	Labourer
May	1886	304	Henry	Angela	3	Lusk	Constable
May	1886	305	Rickard	Margaret	4	Lusk	Deceased
May	1886	306	Toole	Mary	7	Nth Commons	Labourer
May	1886	307	Toole	Anne	7	Nth Commons	Labourer
Oct	1886	311	Dennis	Mary R	4	Lusk	Labourer
Jan	1887	312	Cruise	Esther	4	Lusk	Farmer
Jan	1887	313	Greene	Ellen	4	Lusk	Corn Factor
Jan	1887	314	Collins	Bridget	4	Lusk	Labourer
Feb	1887	315	Meehan	Margaret	4	Lusk	Labourer
Feb	1887	316	Rodgers	Mary	4	Nth Commons	Labourer
Feb	1887	317	Mathews	Jane M	6	Nth Commons	Farmer
Nov	1886	318	Owens	Christina	4	Kingstown	Farmer
Nov	1886	319	Rafferty	Jane	3	Lusk	Labourer
Nov	1886	320	Whelan	Anne	3	Lusk	Labourer
May	1887	327	Brogan	Bridget	5	Nth Commons	Labourer
July	1887	328	Toole	Alicia	5	Lusk	Labourer
Jan	1888	329	Mahon	Mary	5	Lusk	Labourer
Feb	1888	330	Moore	Ellen	5	Lusk	Labourer
Mar	1888	269	Donnelly	Rose	8	Lusk	Labourer
Apr	1888	331	Carroll	Eliza	4	Lusk	Constable
Apr	1888	332	Jenkins	Letitia	4	Lusk	Warder
Apr	1888	333	Devine	Bridget	5	Nth Commons	Labourer
May	1888	334	Clinton	Eliza J	6	Rogerstown	Farmer
May	1888	335	Clinton	Jane J	4	Rogerstown	Farmer
May	1888	336	Clinton	Julia	5	Raheny	Labourer

Appendices

Month Registered in the School	Year	Pupils Register No.	Pupils Surname	First Name	Age last birthday	Residence	Occupation Of Parent/Guardian
May	1888	338	Rickard	Teresa	4	Lusk	Deceased
Oct	1888	339	Donnelly	Margaret	4	Lusk	Ttilor
Oct	1888	342	Kilbride	Kathleen	4	Lusk	Labourer
Oct	1888	343	Devine	Margaret	4	Nth Commons	Labourer
Oct	1888	344	McNally	Esther	3	Lusk	Farmer
Jan	1889	345	Gray	Susan	4	Lusk	Deceased
Mar	1889	347	Whelan	Eliza	4	Lusk	Labourer
Mar	1889	348	Clinton	Mary	3	Lusk	Farmer
Mar	1889	349	Clarke	Margaret	3	Lusk	Farmer
Mar	1889	350	Moore	Ellen	4	Lusk	Farmer
Apr	1889	351	Sweet man	Eliza	4	Lusk	Farmer
Apr	1889	353	Connelly	Julia	4	Lusk	Labourer
Apr	1889	353	Kelly	Mary A	3	Lusk	Labourer
Apr	1889	354	Kean	Mary	4	Lusk	Labourer
Apr	1889	355	Bray	Catherine	6	Nth Commons	Labourer
Apr	1889	356	Mathews	Margaret	6	Nth Commons	Farmer
May	1889	357	Brogan	Ellen	5	Nth Commons	Labourer
July	1889	358	Carton	Catherine G	3	Lusk	Groom
Sept	1889	359	Maypother	Margaret	4	Lusk	Labourer
Oct	1889	360	Carton	Mary J	3	Lusk	Groom
Nov	1889	361	Cruise	Dorothy	3	Lusk	Farmer
Nov	1889	262	McArdle	Annie	4	Nth Commons	Labourer
Jan	1890	262	Barber	Bridget	4	Lusk	Labourer
Jan	1890	264	Mathews	Mary	4	Lusk	Labourer
Mar	1890	366	Clarke	Mary	3	Lusk	Farmer
Apr	1890	367	McGee	Kate	5	Nth Commons	Farmer
Apr	1890	368	Hughes	Margaret	6	Nth Commons	Farmer
Apr	1890	369	Connolly	Annie	4	Lusk	Labourer
Apr	1890	370	Moore	Christina	4	Lusk	Labourer
Apr	1890	371	Skelly	Martha	4	Lusk	Labourer
Apr	1890	372	Rafferty	Ellen	4	Lusk	Labourer

Month Registered in the School	Year	Pupils Register No.	Pupils Surname	First Name	Age last birthday	Residence	Occupation Of Parent/Guardian
June	1890	368	Hughes	Margaret	7	Nth Commons	Farmer
Nov	1890	373	Devine	Alice	4	Lusk	Labourer
Feb	1891	374	Mathews	Josephine	5	Nth Commons	Farmer
Apr	1891	376	Jenkinson	Ellen	5	Newhhaggard	Stewart
Apr	1891	377	Seaver	Mary Anne	5	Nth Commons	Farmer
Apr	1891	378	Caddell	Mary	5	Nth Commons	Farmer
July	1891	380	Natly	Martha	6	Lusk	Sergeant
Sept	1891	230	Kelly	Mary	?	Quickpenny	
Sept	1891	221	Dennis	Anne E	?	Lusk	
Sept	1891	273	O'Hara	Mary	14	Irishtown	Stewart
Sept	1891	274	O'Hara	Annie	15	Irishtown	Stewart
Apr	1891	379	McColl	Isabella	5	Military Farm	Soldier
Aug	1891	381	Aungier	Catherine	4	Lusk	Labourer
Oct	1891	382	McNally	Mary	3	Rahenny	Farmer
Oct	1891	383	Hughes	Mary Julia	5	Lusk	Farmer

Appendices

List of Girls 1892 to 1899

Month Registered in the School	Year	Pupils Register No.	Pupils Surname	First Name	Age last birthday	DOB	Residence	Occupation Of Parent/Guardian	Previous School (if applicable)
Mar	1892	384	Brogan	Jane	6		Nth Commons	Labourer	
Mar	1892	386	Cotton	Beatrice	4		Military Farm	Soldier	
Mar	1892	387	Connolly	Eliza H	4		Lusk	Labourer	
Mar	1892	389	Clinton	Alice	4		Rahenny	Labourer	
Mar	1892	385	Mathews	Sarah	7		Nth Commons	Farmer	
May	1892	390	Moore	Eliza	3		Lusk	Servant	
May	1892	391	Sweetman	Kate	5		Lusk	Farmer	
May	1892	392	Sweetman	Mary Anne	4		Lusk	Farmer	
May	1892	393	Aungier	Kate	4		Lusk	Labourer	
May	1892	394	Farrell	Kate	4		Lusk	Dealer	
May	1892	395	Williams	Mary	4		Lusk	Deceased	
May	1892	396	Moore	Annie	4		Lusk	Labourer	
July	1892	397	Dennis	Bridget R	5		Lusk	Labourer	
Aug	1892	398	Marmion	Jane	5		Lusk	Carpenter	
Oct	1892	402	Clarke	Annie	4		Lusk	Farmer	
Feb	1893	403	Masterson	Mary	4		Lusk	Labourer	
Mar	1893	404	Sweetman	Mary E	4		Lusk	Labourer	
Mar	1893	405	Byrne	Anne	6		Palmerstown	Farmer	
Apr	1893	406	McGuire	Eliza	4		Ballymaguire	Farmer	
May	1893	407	Cluskey	Mary	4		Quickpenny	Farmer	
May	1893	408	Kerrigan	Frances	5		Ballymaguire	Labourer	
Aug	1893	409	Fay	Margaret	5		Rogerstown	Labourer	
Nov	1893	410	Devine	Anne	4		Hayestown	Labourer	
Nov	1893	393	Aungier	Catherine	6		Lusk	Labourer	
Nov	1893	398	Marmion	Jane	7		Lusk	Carpenter	
Nov	1893	364	Mathews	Mary	8		Lusk	Servant	
Nov	1893	402	Clarke	Anne	6		Lusk	Mason	
Jan	1894	411	Halpin	Kate	6		Newhaggard	Carpenter	
Jan	1894	412	Kelly	Esther	4		Lusk	Labourer	
Mar	1894	413	Lambe	Margaret	4		Ballaly	Herd	

Month Registered in the School	Year	Pupils Register No.	Pupils Surname	First Name	Age last birthday	DOB	Residence	Occupation Of Parent/Guardian	Previous School (if applicable)
Apr	1894	414	Sweetman	Margaret	4		Lusk	Farmer	
Apr	1894	415	Thomson	Sarah	4		Nth Commons	Farmer	
Apr	1894	416	Connolly	Mary h	4		Lusk	Labourer	
May	1894	417	McKenna	H	4		Quickpenny	Farmer	
May	1894	418	Dennis	Ellen	3		Lusk	Farmer	
July	1894	419	Baker	Ada l	4		Military Farm	Soldier	
July	1894	420	Masterson	Kate	3		Lusk	Labourer	
July	1894	421	carton	Emily	4		Lusk	Groom	
July	1894	422	Donnelly	Alice	3		Lusk	Tailor	
Aug	1894	423	Whelan	Bridget	4		Lusk	Labourer	
Oct	1894	424	Clinton	Anne	4		Raheny	Labourer	
Oct	1894	425	Devine	Margaret	3		Lusk	Labourer	
Oct	1894	426	Donnelly	Margaret	3		Lusk	Labourer	
Jan	1895	427	Rafferty	Mary	4		Lusk	Labourer	
Mar	1895	428	McNally	Katie	3		Lusk	Farmer	
Mar	1895		Brogan	Mary	10		Nth Commons	Labourer	
Apr	1895	429	Reilly	Bridget	5		Tyrrelstown	Labourer	
June	1895	431	Clarke	Mary Anne	6		Tyrrelstown	Farmer	
Sept	1895	433	Monks	Mary	4		Railway Station	Signalman	
Oct	1895	435	Clarke	Kate	4		Tyrrelstown	Farmer	
Jan	1896	436	Brogan	Maggie	6		Nth Commons	Labourer	
Jan	1896	437	Marmion	Georgina	5		Lusk	Carpenter	
Feb	1896	438	Price	Mary	3		Lusk	R.O.	
Feb	1896	439	Maguire	Bridget	3		Rathmooney	Farmer	
Apr	1896	440	Harper	Ada	4		Military Farm	Soldier	
Apr	1896	441	Owens	Mary A	6		Kingstown	Farmer	
May	1896	442	Caragher	Mary B	4		Chanterland	Stewart	
July	1896	443	Page	Mabel	6		Govt. Farm	Soldier	
June	1896	445	Devine	Kate	3		Lusk	Labourer	
Nov	1896	446	Maguire	Helen	3		Rathmooney	Farmer	
Nov	1896	447	Aungier	Maggie	4		Lusk	Labourer	
Nov	1896	448	Moore	Sarah Mary	4		Lusk	Labourer	

Appendices

Month Registered in the School	Year	Pupils Register No.	Pupils Surname	First Name	Age last birthday	DOB	Residence	Occupation Of Parent/Guardian	Previous School (if applicable)
Nov	1896	449	Power	Ellen	5		Lusk	Labourer	
Nov	1896	450	Halpin	Maggie	5		Nth Commons	Carpenter	
Dec	1896	451	Jenkinson	Mary	4		Newhhaggard	Stewart	
Jan	1897	452	Carton	Gertrude	4		Lusk	Shopkeeper	
Jan	1897	453	Johnston	Susan	4		Lusk	RIC Sergeant	
Mar	1897	455	McCann	Maggie	3		Lusk	Labourer	
Mar	1897	456	Sherry	Mary	3		Lusk	Railway Porter	
Apr	1897	457	Thomson	Elizabeth	5		Nth Commons	Farmer	
May	1897	458	Kiernan	Katie	4		Lusk	Farmer	
May	1897	459	Clarke	Bridget	4		Tyrrelstown	Farmer	
May	1897	460	Lambe	Alice	4		Ballaly	Herd	
Oct	1897	6	Fogarty	Maggie		27-12-1893	Lusk	Blacksmith	
Nov	1897	8	Moore	Johanna	3	17-4-1894	Railway Rd.	Labourer	
Nov	1897	7	McNally	Maggie		4-2-1894	Lusk	Farmer	
Nov	1897	9	Thorne	Annie		20-7-1892	Tyrrelstown	Farmer	
Nov	1897	10	Carton	Lizzie		6-4-1894	Lusk	Labourer	
Jan	1898	11	Kelly	Lizzie		9-1-1895	Lusk	Labourer	
Jan	1898	12	French	Mary k		1-4-1889	Lusk	Constable	
Jan	1898	13	Carton	Teresa		2-12-1894	Lusk	Shopkeeper	
Feb	1898	15	Whelan	Alice		2-12-1894	Near Rail Station	Orphan	
Feb	1898	14	McAneney	Julia		28-8-1886	Woodpark	Farmer	Corduff
Mar	1898	16	French	Maggie		27-1-1895	Lusk	Constable	
Mar	1898	17	Fay	Mary K		27-7-1895	Lusk	Labourer	
Apr	1898	18	Cluskey	Lizzie		27-5-1894	Quickpenny	Farmer	
May	1898	19	Alexander	Lillian		1-4-1886	Lusk	Accountant	Carlingford Co. Louth
May	1898	20	Alexander	Mabel		1-5-1887	Lusk	Accountant	Carlingford Co. Louth
May	1898	21	Alexander	Winifred		6-2-1891	Lusk	Accountant	Carlingford Co. Louth
June	1898	428	McNally	Katie		26-08-1891	Lusk	Farmer	
Aug	1898	22	Boyle	Bridget		17-11-1890	Lusk	Orphan	Kings Inns Dublin
Aug	1898	23	Boyle	Katie		23-9-1887	Lusk	Orphan	Kings Inns Dublin

Month Registered in the School	Year	Pupils Register No.	Pupils Surname	First Name	Age last birthday	DOB	Residence	Occupation Of Parent/Guardian	Previous School (if applicable)
Sept	1898	450	Halpin	Maggie		27-5-1898	Nth. Commons	Carpenter	
Sept	1898	24	Dennis	Lizzie		4-12-1894	Lusk	Labourer	
Sept	1898	25	Alexander	Kathleen		26-2-1894	Lusk	Accountant	
Sept	1898	435	Clarke	Katie	7		Kingstown	Orphan	
Dec	1898	439	Maguire	Brigid	6		Rathmooney	Farmer	
Dec	1898	339	Donnelly	Maggie	7		Lusk	NS Teacher	
Jan	1899	26	Doyle	Jane		3-8-1895	Lusk	Labourer	
Jan	1899	27	Peppard	Anne Mary		14-5-1895	Lusk	Labourer	
Feb	1899	28	Sherry	Katie		12-5-1895	Lusk	Labourer	
Mar	1899	29	Maguire	Alice		25-12-1895	Rathmooney	Farmer	
Mar	1899	30	Monks	Agnes		22-10-1894	R. Station	Signalman	
Mar	1899	31	Gough	Mary A		31-8-1894	Nth. Commons	Labourer	
Mar	1899	32	Seaver	Lizzie		31-3-1894	Nth. Commons	Farmer	
Mar	1899	33	Connolly	Alice		3-6-1895	Lusk	Labourer	
Apr	1899	34	Dixon	Mary J		28-11-1894	Lusk	Soldier	
May	1899	35	Hannon	Mary		19-1-1885	Ratheney	Labourer	Cliffoney, Sligo
June	1899	36	Donnelly	Maggie		20-8-1894	Lusk	Clerk	
June	1899	37	French	Nelly		25-8-1890	Lusk	Constable	
Aug	1899	38	Davis	Alice		11-6-1890	Lusk	Orphan	Balrothery Union Workhouse
Aug	1899	39	Caffrey	Katie		??-8-1891	Lusk	Labourer	Balrothery Union
Sept	1899	40	Murphy	Kathleen		1-3-1893	Ballastrane	Labourer	Hedgestown
Sept	1899	41	Bates	Bridget		??-9-1891	Lusk	Labourer	Balrothery Union
Oct	1899	42	Bambrick	Christine		26-12-1895	Lusk	Constable	
Oct	1899	43	Devine	Mary E		14-5-1895	Lusk	Labourer	
Oct	1899	44	Finnegan	Ellen		5-10-1895	Ballough	Labourer	
Oct	1899	45	Seaver	Alice		14-10-1895	Rellyskeystown	Farmer	
Oct	1899	46	Thomson	Annie		5-3-1895	Nth. Commons	Farmer	
Oct	1899	47	Brogan	Rosanna		28-1-1896	Nth. Commons	Horse Trainer	
Oct	1899	48	Halpin	Lizzie		23-9-1895	Nth. Commons	Carpenter	
Nov	1899	49	Marmion	Annie		23-3-1893	Lusk	Carpenter	
Nov	1899	50	Marmion	Ellie		12-3-1893	Lusk	Carpenter	

Appendices

Month Registered in the School	Year	Pupils Register No.	Pupils Surname	First Name	Age last birthday	DOB	Residence	Occupation Of Parent/Guardian	Previous School (if applicable)
Dec	1899	455	McCann	Maggie		28-2-1893	Lusk	Labourer	
Dec	1899	456	Sherry	Mary		31-3-1893	Lusk	Labourer	
Dec	1899	458	Kiernan	Katie		9-3-1893	Lusk	Farmer	
Dec	1899	460	Lambe	Alice		4-10-1893	Ballaly	Herd	

List of Girls from 1900 to 1970

Month Registered in the School	Year	Pupils Register No.	Pupils Surname	First Name	Dob	Place Of Residence	Occupation Of Parent/Guardian	Previous School (If Applicable)
Jan	1900	51	McGee	Maggie	1-3-1893	Lusk	Store Keeper	Georges Hill, Dublin
Apr	1900	52	Smyth	Sophie	16-6-1891	Lusk	Sexton	Farnham, Cavan
Apr	1900	53	Carton	Mary	24-5-1896	Lusk	Labourer	
Apr	1900	54	Brinn	Edith	2-10-1895	Gov. Farm	Soldier	
Apr	1900	55	Maguire	Kathleen	30-4-1896	Rathmooney	Farmer	
June	1900	56	Snodden	Lizzie	18-4-1892	Gov. Farm	Soldier	
June	1900	57	Snodden	Anna	1-6-1894	Gov. Farm	Soldier	
June	1900	58	Hogg	Isabella	14-7-1891	Gov. Farm	Soldier	
Aug	1900	59	Dixon	Ellen	26-7-1896	Lusk	Soldier	
Aug	1900	60	Doyle	Mary	8-5-1893	Lusk	Shopkeeper	St. Bridgids, Strand St.
Aug	1900	61	Doyle	Maggie	18-3-1892	Lusk	Shopkeeper	
Sept	1900	62	Jenkinson	Lizzie	9-9-1895	Newhaggard	Stewart	
Sept	1900	446	Maguire	Helen		Rathmooney	Farmer	
Apr	1901	63	Kelly	Alice	9-11-1896	Lusk	Labourer	
Apr	1901	64	Austin	Alice	6-5-1896	Lusk	Soldier	
June	1901	65	Mccann	Maggie	4-9-1896	Station, Lusk	Railway Porter	
June	1901	66	Donnelly	Margaret	12-7-1897	Lusk	Postman	
Aug	1901	67	Daly	Alice	7-1-1897	Lusk	Labourer	
Oct	1901	68	Devine	Ellen	7-10-1897	Lusk	Labourer	
Oct	1901	69	Connor	Maggie	3-5-1898	Lusk	Labourer	Gardiner St. Dublin
Oct	1901	70	Connor	Katie	17-10-1894	Lusk	Labourer	
Oct	1901	71	Connor	Lizzie	19-7-1890	Lusk	Labourer	

Month Registered in the School	Year	Pupils Register No.	Pupils Surname	First Name	Dob	Place Of Residence	Occupation Of Parent/Guardian	Previous School (If Applicable)
Jan	1902	72	Fay	Winifred	6-9-1897	Lusk	Labourer	
Jan	1902	73	Clifford	Harriet	22-12-1897	Lusk	Soldier	
Apr	1902	74	Donnelly	Kathleen	10-1-1899	Lusk	Postman	
Apr	1902	75	Murtagh	Kathleen	12-8-1898	Lusk	Constable	St. Marys Balbriggan
Apr	1902	76	Murtagh	Ellen F	10-4-1893	Lusk	Constable	St. Marys Balbriggan
Apr	1902	77	Murtagh	Bridget	2-2-1890	Lusk	Constable	St. Marys Balbriggan
Apr	1902	78	Murtagh	Mary J	3-6-1889	Lusk	Constable	St. Marys Balbriggan
Sept	1902	393	Aungier	Catherine		Lusk	Labourer	
Mar	1903	89	Halpin	Kathleen	7-10-1894	Lusk	Carpenter	Balcunnin
Mar	1903	90	Devine	Bridget	20-3-1893	Hayestown	Orphan	Loughshinny
Apr	1903	91	Mcnally	Elizabeth	9-3-1899	Lusk	Farmer	
Apr	1903	92	Sweetman	Kathleen	20-5-1898	Lusk	Labourer	
May	1903	93	Sherry	Margaret	27-2-1899	Lusk	Labourer	
May	1903	94	Austin	Edith	28-4-1898	Gov. Farm	Soldier	
July	1903	95	Connolly	Teresa	??-6-1899	Lusk	Labourer	
Sept	1903	96	Jenkinson	Bridget	3-9-1897	Newhaggard	Stewart	
Sept	1903	97	Halpin	Jane	30-9-1890	Lusk	Carpenter	
Nov	1903	98	Dowdall	Kate	17-3-1892	Lusk	Drayman	St. Patricks Nth. King St. Dublin
Nov	1903	99	Leonard	Annie	15-6-1891	Nth. Commons	Labourer	Gardiner St. Dublin
Feb	1904	100	Higgins	Sarah T	10-3-1899	Gov. Farm	Soldier	
May	1904	101	Collins	Mary	29-10-1899	Nth. Commons	Labourer	
May	1904	102	Rafferty	Kathleen	9-2-1899	Lusk	Labourer	
May	1904	103	Jenkinson	Josephine	3-3-1899	Newhaggard	Stewart	
June	1904	104	Halpin	Alice	11-10-??	Nth. Commons	Carpenter	
June	1904	105	Morgan	Florence	10/08/1900	Bride Tree	Farmer	
June	1904	106	Sweetman	Bridget	??-9-1899	Lusk	Relieving Officer	
Aug	1904	107	O'Reilly	Annie	??-3-1900	Lusk	Drayman	
Aug	1904	108	Clarke	Christina	12/11/1900	Lusk	Labourer	
Aug	1904	109	Monks	Kathleen	18/10/1900	Railway Station	Signalma,n	
Sept	1904	110	Grimes	Lilly	3-11-1899	Lusk	Labourer	
Sept	1904	111	Groves	Katie	5-10-1896	Rogerstown	Labourer	Hedgestown
Oct	1904	112	Smyth	Mary	29-6-1890	Lusk	Policeman	Straffan, Co. Kildare
Dec	1904	113	Hughes	Bridget	5-9-1892	Railway Station	Signalman	Rush

Appendices

Month Registered in the School	Year	Pupils Register No.	Pupils Surname	First Name	Dob	Place Of Residence	Occupation Of Parent/Guardian	Previous School (If Applicable)
Jan	1905	114	Hughes	Lizzie	5-8-1897	Railway Station	Signalman	Rush
Feb	1905	115	Hogan	Elizabeth	7/10/1900	Lusk	Labourer	
Apr	1905	116	McNally	Bridget	05/02/1900	Lusk	Farmer	
May	1905	117	Mcgann	Annie	27/04/1901	Railway Station	Porter	
May	1905	118	Devine	Kathleen	06/02/1900	Lusk	Labourer	
May	1905	119	Hanratty	Frances	02/08/1900	Lusk	Labourer	Darver, Co. Louth
May	1905	120	Hanratty	Agnes	22-12-1897	Lusk	Labourer	Darver, Co. Louth
May	1905	121	Mescal	Jane	02/08/1900	Lusk	Constable	Naul, Co. Dublin
May	1905	122	Mescal	Susan	27/07/1901	Lusk	Constable	Naul, Co. Dublin
June	1905	123	Halpin	Jane	07/12/1900	Nth. Commons	Carpenter	
June	1905	124	McMahon	Mary A	12/10/1901	Lusk	Labourer	
June	1905	125	Dixon	Agnes	16/12/1901	Lusk	Labourer	
Aug	1905	126	Devine	Annie	14/08/1900	Lusk	Labourer	
Aug	1905	127	Norton	Mary	?-1-1900	Lusk	Soldier	
Aug	1905	128	Mescal	Bridget	24/09/1902	Lusk	Constable	
Sept	1905	129	Kane	Lilly	9-8-1896	Lusk	Labourer	Nth. William St. Dublin
Nov	1905	130	Doyle	Frances	1-10-1893	Lusk	Postman	Ringsend
Mar	1906	131	Maguire	Bridget	13-11-1894	Rogerstown	Labourer	Corduff
Mar	1906	132	Maguire	Kate	31-3-1899	Rogerstown	Labourer	
Apr	1906	133	Healy	Hilda M	4-7-1898	Rogerstown	Farmer	
Apr	1906	134	Barrer	Annie	29-11-1898	Lusk	Groom	Kilbert, Cork
May	1906	135	Jenkinson	Marcella	16/06/1900	Newhaggard	Farmer	
May	1906	136	Sherry	Annie	24/09/1901	Lusk	Labourer	
May	1906	137	Kelly	Anna Maria	19/05/1902	Lusk	Labourer	
July	1906	447	Aungier	Maggie	17-3-1892	Lusk	Car Owner	
July	1906	448	Moore	Sarah	12-9-1892	Lusk	Labourer	
July	1906	451	Jenkinson	Mary	10-9-1892	Newhaggard	Farmer	
July	1906	452	Carton	Gertrude		Lusk	Shopkeeper	
July	1906	445	Devine	Katie	??-9-1892	Lusk	Labourer	
Aug	1906	138	Collins	Alice	03/11/1901	Nth. Commons	Labourer	
Sept	1906	139	Carton	Bridgid	05/07/??	Nth. Commons	Labourer	
Apr	1907	1	Martin	Emily	11/09/1902	Railway Station	Station Master	
Apr	1907	2	Barrett	Bridgid	26/11/1901	Ballaley	Labourer	

Month Registered in the School	Year	Pupils Register No.	Pupils Surname	First Name	Dob	Place Of Residence	Occupation Of Parent/Guardian	Previous School (If Applicable)
June	1907	3	Daly	Maggie	19/09/1901	Lusk	Labourer	
June	1907	4	Grimes	Christina	9/10/??	Lusk	Labourer	
July	1907	1	Price	Annie	23/7/1893	Lusk	Shopkeeper	
Aug	1907	5	Connolly	Kate	11/06/1903	Lusk	Labourer	
Aug	1907	6	Russell	Lizzie	10/12/1903	Railway Road	Labourer	
Aug	1907	7	Donnelly	Mary Ellen	31/08/1903	Lusk	Labourer	
Sept	1907	8	O'Reilly	Gertrude	08/04/1904	Lusk	Drayman	
Nov	1907	9	Dennis	Julia	31/07/1904	Lusk	Labourer	
Nov	1907	10	Seaver	Maggie	10/01/1902	Nth. Commons	Farmer	
Mar	1908	11	Jenkinson	Teresa M	??/10/1901	Newhaggard	Farmer	
Apr	1908	12	Donnelly	Eileen	27/06/1904	Lusk	Postman	
Apr	1908	13	Donnelly	Mary J	05/09/1904	Railway Road	Labourer	
May	1908	14	Norton	Margaret	24/05/1904	Railway Road	Labourer	
May	1908	15	Rafferty	Eileen	05/11/1904	Lusk	Labourer	
May	1908	16	Russell	Lizzie	22-12-1896	Rogerstown	Labourer	
May	1908	17	Brann	Mary Frances	06/05/1903	Gov. Farm	Soldier	
May	1908	18	Browne	Bridgid	4-9-1896	Nth. Commons	Orphan	
May	1908	19	Magee	Lizzie Mary	05/09/1904	Nth. Commons		
Aug	1908	20	Collins	Annie	??-12-1903	Lusk	Labourer	
Aug	1908	21	Barrett	Maggie	31-11-1903	Ballaley	Labourer	
Aug	1908	22	Donnelly	Mary	??-1-1902	Railway Road	Labourer	
Nov	1908	23	McArthur	Jane L	16-10-1899	Gov. Farm	Army Pensioner	
Nov	1908	24	McArthur	Catherine	16/10/1901	Gov. Farm	Army Pensioner	
Nov	1908	25	McArthur	Beatrice	12/08/1904	Gov. Farm	Army Pensioner	
Nov	1908	26	McGavin	Mary	24-12-1896	Railway Road	Labourer	
Feb	1909	27	Gormanly	Mary	28/02/1903	Railway Station	Porter	
Mar	1909	28	Gleeson	Christina	16/12/1900	Lusk	Labourer	
Mar	1909	29	Gleeson	Florence	27/02/1904	Lusk	Labourer	
Mar	1909	30	Gleeson	Mary Kate	22/03/1906	Lusk	Labourer	
May	1909	31	Jenkinson	Magdalen	28/03/1903	Newhaggard	Farmer	

Appendices

Month Registered in the School	Year	Pupils Register No.	Pupils Surname	First Name	Dob	Place Of Residence	Occupation Of Parent/Guardian	Previous School (If Applicable)
June	1909	32	O'Dea	Maura	30/05/1904	Nth. Commons		
June	1909	33	Donovan	Kate	??-??-1897	Rogerstown	Tinker	
June	1909	34	Lenehan	Mary	8-5-1897	Lusk	Farmer	
June	1909	35	Gough	Elizabeth	30/04/1904	Nth. Commons	Labourer	
July	1909	36	Skelly	Elizabeth	13/06/1906	Lusk	Labourer	
Aug	1909	37	O'Reilly	Mary	??/12/1906	Lusk	Drayman	
Aug	1909	38	Daly	Bride	??/8/1903	Lusk	Labourer	
Sept	1909	39	Gallagher	Eileen Mary	05/03/1905	Railway Road	Labourer	
Sept	1909	40	Dixon	Helena	??/6/1905	Lusk	Labourer	
Sept	1909	41	Devine	Mary	10/01/1905	Lusk	Labourer	
Apr	1910	42	Donovan	Eileen	05/04/1905	Rogerstown	Tinker	
Apr	1910	43	Lenehan	Isabella	04/01/1905	Lusk	Farmer	
Apr	1910	44	Magee	Rita	14/01/1906	Nth. Commons	Engineer	
Apr	1910	45	McMahon	Katie	21/10/1906	Lusk	Labourer	
Apr	1910	46	Grimes	Bridget	??/9/1905	Lusk	Labourer	
	1910	47	Russell	Mary F	19/08/1905	Lusk	Labourer	
Apr	1910	48	Donnelly	E Bridget	??/11/1905	Railway Road	Labourer	
May	1910	49	Cruise	Mary	??/2/1906	Lusk	Tailor	
May	1910	50	Mescal	Annie	??/1/1907	Lusk	Policeman	
May	1910	51	Doyle	Mary Anne	??/5/1907	Commons	Labourer	
May	1910	52	McNally	Mary	??/5/1906	Lusk	Farmer	
June	1910	53	Hurley	Kathleen	12/02/1907	Lusk	Labourer	
June	1910	54	Courtney	Annie	??/6/1900	Lusk	Horse-Trainer	
June	1910	55	Groves	E Mary	??/4/1905	Lusk	Labourer	
July	1910	56	Seaver	Mollie	??/4/1906	Nth. Commons	Farmer	
Aug	1910	57	Smeed	Rosie	??/10/1901	Gov. Farm	Soldier	
Aug	1910	58	Gallagher	Annie	26/06/1907	Railway Road	Labourer	
Sept	1910	59	Haslam	Florence	07/02/1907	Lusk	Engineer	
Jan	1911	60	Lawton	Annie	??/3/1905	Lusk	Policeman	
Jan	1911	61	Lawton	Mary H	??/3/1903	Lusk	Policeman	
Jan	1911	62	O'Reilly	Eileen	??/7/1907	Lusk	Drayman	

Month Registered in the School	Year	Pupils Register No.	Pupils Surname	First Name	Dob	Place Of Residence	Occupation Of Parent/Guardian	Previous School (If Applicable)
Mar	1911	63	Hand	Eilis	11/03/1908	Lusk	Farmer	
May	1911	64	Hughes	Mary	??/9/1905	Railway Station	Signalman	
May	1911	65	Mills	Alice V	??/3/1901	Gov. Farm	Sergeant	
May	1911	66	Mills	Irene A	??/8/1902	Gov. Farm	Sergeant	
June	1911	67	Gallagher	Annie	04/06/1907	Lusk	Labourer	
June	1911	68	Daly	Nellie	01/11/1906	Lusk	Labourer	
Aug	1911	69	Brake	Teresa	??/12/1905	Gov. Farm	Soldier	
Aug	1911	70	Mills	Winifred	??/3/1906	Gov. Farm	Sergeant	
Sept	1911	71	Courtney	Margaret	??/6/1908	Lusk	Groom	
Nov	1911	72	Magee	Katie	02/10/1907	Nth. Commons	Engineer	
Mar	1912	73	Carton	Bridgid	??/7/1902	Lusk	Labourer	
May	1912	74	Cruise	Christina	13/12/1907	Lusk	Tailor	
Aug	1912	75	Hogan	Esther	03/04/1907	Lusk	Labourer	
Aug	1912	76	Clifford	Ena	??/3/1906	Lusk	Labourer	
Aug	1912	77	Clifford	Annie	??/7/1903	Lusk	Labourer	
Feb	1913	78	Maguire	Mary	??/5/1906	Union	Deceased	
Apr	1913	79	Owens	Christina	12/11/1909	Lusk	Harness-Maker	
Apr	1913	80	McNally	Maggie	31/03/1909	Lusk	Farmer	
Apr	1913	81	Fay	Bridgid	06/11/1907	Railway Road	Labourer	
Apr	1913	82	Cruise	Kathleen	15/08/1909	Lusk	Tailor	
Apr	1913	83	Jenkinson	Lucy	10/12/1907	Newhaggard	Farmer	
July	1913	84	Cowley	Sinead	07/09/1910	Lusk	Harness-Maker	
July	1913	85	O'Sullivan	Eilis	28/12/1909	Lusk	Farmer	
Sept	1913	86	Magee	Mary	15/10/1910	Nth. Commons	Engineer	
Oct	1913	87	Williams	Nellie	08/10/1907	Lusk	Soldier	
Oct	1913	88	McLoughlin	Mary	26/05/1910	Lusk	Labourer	
Nov	1913	89	Read	Sarah	??/12/1900	Nth. Commons	Labourer	
Jan	1914	90	Seaver	Nellie	??/11/1908	Nth. Commons	Farmer	
Mar	1914	91	Privett	Maud	?/8/1906	Gov. Farm	Soldier	
Mar	1914	92	Myles	Jane M	??/11/1907	Gov. Farm	Soldier	
Mar	1914	93	Clarke	Maggie	02/11/1910	Lusk	Labourer	

Appendices

Month Registered in the School	Year	Pupils Register No.	Pupils Surname	First Name	Dob	Place Of Residence	Occupation Of Parent/Guardian	Previous School (If Applicable)
Apr	1914	94	Simmons	Kathleen	??/4/1908	Lusk	Ex-Soldier	
May	1914	95	Dennis	Bridie	14/11/1910	Lusk	Labourer	
July	1914	96	Peacock	Kathleen	??/4/1901	Gov. Farm	Soldier	
July	1914	97	Peacock	Alice	??/7/1904	Gov. Farm	Soldier	
Aug	1914	98	O'Brien	Maggie	??/10/1904	Union	Orphan	
Oct	1914	99	Skelly	Annie	??/9/1911	Lusk	Dealer	
Mar	1915	100	Davis	Mary	15/06/1911	Lusk	Army Sergeant	
Apr	1915	101	Maguire	Julia	07/10/1910	Railway Road	Orphan	
Apr	1915	102	Simmons	Sheila	??/6/1910	Lusk	Labourer	
May	1915	103	Keane	Florence	??/12/1906	Gov. Farm	Bookkeeper, Gov. Farm	
May	1915	104	Sweetman	Mary	08/09/1911	Lusk	Labourer	
May	1915	105	Owens	Gretta	06/07/1911	Lusk	Soldier	
May	1915	106	Brown	Josephine	??/7/1910	Lusk	Carpenter	
May	1915	107	Cruise	Lizzie	27/05/1911	Lusk	Tailor	
May	1915	108	Magee	Molly	??/7/1911	Nth. Commons	Postman	
June	1915	109	Gosson	Mary	01/12/1910	Nth. Commons	Labourer	
Sept	1915	110	Hand	Kathleen	22/01/1912	Lusk	Farmer	
Sept	1915	111	Groves	Alice	28/08/1910	Lusk	Labourer	
Sept	1915	112	Smith	Kathleen	??/9/1911	Lusk		
Sept	1915	113	Carton	Kathleen	25/09/1912	Lusk	Labourer	
Sept	1915	114	Daly	Maire	27/04/1912	Lusk	Labourer	
Sept	1915	115	McGee	Nellie	12/07/1912	Commons	Electrician	
Sept	1915	116	McLoughlin	Maggie	06/08/1912	Lusk	Labourer	
Oct	1915	117	Keane	Mary	??/8/1903	Gov. Farm	Clerk ???	
Nov	1915	118	Dennis	Annie	??/3/1912	Lusk	Labourer	
Mar	1916	119	Murray	Katie	??/3/1907	Commons	Orphan	
Feb	1916	120	Russell	Mary	08/10/1912	Lusk	Labourer	
May	1916	121	Denis	Annie	??/10/1911	Lusk	Labourer	
May	1916	122	Fay	Mary	04/10/1912	Lusk	Labourer	
May	1916	123	Daly	Kathleen	??/3/1908	Dublin	Labourer	
June	1916	124	McNally	Ellie	28/10/1911	Lusk	Farmer	

Month Registered in the School	Year	Pupils Register No.	Pupils Surname	First Name	Dob	Place Of Residence	Occupation Of Parent/Guardian	Previous School (If Applicable)
Aug	1916	125	Devine	Frances	08/10/1909	Nth. Commons	Soldier	
Aug	1916	126	Wade	Bridgid	??/8/1906	Rogerstown	Labourer	
Aug	1916	127	Wade	Molly	02/09/1907	Rogerstown	Labourer	
Sept	1916	128	Devine	Maggie	06/09/1911	Nth. Commons	Soldier	
Oct	1916	129	Murphy	Eileen	??/11/1912	Lusk	Soldier	
Apr	1917	130	Wade	Rosie	04/11/1910	Rogerstown	Labourer	
May	1917	131	Hogan	Nora	13/09/1911	Lusk	Labourer	
June	1917	132	Deane	May	18/06/1909	Gov. Farm	Blacksmith	
Aug	1917	133	Mills	Lillie	??/8/1911	Lusk	Sergent-Major	
Sept	1917	134	Nickoles	Kathleen	??/3/1909	Lusk	Soldier	
Sept	1917	135	Murphy	Mary M	??/8/19014	Lusk	Soldier	
Oct	1917	136	O'Reilly	Bridie	04/10/1912	Lusk	Labourer	
Oct	1917	137	Denis	Lizzie	??/10/1913	Lusk	Labourer	
Nov	1917	138	Clarke	Alice	06/11/1914	Lusk	Labourer	
Nov	1917	139	Hand	Maureen	??-12-1913	Lusk	Farmer	
Jan	1918	140	Smyth	Teresa	??-10-1907	Whitestown	Herd	
Jan	1918	141	Smyth	Mary	??/4/1911	Whitestown	Herd	
Jan	1918	142	Smyth	Rose	??/5/1913	Whitestown	Herd	
May	1918	143	Connolly	Mollie	15/04/1913	Nth. Commons	Farmer	
May	1918	144	Gough	Clare	??/1/1912	Rogerstown	Sea Captain	
May	1918	145	Owens	Mary	06/09/1912	Lusk	Soldier	
May	1918	146	Magee	Annie	23/12/1914	Nth. Commons	Engineer	
May	1918	147	Dixon	Alice	26/02/1913	Lusk	Soldier	
June	1918	148	Cruise	Dora	08/07/1913	Lusk	Tailor	
June	1918	149	Fay	Sheila	20/03/1914	Railway Station	Soldier	
Aug	1918	150	Kelly	May	??/8/1915	Lusk	Workman	
Mar	1919	151	Gough	Ada	??/3/1913	Rogerstown	Farmer	
Mar	1919	152	Gough	Beatrice	??/5/1914	Rogerstown	Farmer	
Mar	1919	153	Malone	Christina	10/06/1910	Lusk	Labourer	
May	1919	154	Denis	Alice	??/9/1915	Lusk	Labourer	
May	1919	155	Sweetman	Kitty	??/9/1915	Lusk	Baker	

Appendices

Month Registered in the School	Year	Pupils Register No.	Pupils Surname	First Name	Dob	Place Of Residence	Occupation Of Parent/Guardian	Previous School (If Applicable)
May	1919	156	Mcnally	Kathleen	21/07/1914	Lusk	Farmer	
May	1919	157	Seaver	Christina	24/12/1914	Commons	Farmer	
Sept	1919	158	Reilly	May	03/06/1908	Greystones	Soldier	
Sept	1919	159	Maher	Anastia	??/6/1906	Lusk	Orphan	
Sept	1919	160	Maher	Evelyn	??/6/1906	Lusk	Orphan	
Sept	1919	161	Keane	Alice	??/11/1914	Gov. Farm	Clerk	
Sept	1919	162	O'Reilly	Kitty	??/9/1912	Lusk	Labourer	
Sept	1919	163	O'Reilly	Eileen	??/9/1915	Lusk	Labourer	
Sept	1919	164	Boylan	Mary	01/10/1908	Commons	Orphan	
Oct	1919	165	Smith	Kathleen	31/07/1911	Lusk	Asylum Offical	
Jan	1920	166	McMannion	Rose	??/6/1914	Lusk	Farmer	
Jan	1920	167	Denis	Lizzie	06/02/1914	Lusk	Labourer	
Mar	1920	168	White	Mairead	??/4/1906	Lusk	Orphan	
Mar	1920	169	White	Brigid	??/4/1904	Lusk	Orphan	
May	1920	170	MaGee	Teresa	??/11/1916	Nth. Commons		
May	1920	171	Collins	Annie	??/5/1916	Lusk	Orphan	
May	1920	172	Hand	Breed	30/01/1916	Lusk	Farmer	
May	1920	173	Deane	Nellie	01/12/1915	Gov. Farm	Blacksmith	
June	1920	174	Sherwin	Maureen	11/11/1914	Gov. Farm	Groom	
Aug	1920	175	Davis	Mary	15/06/1911	Lusk		
Aug	1920	176	Davis	Kathleen	06/01/1914	Lusk		
Aug	1920	177	Davis	Monica	14/03/1917	Lusk		
Aug	1920	178	O'Sullivan	Maureen	04/04/1916	Lusk	Farmer	
Oct	1920	179	Kiernan	Agnes	20/12/1912	Nth. Commons	Factory Worker, Balbriggan	
Jan	1921	180	Connor	Agnes	01/10/1912	Lusk		
Jan	1921	181	Owens	Sheila	07/03/1917	Lusk	Harness-Maker	
May	1921	182	Brown	Madge	16/10/1916	Lusk	Carpenter	
May	1921	183	McNally	Marcella	21/10/1916	Lusk	Farmer	
May	1921	184	Donnelly	Bridgid	01/09/1917	Commons	Orphan	
June	1921	185	Mills	Edie	??/4/1915	Gov. Farm	Sergeant Major	
Aug	1921	186	Daly	Kathleen	25/12/1917	Lusk	Labourer	

Month Registered in the School	Year	Pupils Register No.	Pupils Surname	First Name	Dob	Place Of Residence	Occupation Of Parent/Guardian	Previous School (If Applicable)
May	1922	187	Devine	Mary-Margaret	03/03/1916	Ratheney	Labourer	
May	1922	188	Devine	Teresa	29/09/1917	Ratheney	Labourer	
Jan	1923	189	Stafford	Winifred	01/03/1912	Remount Depot	Labourer	
Jan	1923	190	O'Connor	Kathleen	20/01/1919			
Jan	1923	191	Booth	Mamie	01/01/1910	Quickpenny		
Apr	1923	192	Maypother	Mary M	10/05/1917	Nth. Commons	Labourer	
Apr	1923	193	Maypother	M. Ellen	04/09/1918	Nth. Commons	Labourer	
Sept	1923	194	Carthy	Teresa	11/09/1919	Nth. Commons	Groom	
Oct	1923	195	Bentley	Rosanna	22/10/1914	Lusk		
Nov	1923	196	Boylan	Lillie	04/04/1919	Lusk	Blacksmith	
Feb	1924	197	Devine	Angela	??/9/1919	Raheny	Labourer	
Apr	1924	198	Denis	Kathleen	03/04/1921	Lusk	Labourer	
June	1924	199	Fay	Teresa	28/12/1919	Railway Station	Labourer	
May	1924	200	Hanratty	Bridie	16/06/1921	Lusk	Soldier	
Sept	1924	201	Wade	Margaret	16/06/1918	Rogerstown	Labourer	
Sept	1924	202	Nulty	Mary T	06/10/1917	Railway Station	Signalman	
Sept	1924	203	Nulty	Bridgid V	08/03/1919	Railway Station	Signalman	
Oct	1924	204	Edwards	Joan	12/06/1924	Lusk	Dressmaker	
Oct	1924	205	Monks	Eileen	26/01/1916	Lusk	Bread Van Driver	
Oct	1924	206	Monks	Anna Maureen	31/05/1914	Lusk	Bread Van Driver	
Feb	1925	207	O'Connor	Eileen	03/02/1920	Lusk	Workman	
Feb	1925	208	Owens	Annie (Nancy)	18/12/1920	Lusk	Harness-Maker	
Mar	1925	209	Sweetman	Catherine	05/03/1920	Lusk	Labourer	
May	1925	210	Browne	Josie	30/06/1914	Gt. Commons	Orphan	
June	1925	211	Nulty	Joan	21/09/1920	Lusk	Signalman	
Sept	1925	212	Byrne	Anne	03/06/1912	Lusk	Labourer	
Sept	1925	213	Hand	Ita	23/12/1919	Lusk	Farmer	
Nov	1925	214	Oglesby	Celia	06/04/1922	Lusk	Jockey	
Jan	1926	215	Derham	Kitty	16/04/1913	Commons	Farmer	
Apr	1926	216	Hoey	Mary	27/09/1921	The Figures	Farmer	

Appendices

Month Registered in the School	Year	Pupils Register No.	Pupils Surname	First Name	Dob	Place Of Residence	Occupation Of Parent/Guardian	Previous School (If Applicable)
Apr	1926	217	Bentley	Esther	19/02/1922	Lusk	Labourer	
May	1926	218	Maypother	Kathleen	18/11/1922	Commons	Labourer	
May	1926	219	Magee	Bridgid	04/05/1923	Commons	Electrician	
May	1926	220	Hanratty	Josie	11/09/1923	Lusk	Ex-Soldier	
May	1926	221	Hughes	May	14/05/1918	Lusk	Labourer	
May	1926	222	McCann	Sarah		Commons	Railway Porter	
Oct	1926	223	Deane	Veronica	22/05/1921	Railway Road	Smith	
May	1927	224	Ferguson	Peggy	04/06/1923	Lusk	Asylum Attendant	
July	1927	225	Rogers	Annie	??/??/1916	Lusk	Sailor	
May	1928	226	Groves	May	02/03/1923	The Figures	Labourer	
May	1928	227	Birmingham	Mary E	23/07/1922	Rogerstown	Dentist	
June	1928	228	Spencer	Brigid E	20/09/1922	Lusk	Asylum Attendant	
May	1928	229	Purcell	Bridgid			Traveller	
May	1928	230	Purcell	Margaret			Traveller	
Sept	1928	231	O'Brien	Winifred	13/09/1922	Lusk - Station		
Sept	1928	232	Llewllyn	May	01/03/1925	Lusk		
Oct	1928	233	Whelan	Florrie	31/10/1915	B'rothery Union	Orphan	
Oct	1928	234	Whelan	Kathleen	01/03/1922	B'rothery Union	Orphan	
Dec	1928	235	O'Brien	Annie	12/12/1915	B'rothery Union	Labourer	
Jan	1929	236	Neary	Lillie	18/10/1923	Rogerstown	Ex-Soldier	
Jan	1929	237	Neary	Teresa	25/10/1920	Rogerstown	Ex-Soldier	
Apr	1929	238	Brogan	Molly	21/03/1924	Lusk	Labourer	
Apr	1929	239	McCann	Maureen	05/12/1924	Lusk	Labourer	
Apr	1929	240	McGuigan	May	01/05/1925	Lusk	Sailor	
May	1929	241	Curtis	Peggy	25/01/1924	Lusk	Boots	
May	1929	242	Curtis	Gabriel	05/03/1925	Lusk		
Sept	1929	243	Bradley	Lillie	02/05/1922	Lusk	Shopkeeper	
Sept	1929	244	Bradley	Maudie	22/09/1923	Lusk	Shopkeeper	
Sept	1929	245	Crosbie	Maggie	??/5/1919	B'rothery Union	Labourer	
Nov	1929	246	McKenna	Kathleen	24/02/1918	Lusk	Engineer	

Month Registered in the School	Year	Pupils Register No.	Pupils Surname	First Name	Dob	Place Of Residence	Occupation Of Parent/Guardian	Previous School (If Applicable)
Jan	1930	247	McLoughlin	Christina	23/12/1918	Rogerstown	Labourer	
Feb	1930	248	O'Reilly	Kathleen	05/12/1923	Rogerstown	Labourer	
Mar	1930	249	Devine	Maureen	19/11/1924	Ratheney	Labourer	
Mar	1930	250	Byrne	Joan	07/09/1920	Lusk	Railway Porter	
Apr	1930	251	McNally	Mary	11/02/1925	Lusk	Farmer	
Apr	1930	252	McCann	Sarah	19/08/1926	Lusk	Labourer	
May	1930	253	Byrne	Una	30/03/1925	Lusk	Railway Porter	
May	1930	254	O'Brien	Maureen	20/05/1924	Lusk	Signalman	
July	1930	255	Hanratty	Hilda	01/09/1926	Lusk		
Sept	1930	256	Hussey	Maureen	06/01/1927	Lusk	Orphan	
Sept	1930	257	Connor	Philomena	12/12/1926	B R Road	Labourer	
Sept	1930	258	Connor	Kathleen	07/03/1920	Railway Road	Labourer	
Sept	1930	259	Connor	Rosaleen	30/07/1918	Railway Road	Labourer	
Sept	1930	260	Hoey	Alice	01/07/1925	The Figures	Labourer	
Sept	1930	261	Clarke	Bridie	22/04/1925	B'rothery Union	Orphan	
Sept	1930	262	Whelan	Jane	29/12/1925	B'rothery Union	Orphan	
Sept	1930	263	Groves	Kathleen	22/01/1925	Rathmooney	Labourer	
Nov	1930	264	Woods	Maureen	19/11/1923	Railway Station	Porter	
Nov	1930	265	Woods	Peggy	18/11/1924	Railway Station	Porter	
Feb	1931	266	Maypother	Margaret	23/07/1918	Tyrrelstown	Labourer	
Feb	1931	267	Maypother	Carmel	12/07/1920	Tyrrelstown	Labourer	
Feb	1931	268	Maypother	Kathleen	15/07/1921	Tyrrelstown	Labourer	
Feb	1931	269	Maypother	Pauline	29/06/1923	Tyrrelstown	Labourer	
Apr	1931	270	Maypother	Christina	07/12/1925	Commons	Labourer	
May	1931	271	Greany	Anastia		Lusk	Labourer	
June	1931	272	Kiely	Annie		B'rothery Union	Labourer	
July	1931	273	Corcoran	Winifred		B'rothery Union	Labourer	
July	1931	274	Corcoran	Lilly		B'rothery Union	Labourer	
July	1931	275	Corcoran	Phyllis		B'rothery Union	Labourer	
Sept	1931	276	Oglesby	Rose		Lusk	Labourer	
Oct	1931	277	Kavanagh	Eileen		Lusk	Labourer	

Appendices

Month Registered in the School	Year	Pupils Register No.	Pupils Surname	First Name	Dob	Place Of Residence	Occupation Of Parent/Guardian	Previous School (If Applicable)
Jan	1932	278	McCann	Eileen		Lusk	Labourer	
Jan	1932	279	McCann	Gretta		Lusk	Labourer	
Jan	1932	280	Neary	Phyllis		Rogerstown	Ex-Soldier	
Apr	1932	281	Devine	Mary A		Gt. Commons	Ex-Soldier	
May	1932	282	Murray	Elizabeth M		Lusk	Publican	
June	1932	283	Connor	Teresa Anne		Railway Station	Labourer	
July	1932	284	O'Brien	Evelyn		Railway Station	Signalman	
Sept	1932	285	Jenkinson	Mary		Lusk	Co. Co. Clerk	
Nov	1932	286	Crosby	Brigid		B'rothery Union		
Jan	1933	287	Neary	Marian		Rogerstown	Ex-Soldier (B'smith)	
May	1933	288	Wright	Jane M		Lusk	Labourer	
Sept	1933	289	Clare	Mary M		Lusk	Carpenter	
Sept	1933	290	Gaffney	Sarah J		Commons	Labourer	
Sept	1933	291	Clare	Cait		Lusk	Carpenter	
Sept	1933	292	Spencer	Lillie		Lusk	Attendant	
Jan	1934	293	Sweetman	Mary		Lusk	Labourer	
Feb	1934	294	Dunne	Joan		Lusk	Nat. Teacher	
Apr	1934	295	Donnelly	Brigid		B'rothery Union	Labourer	
Apr	1934	296	Wright	Kathleen		Lusk	Labourer	
Apr	1934	297	Curtis	Maureen		Lusk	Boots	
May	1934	298	McGuigan	Kathleen		Lusk	Sailor	
June	1934	299	Devine	Ellen E		Quickpenny	Labourer	
Sept	1934	300	Kelly	Maureen		Lusk	Motor Mechanic	
Jan	1935	301	Oglesby	Anna M		Lusk	Labourer	
Jan	1935	302	Brogan	Annie		Commons	Labourer	
Jan	1935	303	Neary	Clare		Rogerstown	Blacksmith	
Jan	1935	304	O'Brien	Mabel		Railway Station	Signalman	
Feb	1935	305	Cusack	Kathleen		Lusk	Doctor	
Feb	1935	306	Cusack	Felicitie		Lusk	Doctor	
Feb	1935	307	Magee	Brigid V		Commons		

Month Registered in the School	Year	Pupils Register No.	Pupils Surname	First Name	Dob	Place Of Residence	Occupation Of Parent/Guardian	Previous School (If Applicable)
Apr	1935	308	Hoey	Teresa		The Figures		
May	1935	309	Moore	Annie C		Lusk		
May	1935	310	McGonagle	Mona		Lusk		
May	1935	311	Boylan	Margaret		Rogerstown		
May	1935	312	Hanratty	Rose		Rogerstown		
May	1935	313	Kiely	Margaret		B'rothery Union		
Sept	1935	314	Murray	Margaret M		Lusk	Publican	
Nov	1935	315	Clare	Irene		Lusk	Carpenter	
Jan	1936	316	O'Brien	Peggy		Commons	Labourer	
Jan	1936	317	Dennigan	Kathleen		Irishtown	Farmer	
May	1936	318	Gilsenan	Lillie		Knock Co. Dublin	Farmer	
May	1936	319	Treacy	Lilian		Ballaly	Farmer	
May	1936	320	Gaffney	Maire P		Commons	Labourer	
Aug	1936	321	Maypother	Bernadette		Tyrrelstown	Labourer	
Sept	1936	322	Oglesby	Maura		Newhaggard	Labourer	
Sept	1936	323	Murray	Marie		Lusk	Publican	
Sept	1936	324	Wright	Mary		Lusk	Labourer	
Nov	1936	325	Sweetman	Pam		Lusk	Farmer	
Feb	1937	326	Clare	Brigid		The Green	Carpenter	
May	1937	327	Smith	Brigid		The Green	Labourer	
May	1937	328	Fulham	Mary		Newhaggard	Dairyman	
Aug	1937	329	Nolan	Josephine		Commons	Orphan	
Aug	1937	330	O'Brien	Marcella		Commons	Labourer	
Aug	1937	331	Grimes	Brigid		Lusk	Labourer	
Aug	1937	332	Lawlor	Brigid		Station Rd	Labourer	
Sept	1937	333	Sherwin	Kathleen		Newhaggard	Labourer	
Sept	1937	334	Jacob	Mary C		Lusk	N.C. Officer	
Sept	1937	335	Jacob	Patricia C		Lusk	N.C. Officer	
Sept	1937	336	Kelly	Gertrude		Lusk		
Mar	1938	337	Wright	Brigid M		Lusk	Labourer	
Mar	1938	338	Harte	Margaret M		Lusk	Orphan	

Appendices

Apr	1938	339	Coileain	Teresa		The Figures	Labourer	
May	1938	340	Clare	Bernadette		Lusk	Carpenter	
May	1938	341	Donnelly	Pauline		Rogerstown	Labourer	
May	1938	342	Rogan	Christina M		Dublin Rd	Farmer	
May	1938	343	Tyrrell	Mary (Lucy)		The Green	Orphan	
May	1938	344	Martin	Mary		Lusk	Labourer	
Sept	1938	345	O'Malley (Gough)	Eileen		Gov. Farm	Labourer	
Sept	1938	346	Micheau	Monica		Rogerstown	Chair-Maker	
Sept	1938	347	Gough	May		Gov. Farm	Labourer	
Sept	1938	348	Sweetman	Anna		Newhaggard	Labourer	
Sept	1938	349	Gaffney	Christina		Commons	Labourer	
Sept	1938	350	Molloy	Maire		Ballough	Orphan	
Apr	1939	351	Gosson	Kathleen		Raheny	Labourer	
May	1939	352	Carroll	Maire C		Johnstown	Labourer	
May	1939	353	Denis	Maura		Ballaly	Labourer	
May	1939	354	Dennigan	Lucy		Irishtown	Farmer	
May	1939	355	Garrigan	Maureen		Lusk	Attendant	
May	1939	356	Clarke	Maureen		Rogerstown Lane	Labourer	
May	1939	357	Brophy	Miriam A		Lusk	Ex-Army Colonel	
Sept	1939	358	Kavanagh	Kathleen		Lusk	Labourer	
Sept	1939	359	Peters	Josephine		Lusk	Labourer	
Sept	1939	360	Grimes	Kathleen		Lusk	Van Driver	
Sept	1939	361	O'Toole	Eileen		Lusk	Upholsterer	
Sept	1939	362	Gaffney	Eileen		Lusk	Labourer	
Feb	1940	363	Sweetman	Harriet		Newhaggard	Labourer	
Apr	1940	364	Connor	Eileen		Newhaggard	Labourer	
May	1940	365	Kelly	Rose		Newhaggard	Labourer	
May	1940	366	Brady	Mary		Raheny	Labourer	
June	1940	367	Hogan	Mary		Lusk	Labourer	
Oct	1940	368	Dunne	Deirdre Anne		Ballough	N. Teacher	
Nov	1940	369	Patterson	May J		Lusk	Labourer	
Sept	1940	370	Carroll	Madge		Irishtown	Labourer	

Month Registered in the School	Year	Pupils Register No.	Pupils Surname	First Name	Dob	Place Of Residence	Occupation Of Parent/Guardian	Previous School (If Applicable)
Apr	1940	371	Ebbs	Annie		Rogerstown	Soldier	
Apr	1941	372	Bentley	Nancy		Lusk		
Apr	1941	373	McDonnell	Mary B		Lusk		
Apr	1941	374	Kelly	Mary A		Rogerstown		
May	1941	375	Taylor	Bernadette		Commons		
Sept	1941	376	Kelly	Eileen		Square, Lusk		
Sept	1941	377	Micheau	Margaret		Rogerstown		
Sept	1941	378	Connor	Alice		Newhaggard		
Sept	1941	379	Ardiff	Teresa		Station Rd		
Oct	1941	380	Ebbs	Lily		Rogerstown		
Oct	1941	381	Kelly	Margaret		Rogerstown		
Apr	1942	382	Kavanagh	Maureen		Lusk		
Apr	1942	383	Gough	Kathleen		Remount Farm		
Apr	1942	384	Kelly	Deirdre		Rogerstown		
Apr	1942	385	O'Brien	Margaret		Raheny		
Apr	1942	386	Matthews	Mary		Commons		
May	1942	387	White	Violet		Rogerstown		
June	1942	388	Moloney	Margaret		Dublin Rd		
Sept	1942	389	Kelly	Kathleen E		Newhaggard		
Nov	1942	390	Grimes	Margaret		Lusk		
Apr	1943	391	Mcnally	Margaret		Lusk		
May	1943	392	Bentley	Helen		Lusk		
May	1943	393	Dennis	Mary		Lusk		
May	1944	394	Gaffney	Rosaleen		Lusk		
May	1944	395	Mullally	Peggie		Lusk (Mrs Rogan)		
May	1944	396	Gaffney	Mary		Lusk (Mrs Rogan)		
June	1944	397	Fennell	Ursula		Lusk (Mrs Rogan)		
May	1944	398	Connor	Maura		Newhaggard		
Sept	1944	399	Rogan	Gertie		Lusk		
Sept	1944	400	Oglesby	Alice		Newhaggard		
Sept	1944	401	Kavanagh	Annie (Nan)		Lusk		

Appendices

Month Registered in the School	Year	Pupils Register No.	Pupils Surname	First Name	Dob	Place Of Residence	Occupation Of Parent/Guardian	Previous School (If Applicable)
Sept	1944	402	Monks	Margaret M		Lusk		
Oct	1944	403	Dennis	Mary		Lusk		
Mar	1945	404	Donnelly	Monica M		Lusk		
Apr	1945	405	Donnelly	Noleen		Rogerstown		
Apr	1945	406	Hynes	Maureen		Commons		
Apr	1945	407	Markey	Concepta		Rogerstown		
Apr	1945	408	Sherry	Brigid		Lusk		
Apr	1945	409	Mccann	Nellie		Lusk		
May	1945	410	Neary	Olive		Lusk		
May	1945	411	Brown	Margaret		Lusk		
May	1945	412	Daly	Margaret (Rita)		Lusk		
Aug	1945	413	Wright	Margaret		Lusk		
Sept	1945	414	Knott	Angela		Rogerstown		
Feb	1946	415	Rogan	Bernie		Lusk		
Mar	1946	416	Hurley	Kathleen		Lusk		
Mar	1946	417	Hurley	Aileen		Lusk		
May	1945	418	Brown	Frances		Post Office Road		
May	1945	419	Fitzgerald	Mary		Skerries Road		
May	1945	420	Brogan	Brigid		The Commons		
June	1946	421	McNally	Angela		Main St.		
Sept	1946	422	Dennis	Ann		Lusk		
Oct	1946	423	Neary	Philomena		Lusk		
Oct	1946	424	Markey	Margaret M		Rogerstown		
Apr	1947	425	O'Connor	Kathleen		Newhaggard		
Apr	1947	426	Donnelly	Marion		Rogerstown		
Apr	1947	427	Butler	Margaret		The Commons (Mrs Mcgee)		Balrothery School
Apr	1947	428	Butler	Elizabeth		The Commons (Mrs Mcgee)		Balrothery School
May	1947	429	Murphy	Lena		Lusk (Mrs Browne)		
May	1947	430	Daly	Elizabeth		Skerries Road		
June	1947	431	Shortt	Mai		Station Rd		

Month Registered in the School	Year	Pupils Register No.	Pupils Surname	First Name	Dob	Place Of Residence	Occupation Of Parent/Guardian	Previous School (If Applicable)
June	1947	432	Shortt	Kathleen		Station Rd		
Sept	1947	433	Sherry	Pearl		Main St.		
Sept	1947	434	Kelly	Mary		Newhaggard		
Oct	1947	435	Schuller	Margaret		Station Rd. (Mrs Cusack)		
Sept	1947	436	Knott	Philomena		Rogerstown		
Nov	1947	437	Rogan	Marie		Lusk		
Nov	1947	438	Kelly	Dymphna		The Square		
Apr	1948	439	Clarke	Teresa		Rogerstown		
May	1948	440	Scally	Mary Annie		Post Office Road		
May	1948	441	Donnelly	Betty		Rogerstown		
May	1948	442	Garrigan	Oonagh		Station Rd		
May	1948	443	Ryan	Sheila		The Green		
May	1948	444	Grimes	Betty		Lusk		
June	1948	445	Bentley	Maud		Lusk		
Sept	1948	446	Knott	Anna		Lusk		
Sept	1948	447	Daly	Marie		Lusk		
Oct	1948	448	Wright	Ena		Lusk		
Jan	1949	449	Kavanagh	Madge		Lusk		
Jan	1949	450	Fitzgerald	Joan		Lusk		
Feb	1949	451	Mullen	Madeline Ann		Lusk		
Mar	1949	452	Clarke	Mary Bridget		Commons		
Apr	1949	453	Grimes	Marie		The Square		
Apr	1949	454	Knott	Anita		Rogerstown		
Apr	1949	455	Garrigan	Fidelma		Lusk		
May	1949	456	Dennis	Bernadette		Lusk		
May	1949	457	McNally	Marie		Lusk		
May	1949	458	Boyle	Margery		Lusk		
June	1949	459	Clarke	Angela		Raheney		
Sept	1949	460	Scally	Jean		Post Office Road		
May	1949	461	Donnelly	Colette		Station Rd		

Appendices

Month Registered in the School	Year	Pupils Register No.	Pupils Surname	First Name	Dob	Place Of Residence	Occupation Of Parent/Guardian	Previous School (If Applicable)
Jan	1950	462	Hurley	Bridget		The Green		
Apr	1950	463	Ryan	Anne-Marie		The Green		
Apr	1950	464	Murphy	Maura		The Commons		
June	1950	465	Wall	Brenda Mary		Main St.		
June	1950	466	Clarke	Christina		Raheney		
Sept	1950	467	Byrne	Kathleen		The Square		
Sept	1950	468	Grimes	Carmel		The Square		
Oct	1950	469	Cruise	Maire Aine		Lusk		
Oct	1950	470	Cowley	Eilis		Lusk		
Oct	1950	471	Oglesby	Emer		Newhaggard		
Apr	1951	472	Jenkinson	Margaret		Lusk		
Apr	1951	473	Boyle	Ann		Lusk		
Sept	1951	474	Bentley	Brigid		Lusk		
Sept	1951	475	Gough	Teresa		The Farm, Lusk		
Apr	1952	476	McDonnell	Rose		Skerries Road		
Apr	1952	477	Neary	Barbara		Lusk		
Apr	1952	478	Russell	Kathleen		Lusk		
Apr	1952	479	Ryan	Vera		Lusk		
Apr	1952	480	Daly	Patricia		Lusk		
Apr	1952	481	O'Brien	Joyce		The Square		
May	1950	482	Knott	Maureen		Lusk		
July	1952	483	Peters	Elizabeth		Newhaggard		
Sept	1952	484	Scally	Patricia		Lusk		
Sept	1952	485	Rogan	Siobain		The Square		
Sept	1952	486	Hanratty	Anne M		The Green		
Feb	1953	487	Connor	Joan		Newhaggard		
Apr	1953	488	Garrigan	Nuala		Station Rd		
Apr	1953	489	Carton	Margaret		The Square		
Apr	1953	490	Kiernan	Margaret		Station Rd		
Apr	1953	491	Cruise	Dorothy		The Green		

Month Registered in the School	Year	Pupils Register No.	Pupils Surname	First Name	Dob	Place Of Residence	Occupation Of Parent/Guardian	Previous School (If Applicable)
Apr	1953	492	Ryan	Una		The Green		
Apr	1953	493	Hughes	Carl		Rush Rd.		
Apr	1953	494	Boyle	Kathleen		Garda Stn.		
Apr	1953	495	Doyle	Patricia		Dublin Rd		
Apr	1953	496	Doyle	Jean		Dublin Rd		
Sept	1953	497	Scally	Maureen		Post Office Road		
Sept	1953	498	Kinsella	Elizabeth		Back Rd.		
Jan	1954	499	Jenkinson	Ann		Post Office		
Mar	1954	500	Browne	Etna		The Brewery		
Mar	1954	501	Dennis	Margaret		The Green		
Mar	1954	502	Hurley	Mary		Lusk		
May	1954	503	Kiernan	Kathleen		Lusk		
June	1954	504	Clarke	Margaret (Rita)		Lusk		
Sept	1954	506	Bentley	Esther		Lusk		
Sept	1954	507	Donnelly	Dymphna		Lusk		
Oct	1954	508	Doyle	Margaret		Dublin Rd		
Oct	1954	505	Peters	Marcella		Newhaggard		
Nov	1954	509	Derham (Pigott)	Philomena		Commons		
Jan	1955	510	Ryan	Mairin		Lusk		
Mar	1955	511	Brown	Mary		Lusk		
Mar	1955	512	Neary	Marie		Lusk		
Apr	1955	513	Boyle	Jennie		Lusk		
Apr	1955	514	Clare	Emer		Lusk		
Sept	1955	515	Bentley	Anne Marie		Lusk		
Sept	1955	516	Hanberry	Eileen		Colecot		
Sept	1955	517	Russell	Ann		Station Rd		
Sept	1955	518	Scally	Attracta		Post Office Road		
Nov	1955	519	Scally	Patricia		Post Office Road		
Jan	1956	520	Dennis	Doreen		Post Office Road		
Jan	1956	521	Llewellan	Teresa		Post Office Road		

Appendices

Month Registered in the School	Year	Pupils Register No.	Pupils Surname	First Name	Dob	Place Of Residence	Occupation Of Parent/Guardian	Previous School (If Applicable)
Apr	1956	522	Neary	Joan		Post Office Road		
Apr	1956	523	Mcgee	Peggie		Commons		
Apr	1956	524	Ryan	Mary		The Green		
Apr	1956	525	Jenkinson	Rosalyeen		Iona'		
Apr	1956	526	Brown	Concepta		The Brewery		
May	1956	527	O'Brien	Philomena		The Square		
May	1956	528	Wall	Kathryn		Skerries Road		
June	1956	529	Byrne	Patricia		Ballough		
Sept	1956	530	Sherry	Dymphna		Lusk		
Sept	1956	531	Daly	Mona		Newhaggard		
Sept	1956	532	Grimes	Frances		Lusk		
Sept	1956	533	Bentley	Frances		Lusk		
Sept	1956	534	Hughes	Mary		Newhaggard		
May	1957	535	Scally	Margaret		Lusk		
May	1957	536	Connor	Aubrey		Newhaggard		
May	1957	537	Monks	Phyllis		Lusk		
May	1957	538	Rooney	Bridget		Quickpenny		
June	1957	539	McGee	Bridget		The Commons		
June	1957	540	Cowley	Carmel		Skerries Road		
June	1957	541	Griffin	Noelin		Chapel Lane		
July	1957	542	Carton	Angela		The Square		
Sept	1957	543	Dennis	Miriam		Rush Rd.		
Sept	1957	545	Brennan	Maire		Rush Rd.		
Sept	1957	546	Brennan	Felicitie		Rush Rd.		
Dec	1957	547	Wynne	Dorothy		Commons		
Feb	1958	548	Jenkinson	Elizabeth		Iona'		
Apr	1958	549	Hughes	Patricia		Newhaggard		
Apr	1958	550	Morgan	Marie		The Commons		
Apr	1958	551	McGee	Cathrine		The Commons		
Apr	1958	552	Clare	Patricia		The Green		
July	1958	553	Neary	Patricia		Post Office Road		

Month Registered in the School	Year	Pupils Register No.	Pupils Surname	First Name	Dob	Place Of Residence	Occupation Of Parent/Guardian	Previous School (If Applicable)
Sept	1958	554	Dennis	Irene		Ballaly		
June	1959	555	Connor	Georgina		Newhaggard		
June	1959	556	Hughes	Teresa		Newhaggard		
June	1959	557	Hanberry	Sheila		Colecot		
July	1959	558	Doyle	Margaret		Brides Tree		
July	1959	559	Andrews	Miriam		Lusk		
Feb	1960	560	Cruise	Concepta		Lusk		
Apr	1960	561	Boylan	Margaret		The Square		
Apr	1960	562	Sheridan	Mary		Quickpenny Rd.		
May	1960	563	Harford	Imelda		Hill House		
May	1960	564	McGee	Colette		Post Office Road		
July	1960	565	Clarke	Monica		St Josephs Ave.		
July	1960	566	Ryan	Kathryn		The Green		
Sept	1960	567	Seaver	Mary		The Commons		
Sept	1960	568	McGee	Monica		The Commons		
Sept	1960	569	Groves	Ann		The Figures		
Oct	1960	570	Garvey	Sheila		Swords		
Oct	1960	571	Garvey	Maura		Swords		
Apr	1961	572	Dennis	Lorraine		Ballaly		
Sept	1961	573	Jenkinson	Rhona		Lusk		
Sept	1961	574	Dennis	Pauline		Lusk		
Feb	1962	575	Clarke	Anne		Lusk		
May	1962	576	McGee	Mary A		The Commons		
May	1962	577	Bentley	Marion		Ballaly		
July	1962	578	Boylan	Colette		The Square		
July	1962	579	McGuinness	Bernadette		Skerries Road		
Feb	1963	580	Mcgee (Hughes)	Kathleen		Newhaggard		
Apr	1963	581	Bennett	Elaine		Post Office Road		
Apr	1963	582	Brown	Kathleen		The Brewery		
Apr	1963	583	Monks	Rosaleen		Barrrack Rd.		
Apr	1963	584	Gordon	Ide		The Commons		

Appendices

Month Registered in the School	Year	Pupils Register No.	Pupils Surname	First Name	Dob	Place Of Residence	Occupation Of Parent/Guardian	Previous School (If Applicable)
May	1963	585	O'Rourke	Bridget		Lusk		
July	1963	586	McGuinness	Maureen		Lusk		
July	1963	587	Sheridan	Kathleen		Ballymaguire		
July	1963	588	Mcgee	Bernadette		Commons		
July	1963	589	Brown	Bernadette		Lusk		
Sept	1963	590	Murray	Elizabeth		Lusk		
Oct	1963	591	Hand	Philomena		The Green		
Oct	1963	592	Gerrard	Paula		The Square		
Nov	1963	593	McCann	Maura		Lusk		
Jan	1964	594	Brown	Margaret		Treen Hill		
Apr	1964	595	Sherwin	Philomena		Lusk		
Apr	1964	596	Butterly	Philomena		Ballaly		
July	1964	597	Daly	Dolores		Lusk		
July	1964	598	Kavanagh	Ann		Lusk		
July	1964	599	Brown	Jennie		Lusk		
Sept	1964	600	Sweetman	Margaret		Lusk		
Sept	1964	601	Hogan	Kathleen		The Green		
Sept	1964	602	Sherwin	Bernadette		Lusk		
July	1965	603	O'Hara	Mary		Lusk		
July	1965	604	Murray	Lorretto		Lusk		
July	1965	605	Cruise	Christine		Lusk		
July	1965	606	McDonnell	Elaine		Lusk		
July	1965	607	Bentley	Fiona		Lusk		
July	1965	608	O'Rourke	Maeve		Lusk		
July	1965	609	Devine	Catherine		Lusk		
July	1965	610	Clare	Ann		Lusk		
Sept	1965	611	Gordon	Georgina		Commons		
Sept	1965	612	Fay	Caroline		Lusk		
Feb	1966	613	Doherty	Moya		Clontarf		
Feb	1966	614	Doherty	Niamh		Clontarf		
Mar	1966	615	Ni Dasan	Aine		Lusk		

Month Registered in the School	Year	Pupils Register No.	Pupils Surname	First Name	Dob	Place Of Residence	Occupation Of Parent/Guardian	Previous School (If Applicable)
Mar	1966	616	Ni Dasan	Siobhain		Lusk		
Apr	1966	617	Doherty	Nuala		Clontarf		
July	1966	618	Browne	Miriam		Lusk		
July	1966	619	O'Hara	Ann		Lusk		
July	1966	620	Dennis	Sandra		Lusk		
July	1966	621	Sherwin	Angela		Lusk		
July	1966	622	Bentley	Ann		Ballay		
July	1966	623	Bentley	Bridgid		Ballay		
July	1966	624	Boylan	Ann		Lusk		
July	1966	625	McGee	Ann		Commons		
July	1966	626	Neary	Julie		Lusk		
July	1966	627	Russell	Maire		Lusk		
July	1966	628	McNally	Maria		Lusk		
July	1966	629	McCann	Geraldine		Lusk		
July	1967	630	Harford	Mairead		Commons		
July	1967	631	Harford	Frances		Commons		
July	1967	632	Harford	Olive		Commons		
July	1967	633	Scally	Kathleen		Station Rd		
July	1967	634	Westacott	Teresa		Newhaggard		
July	1967	635	Kelly	Mary		Kilhedge Lane		
July	1967	636	Mcphilips	Mary		Lusk		
July	1967	637	Brogan	Brid		The Commons		
July	1967	638	Boylan	Christine		The Square		
Feb	1968	639	Cawley	Kathleen		The Station		
Feb	1968	640	Cawley	Margaret		The Station		
Feb	1968	641	Cawley	Helen		The Station		
Feb	1968	642	Cawley	Elizabeth		The Station		
July	1968	643	Austin	Jacquiline		Station Rd		
July	1968	644	Boylan	Ann		Ash Grove		
July	1968	645	O'Hara	Margaret		The Green		
July	1968	646	Browne	Susan		Treen Hill		

Appendices

Month Registered in the School	Year	Pupils Register No.	Pupils Surname	First Name	Dob	Place Of Residence	Occupation Of Parent/Guardian	Previous School (If Applicable)
July	1968	647	Jenkinson	Regina		Iona'		
July	1968	648	Bentley	Valerie		Treen Hill		
July	1968	649	O'Rourke	Elizabeth		Dublin Rd		
July	1968	650	Devine	Sarah		The Square		
July	1968	651	Mcphilips	Geraldine		Dublin Rd		
July	1968	652	Sherwin	Paula		Station Rd		
July	1968	653	O'Rourke	Patricia		Lusk		
Aug	1968	654	O'Leary	Brigid		Newhaggard		
Jan	1969	654A	Fay	Imelda		Lusk		
July	1969	655	Russell	Dolores		Dublin Rd		
July	1969	656	Bentley	Linda		Dublin Rd		
July	1969	657	Kelly	Elaine		Dublin Rd		
July	1969	658	Peters	Michelle		Back Lane		
July	1969	659	Sweetman	Sandra		Station Rd		
July	1969	660	Browne	Fiona		Treen Hill		
July	1969	661	Boylan	Cathleen		Ash Grove		
July	1969	662	Gilmartin	Ann		Kelly Park		
July	1970	663	O'Leary	Margaret		Newhaggard		
July	1970	664	O'Leary	Nan		Newhaggard		
July	1970	664A	Bentley	Colette		Treen Hill		
July	1970	665	Seaver	Mary		Commons		
July	1970	666	McGee	Elizabeth		Commons		
July	1970	667	O'Connor	Ann		Kelly Park		
July	1970	668	Green	Eileen		Commons		
July	1970	669	Devine	Deirdre		Commons		
July	1970	670	Kelly	Allison		Dublin Rd.		
July	1970	671	Sweetman	Bernadette		Main St.		
July	1970	672	Foster	Mary		Skerries Rd.		
July	1970	673	McBride	Margaret		Lusk		
Aug	1970	674	Sheridan	Elizabeth		Ministers Rd.		
Aug	1970	675	Sheridan	Catherine		Ministers Rd.		

Month Registered in the School	Year	Pupils Register No.	Pupils Surname	First Name	Dob	Place Of Residence	Occupation Of Parent/Guardian	Previous School (If Applicable)
Sept	1970	676	Haugh	Nora		Church View		
Sept	1970	677	Haugh	Helen		Church View		
Sept	1970	678	Haugh	Louise		Church View		
Dec	1970	679	Carty	Vivienne		Lusk		

List of Girls 1971 to 1992

Month registered in the School	Year	Pupils Register No.	Pupils Surname	First Name	Address
June	1971	680	Leonard	Deirdre	Oberstown
June	1971	681	Leonard	Patricia	Oberstown
July	1971	682	Doyle	Ellen	Dublin Rd
July	1971	683	Doyle	Susan	Dublin Rd
July	1971	684	Clarke	Martina	St. Josephs Ave.
July	1971	685	Fay	Denise	The Green
July	1971	686	Neary	Michelle	The Green
July	1971	687	Austin	Aishling	Raheny
July	1971	688	Neary	Ann	Station Rd
July	1971	689	Hughes	Ann	Newhaggard
July	1971	690	Browne	Ann	The Green
July	1971	691	Skelly	Linda	Station Rd
July	1971	692	Sweetman	Denise	P.O. Road
July	1971	693	Gordon	Anne	The Commons
July	1971	694	O'Rourke	Margaret	Dublin Rd
July	1971	695	Gerrard	Brigid	Church View
July	1971	696	Brogan	Loraine	The Commons
July	1971	697	O'Toole	Helen	The Square
July	1971	698	Grimes	Frances	Ash Grove
July	1971	699	Brogan	Suzanne	The Commons
July	1971	700	Thornton	Marion	Ash Grove
July	1971	701	O'Reilly	Jacqualine	St Macculins Close

Appendices

Month registered in the School	Year	Pupils Register No.	Pupils Surname	First Name	Address
July	1971	702	Haugh	Denise	Back Lane
Sept	1971	703	McNally	Nuala	Ministers Rd.
Nov	1971	704	Weston	Mary	The Green
Nov	1971	705	Weston	Ann Julie	The Green
Feb	1972	706	Finnegan	Geraldine	Main St.
Feb	1972	707	Finnegan	Elizabeth	Lusk
Sept	1972	708	Traynor	Mary	Lusk
Sept	1972	709	Traynor	Brigid	Lusk
July	1972	710	Herlihy	Sinead	Lusk
Aug	1972	711	O'Dell	Patricia	Lusk
Mar	1972	712	Doyle	Josephine	Lusk
Mar	1972	713	Bentley	Lorna	Ballaly
Mar	1972	714	Plunkett	Elizabeth	Dublin Rd
Mar	1972	715	Plunkett	Ann	Dublin Rd
Mar	1972	716	Clare	Charlotte	St Josephs Ave
Mar	1972	717	Neary	Lorainne	Dublin Rd
Mar	1972	718	Brogan	Sharon	The Commons
Mar	1972	719	Hoey	Ann Marie	Rathmooney
July	1972	720	Ryan	Eileen	Main St.
July	1972	721	O'Toole	Teresa	Kelly Pk.
July	1972	722	Kelly	Beverly	Dublin Rd
July	1972	723	Cruise	Sandra	Ash Grove
July	1972	724	Greene	Ann	The Commons
July	1972	725	Clare	Caroline	Ash Grove
July	1972	726	Knott	Jacinta	St Macculins Close
July	1972	727	Skelly	Linda	
July	1972	728	O'Rourke	Margaret	
July	1972	729	Grimes	Frances	
July	1972	730	Gordon	Ann	
Aug	1972	731	Westacott	Caroline	Newhaggard
Aug	1972	732	Cross	Dolores	Kelly Pk.
Aug	1972	733	Weldon	Linda	Ash Grove

Month registered in the School	Year	Pupils Register No.	Pupils Surname	First Name	Address
May	1974	734	Greene	Brenda	Kelly Pk.
May	1974	735	Greene	Philomena	Kelly Pk.
Sept	1973	736	Cardiff	Miriam	Dublin Rd
July	1973	737	Bentley	Louise	Treen Hill
July	1973	738	O'Herlihy	Catherine	Station Rd
July	1973	739	Fay	Carmel	Chapel Lane
July	1973	740	O'Rourke	Edel	Dublin Rd
July	1973	741	Brogan	Lorna	The Commons
July	1973	742	Weldon	Carole	Ash Grove
July	1973	743	Delaney	Amanda	Ash Grove
July	1973	744	Neary	Denise	Dublin Rd
July	1973	745	Clare	Jacinta	St Josephs Ave
July	1973	746	Dennis	Caroline	P.O. Road
Sept	1973	747	Seaver	Ann	The Commons
Oct	1973	748	Grimes	Sharon	Ash Grove
May	1974	749	Monks	Margaret	Kelly Pk.
July	1974	750	Trainor	Julie	Kelly Pk.
July	1974	751	Gaffney	Geraldine	The Commons
July	1974	752	Donnelly	Eileen	Kelly Pk.
July	1974	753	Weldon	Geraldine	Kelly Pk.
July	1974	754	Weldon	Catriona	Kelly Pk.
July	1974	755	O'Brien	Louise	Main St.
July	1974	756	McNally	Mary	P.O. Road
July	1974	757	Moore	Sarah	The Commons
July	1974	758	Stafford	Miriam	Kelly Pk.
July	1974	759	Thornton	Paula	Ash Grove
July	1974	760	Clare	Fiona	The Green
July	1974	761	Russell	Yvonne	Kelly Pk.
July	1974	762	Skelly	Deborah	P.O. Road
July	1974	763	Clare	Youlande	Ash Grove
July	1974	764	Greene	Brenda	Kelly Pk.
May	1974	765	Monks	Ann	Kelly Pk.

Appendices

Month registered in the School	Year	Pupils Register No.	Pupils Surname	First Name	Address
Sept	1974	766	O'Leary	Kathleen	
Sept	1974	767	Ferguson	Paula	Kelly Pk.
Sept	1974	768	McArdle	Denise	Dublin Rd
Sept	1974	769	Flynn	Sinead	Dublin Rd
Sept	1974	770	Delaney	Sandra	Kelly Pk.
Sept	1974	771	Flynn	Dervela	Dublin Rd
Sept	1974	772	Dennis	Audrey	Kelly Pk.
Oct	1974	773	Fletcher	Dorothy	Chapel Lane
July	1975	775	Howard	Sharon	Kelly Pk.
July	1975	774	Farrell	Helen	Kelly Pk.
July	1975	776	Donnelly	Victoria	Kelly Pk.
July	1975	777	Daly	Ann	Kelly Pk.
July	1975	778	McKitterick	Helen	Kelly Pk.
July	1975	779	Traynor	Ann	Kelly Pk.
July	1975	780	Donnelly	Geraldine	Kelly Pk.
July	1975	781	Healy	Helen	Kelly Pk.
July	1975	782	Dennis	Carolynn	Kelly Pk.
July	1975	783	Weldon	Louise	Kelly Pk.
July	1975	784	Delaney	Brenda	Kelly Pk.
July	1975	785	Lawlor	Caroline	Kelly Pk.
July	1975	786	Clare	Niamh	Dublin Rd
July	1975	787	O'Rourke	Laura	Dublin Rd
July	1975	788	Plunkett	Valerie	Dublin Rd
July	1975	789	Dennis	Eithne	P.O. Road
July	1975	790	McDonell	Joanne	The Square
July	1975	791	Ryan	Caitrona	Main St.
July	1975	792	Hogan	Annette	Ash Grove
July	1975	793	Brogan	Linda	The Commons
July	1975	794	O'Herlihy	Eimear	Station Rd
July	1975	795	Stafford	Fioan	Kelly Pk.
July	1975	796	Greene	Maria	Kelly Pk.
July	1975	797	Clinton	Evelyn	Tyrrellstown

Month registered in the School	Year	Pupils Register No.	Pupils Surname	First Name	Address
July	1975	798	Mcgee	Jacqualine	P.O. Road
Jan	1976	799	Sherwin	Jacinta	Ballaly
Jan	1976	800	Jenkinson	Elaine	Dublin Rd
Jan	1976	801	Jenkinson	Audrey	Dublin Rd
July	1976	802	Brogan	Gillian	The Commons
July	1976	803	Ryan	Sharon	Main St.
July	1976	804	Clare	Deirdre	The Green
July	1976	805	Gilmartin	Joan	Kelly Pk.
July	1976	806	Cruise	Precilla	Ash Grove
July	1976	807	Mcgrath	Geraldine	Kelly Pk.
July	1976	808	Weldon	Evelyn	Ash Grove
July	1976	809	Theresa	Mcgee	Kelly Pk.
July	1976	810	Hughes	Catherine	
July	1976	811	Dennis	Fidelma	
July	1976	812	Peters	Tracy	
July	1976	813	Plunkett	Rachael	
Oct	1976	814	Daly	Deirdre	Ministers Rd.
Oct	1976	815	McCann	Kathleen	Ministers Rd.
Oct	1976	816	McCann	Mary	Ministers Rd.
Oct	1976	817	Wogan	Elizabeth	Kelly Pk.
Dec	1976	818	Wogan	Carmel	Kelly Pk.
June	1977	819	Hughes	Elaine	Kelly Pk.
June	1977	820	Moylan	Hazel	Kelly Pk.
July	1977	821	Crudden	Jennifer	Kelly Pk.
July	1977	822	Howard	Emma	Kelly Pk.
July	1977	823	Finnegan	Helena	The Commons
July	1977	824	Pullan	Corina	Kelly Pk.
July	1977	825	Turner	Ellen	Kelly Pk.
July	1977	826	Blessing	Donna	Ash Grove
July	1977	827	Skelly	Mellisa	P.O. Road
July	1977	828	Daly	Susan	Ministers Rd.
July	1977	829	Daly	Lorraine	Kelly Pk.

Appendices

Month registered in the School	Year	Pupils Register No.	Pupils Surname	First Name	Address
July	1977	830	Byrne	Caroline	Kelly Pk.
July	1977	831	Gerrard	Aileen	The Square
July	1977	832	Clare	Yvonne	St Josephs Ave
July	1977	833	Keelan	Severena	Kelly Pk.
July	1977	834	Cruise	Jennifer	Ash Grove
July	1977	835	Christie	Victoria	Kelly Pk.
July	1977	836	Christie	Tara	Kelly Pk.
July	1977	837	McKenna	Deirdre	Kelly Pk.
July	1977	838	Brogan	Jennifer	The Commons
July	1977	839	Moylan	Bernice	Kelly Pk.
July	1977	840	Barry	Linda	Ministers Rd.
July	1977	841	McClafferty	Karen	Ministers Rd.
July	1977	842	McClafferty	Jacqueline	Ministers Rd.
July	1977	843	McClafferty	Siobhan	Ministers Rd.
July	1977	844	McClafferty	Martina	Ministers Rd.
July	1977	845	McGealy	Mary	Kelly Pk.
July	1977	846	Watson	Rachel	Kelly Pk.
July	1977	847	Cruise	Camilla	
July	1977	848	O'Donnell	Lisa	
Apr	1978	849	O'Rourke	Yvonne	Orlynn Pk.
July	1978	850	Fallon	Geraldine	Rogerstown
Sept	1978	851	Farrell	Margaret	Kelly Pk.
Sept	1978	852	O'Donnell	Valerie	Ministers Rd.
Sept	1978	853	De Jong	Emer	Church Rd.
Sept	1978	854	Sherry	Orla	Church Rd.
Sept	1978	855	Murphy	Lisa	Kelly Pk.
Sept	1978	856	Cahill	Rhoda	Ratheny
Sept	1978	857	Turner	Olive	Kelly Pk.
Sept	1978	858	Gaffney	Anne	Skerries Rd.
Sept	1978	859	Healy	Teresa	Kelly Pk.
Sept	1978	860	Dennis	Elizabeth	Chapel Green
Sept	1978	861	Jones	Elizabeth	The Green

Month registered in the School	Year	Pupils Register No.	Pupils Surname	First Name	Address
Sept	1978	862	Weldon	Barbara	Kelly Pk.
Sept	1978	863	Weldon	Olivia	Kelly Pk.
Sept	1978	864	Sherwin	Amanda	Reamount
Sept	1978	865	Daly	Sharon	Kelly Pk.
Sept	1978	866	Sherry	Elizabeth	Main St.
Sept	1978	867	Sandford	Nicola	Kelly Pk.
Sept	1978	868	Moore	Mary	The Commons
Sept	1978	869	McDonnell	Lara	The Square
Sept	1978	870	Ledwidge	Annemarie	Kelly Pk.
Sept	1978	871	Peters	Mandy	St. Macullins Close
Oct	1978	872	Sugrue	Michelle	Dublin Rd
Nov	1978	873	McGrath	Catherine	Orlynn Pk.
Nov	1978	874	McGuire	Louise	Orlynn Pk.
Nov	1978	875	McGrath	Brenda	Orlynn Pk.
Apr	1979	876	Milligan	Jennifer	Orlynn Pk.
Feb	1979	877	Fay	Nicola	
Mar	1979	878	Kane	Fiona	P.O. Road
Jan	1979	879	Ryan	Irene	Dublin Rd
Sept	1979	880	Weir	Rachel	The Commons
Sept	1979	881	Fox	Hilary	Orlynn Pk.
Sept	1979	882	Weir	Naomi	The Commons
Jan	1980	883	Timothy	Karina	Orlynn Pk.
Sept	1979	884	O'Neill	Audrey	Kelly Pk.
Sept	1979	885	Clare	Nuala	The Green
Sept	1979	886	Christie	Concepta	Kelly Pk.
Sept	1979	887	Cowley	Elaine	Kelly Pk.
Sept	1979	888	Finnegan	Annmarie	The Commons
Sept	1979	889	Bentley	Vivian	Treen Hill
Sept	1979	890	Peters	Karen	Ballaly Lane
Sept	1979	891	Skelly	Sharon	P.O. Road
Sept	1979	892	Murphy	Sinead	Kelly Pk.
Sept	1979	893	Jenkinson	Lynne	Dublin Rd

Appendices

Month registered in the School	Year	Pupils Register No.	Pupils Surname	First Name	Address
Sept	1979	894	Dennis	Louise	
Sept	1979	895	McGee	Michelle	P.O. Road
Sept	1979	896	Pullen	Victoria	Kelly Pk.
Sept	1979	897	Turner	Yvonne	Kelly Pk.
Sept	1979	898	Carroll	Elaine	Ministers Rd.
Sept	1979	899	Dennis	Tracey	Ballaly Lane
Sept	1979	900	McNally	Fiona	Main St.
Sept	1979	901	Rogan	Majella	Kelly Pk.
Sept	1979	902	Cruise	Eithne	The Green
Sept	1979	903	McGrath	Caroline	Ministers Rd.
Sept	1979	904	Weston	Patricia	The Green
Sept	1979	905	Fay	Adrianne	Chapel Lane
Sept	1979	906	Hogan	Maria	Dublin Rd
Sept	1979	907	McDonell	Denise	Church Rd.
Sept	1979	908	Peters	Edel	Ballaly Lane
Sept	1979	909	Carton	Tracey	Corduff
Sept	1979	910	Thornton	Deirdre	Kelly Pk.
Sept	1979	911	Crowley	Edel	Orlynn Pk.
May	1980	912	Synnott	Jennifer	Orlynn Pk.
Sept	1980	913	Daly	Robina	Orlynn Pk.
Sept	1980	914	Creegan	Caroline	Orlynn Pk.
Sept	1980	915	Creegan	Fiona	Orlynn Pk.
Sept	1980	916	Sherry	Michelle	Church Rd.
Sept	1980	917	McGee	Rachel	Chapel Lane
Sept	1980	918	Sullivan	Lisa	Kelly Pk.
Sept	1980	919	Milligan	Catherine	Orlynn Pk.
Sept	1980	920	Sherry	Rebecca	Main St.
Sept	1980	921	McGrath	Linda	Ministers Rd.
Sept	1980	922	Connerney	Ciara	Orlynn Pk.
Sept	1980	923	O'Rourke	Deirdre	Orlynn Pk.
Sept	1980	924	Russell	Mary	Kelly Pk.
Sept	1980	925	Peters	Lisa	Kelly Pk.

Month registered in the School	Year	Pupils Register No.	Pupils Surname	First Name	Address
Sept	1980	926	Monks	Lorraine	Ministers Rd.
Sept	1980	927	Healy	Deirdre	Kelly Pk.
Sept	1980	928	McBride	Catherine	St. Macullins Close
Sept	1980	929	Devine	Noreen	The Commons
Sept	1980	930	Boylan	Suzanne	Ministers Rd.
Sept	1980	931	O'Neill	Jacqueline	Kelly Pk.
Sept	1980	932	Culleton	Frances	Orlynn Pk.
Sept	1980	933	Dennis	Rosemary	Chapel Green
Sept	1980	934	Daly	Janet	Kelly Pk.
Sept	1980	935	Brogan	Annette	Skerries Rd.
Sept	1980	936	O'leary	Sinead	Orlynn Pk.
Sept	1980	937	Daly	Johanne	Orlynn Pk.
Sept	1980	938	Browne	Marissa	Orlynn Pk.
Sept	1980	939	Sherry	Karen	Barrack Rd.
Sept	1980	940	Byrne	Olive	Kelly Pk.
Dec	1980	941	Hogan	Michelle	Kelly Pk.
Sept	1980	942	Sammon	Aine	Orlynn Pk.
Dec	1980	943	Rundle	Andrea	Orlynn Pk.
Dec	1980	944	Rundle	Tracy	Orlynn Pk.
Dec	1981	945	Rosney	Nichola	Orlynn Pk.
Sept	1981	946	Dennis	Maria	P.O. Road
Sept	1981	947	Fleming	Deborah	Ministers Pk.
Jan	1981	948	O'Brien	Fiona	Kelly Pk.
Apr	1981	949	Gribben	Kim	St. Conards
May	1981	950	Gallagher	Olwyn	Orlynn Pk.
Oct	1981	951	Corbally	Sharon	Orlynn Pk.
Feb	1982	952	O'Gorman	Helen	Ministers Rd.
Sept	1981	953	Bachley	Marian	Tower View
Nov	1981	954	McGratten	Gail	Orlynn Pk.
Apr	1982	955	Gribben	Debbie	St. Conards
Sept	1981	956	Butterly	Anita	Orlynn Pk.
Sept	1981	957	O'Connor	Rachel	Orlynn Pk.

Appendices

Month registered in the School	Year	Pupils Register No.	Pupils Surname	First Name	Address
Sept	1981	958	Mcgrath	Karen	Kelly Pk.
Sept	1981	959	McGealy	Martina	Kelly Pk.
Sept	1981	960	Brogan	Barbara	The Commons
Sept	1981	961	Cruise	Linda	The Green
Sept	1981	962	Cruise	Esther	Ministers Rd.
Sept	1981	963	Ryan	Jill	Regeens
Sept	1981	964	O'Donnell	Irene	Kelly Pk.
Sept	1981	965	O'Donovan	Eimear	Orlynn Pk.
Sept	1981	966	McNally	Theresa	P.O. Road
Sept	1981	967	Doran	Emma	Dublin Rd
Sept	1981	968	Hegarty	Sarah	Orlynn Pk.
Sept	1981	969	Lewis	Christina	Dublin Rd
Sept	1981	970	Weir	Melanie	The Commons
Sept	1981	971	O'Sullivan	Sandra	Kelly Pk.
Sept	1981	972	McKitterick	Collette	Ministers Rd.
Sept	1981	973	Farrell	Lisa	Kelly Pk.
Sept	1982	974	McGrath	Brenda	Kelly Pk.
Sept	1982	975	Kane	Sarah	P.O. Road
Sept	1982	976	Kane	Paula	P.O. Road
Sept	1982	977	Morgan	Karina	Kelly Pk.
Sept	1982	978	White	Ciara	Orlynn Pk.
Sept	1982	979	Bird	Deirdre	Orlynn Pk.
Sept	1982	980	Murphy	Valerie	Orlynn Pk.
Sept	1982	981	Stafford	Brenda	Kelly Pk.
Sept	1982	982	Murphy	Louise	Ministers Rd.
Sept	1982	983	Daly	Elizabeth	Kelly Pk.
Sept	1982	984	Sugrue	Siobhan	Dublin Rd
Sept	1982	985	Carroll	Christina	Ministers Rd.
Sept	1982	986	Synnott	Gillian	Orlynn Pk.
Sept	1982	987	McCormack	Pauline	Orlynn Pk.
Sept	1982	988	Watson	Sabrina	Newhaggard
Sept	1982	989	O'Rourke	Gwendoline	Main St.

Month registered in the School	Year	Pupils Register No.	Pupils Surname	First Name	Address
Sept	1982	990	Lynch	Susan	Ministers Rd.
Sept	1982	991	Daly	Eileen	Kelly Pk.
Sept	1982	992	Cruise	Caroline	Ministers Rd.
Sept	1982	993	Farrell	Lara	Kelly Pk.
Sept	1982	994	Peters	Lynn	Ballaly Lane
Sept	1982	995	Daly	Claire	Chapel Rd.
Sept	1982	996	Teeling	Vivian	Kelly Pk.
Sept	1982	997	Dryden	Angela	Orlynn Pk.
Oct	1982	998	Carr	Donna	Chapel Lane
Sept	1982	999	Dryden	Cecilia	Orlynn Pk.
June	1982	1000	Burke	Aishling	Orlynn Pk.
Sept	1982	1001	Darcy	Shannon	Orlynn Pk.
Sept	1982	1002	Mulligan	Anne	Skerries Rd.
Oct	1982	1003	Farrell	Verna	Orlynn Pk.
Apr	1983	1004	Quinn	Elizabeth	Orlynn Pk.
May	1983	1005	Hoare	Lorraine	Orlynn Pk.
Apr	1983	1006	Quinn	Antoinette	Orlynn Pk.
Jan	1983	1007	Byrne	Kate	Orlynn Pk.
May	1983	1008	Hamilton	Alice	Orlynn Pk.
May	1983	1009	Cronin	Deirdre	Ministers Rd.
Jan	1983	1010	Byrne	Sarah	Orlynn Pk.
Apr	1983	1011	Quinn	Louise	Orlynn Pk.
May	1983	1012	Crowe	Evelyn	Rathmooney
Sept	1983	1013	Mcgee	Estelle	P.O. Road
May	1984	1014	Crowe	Claire	Rathmooney
Sept	1983	1015	McGee	Lynette	P.O. Road
May	1984	1016	Crowe	Helen	Rathmooney
Sept	1983	1017	Dennis	Vivienne	Racecourse Commons
Sept	1983	1018	Farrell	Caroline	
Sept	1983	1019	Byrne	Evelyn	Orlynn Pk.
Sept	1983	1020	O'Rourke	Tracy	Reamount
Sept	1983	1021	Maguire	Claire	Orlynn Pk.

Appendices

Month registered in the School	Year	Pupils Register No.	Pupils Surname	First Name	Address
Sept	1983	1022	Dennis	Eleanor	Chapel Green
Sept	1983	1023	Ryan	Claire	Regeens
Sept	1983	1024	Delaney	Lillian	Minsters Pk.
Sept	1983	1025	Taylor	Lorraine	Chapel Farm
Sept	1983	1026	Gill	Ruth	Old Vicarage, Donabate
Sept	1983	1027	Hegarty	Ruth	Orlynn Pk.
Sept	1983	1028	Finnegan	Marguerite	The Commons
Sept	1983	1029	Sherry	Fidelma	Barrack Rd.
Sept	1983	1030	Walsh	Karen	Ash Grove
Sept	1983	1031	Murphy	Victoria	Ministers Rd.
Sept	1983	1032	O'Connor	Ruth	Orlynn Pk.
Sept	1983	1033	Cox	Jennifer	Orlynn Pk.
Sept	1983	1034	O'Donnell	Sandra	Ministers Rd.
Sept	1983	1035	Christie	Leona	Kelly Pk.
Sept	1983	1036	Derham	Nicola	The Commons
Sept	1983	1037	Murphy	Richella	Orlynn Pk.
Sept	1983	1038	Donnelly	Sarah	Orlynn Pk.
Sept	1983	1039	Ryan	Tanya	Dublin Rd
Sept	1983	1040	Browne	Leona	Orlynn Pk.
Sept	1983	1041	White	Aideen	Orlynn Pk.
Sept	1983	1042	Burke	Pamela	Ministers Rd.
Jan	1985	1043	Collins	Leona	Minsters Pk.
Sept	1984	1044	Kelly	Rhona	Dublin Rd
Sept	1984	1045	Synnott	Jacqueline	Orlynn Pk.
Sept	1984	1046	Marry	Sharon	Ministers Rd.
Sept	1984	1047	McGealy	Miranda	Kelly Pk.
Sept	1984	1048	McGealy	Michelle	Kelly Pk.
Sept	1984	1049	O'Brien	Edel	The Green
Sept	1984	1050	Bonner	Anne	Orlynn Pk.
Sept	1984	1051	Kernan	Aoife	Orlynn Pk.
Sept	1984	1052	Horgan	Aoife	Barrack Rd.
Sept	1984	1053	Daly	Patricia	Kelly Pk.

Month registered in the School	Year	Pupils Register No.	Pupils Surname	First Name	Address
Sept	1984	1054	Hogan	Tracey	Minsters Pk.
Sept	1984	1055	Carroll	Fiona	Minsters Pk.
Sept	1984	1056	Cruise	Sarah	Minsters Pk.
Sept	1984	1057	Murphy	Eadaoin	Orlynn Pk.
Sept	1983	1058	Hegarty	Ruth	Orlynn Pk.
Sept	1894	1059	Lewis	Jennifer	Dublin Rd
Sept	1984	1060	Kearns	Julie	Orlynn Pk.
Sept	1984	1061	Doolin	Niamh	Orlynn Pk.
Sept	1984	1062	McGee	Yvonne	The Commons
Sept	1984	1063	Foxton	Orla	The Green
Sept	1984	1064	Kavanagh	Emma	Kelly Pk.
Sept	1984	1065	Bentley	Carol	Minsters Pk.
Apr	1985	1066	McAnaney	Mariesa	Orlynn Pk.
Sept	1985	1067	Deeb	Seren	Collinstown
Apr	1985	1068	Holmes	Sonya	Orlynn Pk.
Sept	1985	1069	Evans	Susan	Orlynn Pk.
Sept	1985	1070	Deeb	Yvette	Collinstown
Sept	1985	1071	Stears	Aisling	Orlynn Pk.
Sept	1985	1072	Evans	Samantha	Orlynn Pk.
Sept	1985	1073	Deeb	Nyssan	Collinstown
Sept	1985	1074	Campbell	Diane	Kelly Pk.
Sept	1985	1075	Keelan	Alwin	Kelly Pk.
Sept	1985	1076	McKeon	Donna	Ministers Drive
Sept	1985	1077	Daly	Pamela	Chapel Rd.
Sept	1985	1078	Murphy	Mellisa	Kelly Pk.
Sept	1985	1079	Murphy	Debbie	Minsters Pk.
Sept	1985	1080	Hurley	Deirdre	Regles
Sept	1985	1081	Foran	Kara	Minsters Pk.
Sept	1985	1082	Lenehan	Stephanie	Orlynn Pk.
Sept	1985	1083	Teeling	Debbie	Minsters Pk.
Sept	1985	1084	Kee	Lorna	Iona, Ministers Rd.
Sept	1985	1085	Leetch	Gillain	Orlynn Pk.

Appendices

Month registered in the School	Year	Pupils Register No.	Pupils Surname	First Name	Address
Sept	1985	1086	Ryan	Stephanie	Dublin Rd
Sept	1985	1087	Lowrey	Geraldine	Chapel Green
Sept	1985	1088	Cruise	Carolyn	Ministers Rd.
Sept	1985	1089	Boylan	Karen	Ministers Rd.
Sept	1985	1090	Clarke	Ann-Marie	Ministers Rd.
Sept	1985	1091	Browne	Natalie	Orlynn Pk.
Sept	1985	1092	Rosney	Jennifer	Orlynn Pk.
Sept	1985	1093	O'Connor	Reidin	
Sept	1985	1094	McCormack	Elaine	Orlynn Pk.
Sept	1985	1095	Dennis	Julie	P.O. Road
Sept	1985	1096	McQuillan	Lyndsey	Kelly Pk.
Sept	1985	1097	Betts	Emma	The Commons
Sept	1985	1098	Deeb	Kyma	The Commons
Sept	1985	1099	Fraher	Pamela	Orlynn Pk.
Sept	1985	1100	Howlin	Sarah	Minsters Pk.
Sept	1985	1101	Fleming	Arlene	Margaretstown
Sept	1985	1102	Boylan	Nathlie	The Square
Sept	1985	1103	Farrell	Geraldine	Orlynn Pk.
Sept	1986	1104	McNally	Susan	Orlynn Pk.
Sept	1986	1105	Evans	Lindsay	Orlynn Pk.
Sept	1986	1106	Hurley	Susan	Regles
Sept	1986	1107	Rooney	Jean	Orlynn Pk.
Sept	1986	1108	Delaney	Catriona	Kelly Pk.
Sept	1986	1109	Boylan	Camilla	Ministers Rd.
Sept	1986	1110	Blessing	Pamela	Ash Grove
Sept	1986	1111	Delaney	Jennifer	Ministers Rd.
Sept	1986	1112	Byrnes	Maria	Kelly Pk.
Sept	1986	1113	O'Hara	Clare	Orlynn Pk.
Sept	1986	1114	McMahon	Tanya	Minsters Pk.
Sept	1986	1115	Daly	Collette	Kelly Pk.
Sept	1986	1116	Fay	Audrey	Chapel Lane

Month registered in the School	Year	Pupils Register No.	Pupils Surname	First Name	Address
Sept	1986	1117	Russell	Joanne	Ministers Rd.
Sept	1986	1118	O'Neill	Denise	Orlynn Pk.
Sept	1986	1119	Sherry	Katy	Main St.
Sept	1986	1120	Beatty	Olga	The Commons
Dec	1987	1121	Vaughan	Deborah	Orlynn Pk.
Dec	1987	1122	Geraghty	Elaine	P.O. Road
Sept	1987	1123	Caffrey	Cloda	Hampton Cove
Nov	1987	1124	Vaughan	Louise	Orlynn Pk.
Sept	1987	1125	Fitzpatrick	Carla	
Sept	1988	1126	McNamara	Andrea	Orlynn Pk.
Sept	1987	1127	Leetch	Miriam	Orlynn Pk.
Sept	1987	1128	Farrell	Fiona	Orlynn Pk.
Sept	1987	1129	Wyse	Suzanne	Orlynn Pk.
Sept	1987	1130	McMahon	Michelle	Orlynn Pk.
Sept	1987	1131	Walsh	Annmarie	Minsters Pk.
Sept	1987	1132	Watson	Marina	Newhaggard
Sept	1987	1133	Lewis	Amanda	Dublin Rd
Sept	1987	1134	Cruise	Mildred	Ash Grove
Sept	1987	1135	McGealy	Tanya	Kelly Pk.
Sept	1988	1136	Cawley	Joanne	Kelly Pk.
Sept	1988	1137	Carroll	Niamh	Orlynn Pk.
Sept	1988	1138	O'Donovan	Aine	Orlynn Pk.
Sept	1988	1139	Kilmurry	Siobhan	Orlynn Pk.
Sept	1988	1140	O'Reilly	Lorraine	Orlynn Pk.
Sept	1988	1141	Fay	Laura	Chapel Lane
Sept	1988	1142	Madigan	Laura	Orlynn Pk.
Sept	1988	1143	Murphy	Samantha	Ministers Rd.
Sept	1988	1144	Sweetman	Amanda	P.O. Road
Sept	1988	1145	Daly	Joanne	Ministers Rd.
Sept	1988	1146	Betts	Sarah	The Commons
Sept	1988	1147	Dunne	Gillian	Ministers Rd.
Sept	1988	1148	McCormack	Clare	Orlynn Pk.

Appendices

Month registered in the School	Year	Pupils Register No.	Pupils Surname	First Name	Address
Sept	1987	1149	Sheridan	Sharon	Kelly Pk.
Sept	1988	1150	Danagher	Marie	
Sept	1988	1151	O'Connell	Clare	Orlynn Pk.
Jan	1989	1152	Dayman	Michelle	Orlynn Pk.
Sept	1988	1153	Bird	Aibheann	Orlynn Pk.
Sept	1988	1154	Healy	Margaret	Kelly Pk.
Sept	1987	1155	Maguire	Elaine	Orlynn Pk.
Sept	1988	1156	Hogan	Gillian	Ministers Rd.
Sept	1988	1157	Hurley	Niamh	Regles
Sept	1988	1158	Cox	Louise	Orlynn Pk.
Sept	1988	1159	Carroll	Eimear	Orlynn Pk.
Sept	1988	1160	Deeb	Ryam	Skerries Rd.
Sept	1988	1161	O'Sullivan	Eidin	Orlynn Pk.
Sept	1988	1162	Teeling	Andrina	Ministers Rd.
Sept	1988	1163	Carroll	Alison	Ministers Rd.
Sept	1988	1164	Doyle	Suzanne	Orlynn Pk.
Sept	1988	1165	Foran	Kerry-Ann	Orlynn Pk.
Sept	1988	1166	Daly	Regina	Kelly Pk.
Sept	1988	1167	Wyse	Orna	Orlynn Pk.
Sept	1988	1168	McAnaney	Andrea	Orlynn Pk.
Sept	1988	1169	O'Donovan	Oonagh	Orlynn Pk.
Sept	1991	1170	McMahon	Patrice	Ministers Rd.
June	1989	1171	Daly	Allison	Ministers Rd.
Jan	1987	1172	Harrington	Amanda	
Sept	1989	1173	Ryan	Aine	Regeens
Sept	1989	1174	Cowley	Tanya	Minsters Pk.
Sept	1989	1175	Hayes	Sinead	Orlynn Pk.
Sept	1989	1176	Brick	Lorraine	Orlynn Pk.
Sept	1989	1177	Kelly	Karen	Minsters Pk.
Sept	1989	1178	O'Connell	Clare	Orlynn Pk.
Sept	1989	1179	Rosney	Caroline	Orlynn Pk.
Sept	1989	1180	Doyle	Catherine	Orlynn Pk.

Month registered in the School	Year	Pupils Register No.	Pupils Surname	First Name	Address
Sept	1989	1181	Synnott	Nicola	Orlynn Pk.
Sept	1989	1182	Nichols	Amy	Orlynn Pk.
Sept	1989	1183	Dunne	Kayleigh	Orlynn Pk.
Sept	1989	1184	Hoare	Niamh	Orlynn Pk.
Sept	1989	1185	Dunne	Finola	Minsters Pk.
Sept	1989	1186	Daly	Aoife	Kelly Pk.
Sept	1989	1187	Darcy	Sarah	Orlynn Pk.
Sept	1989	1188	McGlew	Barbara	Orlynn Pk.
Sept	1989	1189	Molony	Karen	Orlynn Pk.
Sept	1989	1190	Reilly	Deirdre	Orlynn Pk.
Sept	1989	1191	Ryan	Ailbhe	Orlynn Pk.
Sept	1989	1192	Sheridan	Audrey	Kelly Pk.
Sept	1989	1193	Skelly	Grainne	P.O. Road
Sept	1989	1194	Skelly	Pamela	Skerries Rd.
Sept	1989	1195	Skelly	Sinead	P.O. Road
Sept	1989	1196	Stapelton	Grainne	Orlynn Pk.
Jan	1990	1197	O'Hehir	Nicola	Orlynn Pk.
Sept	1989	1198	Cowley	Grace	Orlynn Pk.
Mar	1990	1199	Phipps	Danielle	Orlynn Pk.
Sept	1989	1200	Cowley	Ruth	Orlynn Pk.
Sept	1989	1201	Aupy	Clare	Orlynn Pk.
Sept	1989	1202	Halpin	Ciara	Orlynn Pk.
Sept	1989	1203	Harold	Christine	Balleally East
		1204	Goulding	Jennifer	Orlynn Pk.
Sept	1990	1205	McGrath	Antoinette	Ministers Rd.
Sept	1990	1206	O'Connor	Aoife	The Commons
Oct	1990	1207	Gregory	Lisa	Orlynn Pk.
Nov	1990	1208	Redmond	Ciara	Orlynn Pk.
Sept	1990	1209	McGrath	Pauline	Ministers Rd.
Sept	1990	1210	Courtney	Jennifer	Orlynn Pk.
Nov	1990	1211	Devane	Laura	Orlynn Pk.
Nov	1990	1212	Baldwin	Sarah	

Appendices

Month registered in the School	Year	Pupils Register No.	Pupils Surname	First Name	Address
Sept	1990	1213	Kernan	Niamh	Orlynn Pk.
Sept	1990	1214	Atherton	Zara	Orlynn Pk.
Sept	1990	1215	Nolan	Fiona	Orlynn Pk.
Sept	1990	1216	Butterly	Caroline	Orlynn Pk.
Sept	1990	1217	Farrell	Anneliese	Kelly Pk.
Sept	1990	1218	Fay	April	Chapel Lane
Sept	1990	1219	O'Kelly	Alison	The Commons
Sept	1990	1220	Peters	Lorraine	St. Macullins Close
Sept	1990	1221	Skelly	Samantha	Skerries Rd.
Sept	1990	1222	O'Donovan	Miriam	Orlynn Pk.
Sept	1990	1223	Fraher	Alison	Orlynn Pk.
Sept	1990	1224	Kealy	Geninne	Orlynn Pk.
Sept	1990	1225	Callan	Mellisa	Ministers Rd.
Sept	1990	1226	Darcy	Elizabeth	Orlynn Pk.
Sept	1990	1227	Dennnis	Emma	P.O. Road
Sept	1990	1228	Dunne	Andrea	Orlynn Pk.
Sept	1990	1229	Kelly	Louise	Minsters Pk.
Sept	1990	1230	Maguire	Niamh	Orlynn Pk.
Sept	1990	1231	McGealy	Anne Marie	Kelly Pk.
Sept	1990	1232	McCullough	Catherine	Orlynn Pk.
Sept	1990	1233	McKeon	Sandra	Minsters Pk.
Sept	1990	1234	Rooney	Linda	Orlynn Pk.
Sept	1990	1235	Ryan	Amanda	Dublin Rd
Sept	1990	1236	Ryan	Helen	Regeens
Sept	1990	1237	Ryan	Kellyanne	Orlynn Pk.
Sept	1990	1238	Savage	Nicola	Minsters Pk.
Sept	1990	1239	Skelly	Paula	
Jan	1991	1240	Hennessey	Clare	Newhaggard
Oct	1991	1241	Cruise	Tanya	St. Catherines Green
Nov	1991	1242	Doyle	Eileen	Brides Tree
Sept	1991	1243	Clarke	Niamh	Orlynn Pk.
Sept	1991	1244	Cowley	Alison	Minsters Pk.

Month registered in the School	Year	Pupils Register No.	Pupils Surname	First Name	Address
Sept	1991	1245	Donnelly	Laura	Station Rd.
Sept	1991	1246	Duignan	Gillian	Orlynn Pk.
Sept	1991	1247	Smith	Deirdre	Orlynn Pk.
Sept	1991	1248	Walsh	Emma	Minsters Pk.
Sept	1991	1249	Lynch	Laura	The Green
Sept	1991	1250	Molony	Jennifer	Orlynn Pk.
Sept	1991	1251	Marshall	Frances	Orlynn Pk.
Sept	1991	1252	McGarry	Shona	Orlynn Pk.
Sept	1991	1253	O'Reilly	Laura	Orlynn Pk.
Sept	1991	1254	Rooney	Amy	Orlynn Pk.
Sept	1991	1255	Doyle	Madeleine	Minsters Pk.
Sept	1991	1256	Hughes	Fiona	Orlynn Pk.
Sept	1991	1257	Teeling	Stacy	Kelly Pk.
Sept	1991	1258	Doyle	Charlene	Ministers Rise
Sept	1991	1259	Shanahan	Jacqueline	Orlynn Pk.
Sept	1991	1260	O'Toole	Stephanie	Minsters Pk.
Sept	1991	1261	Tips	Marei-Claire	Orlynn Pk.
Sept	1991	1262	Cleary	Meave	Orlynn Pk.
Sept	1991	1263	Kilmurry	Deirdre	Orlynn Pk.
Sept	1991	1264	Cruise	Maria	St. Macullins Close
Sept	1991	1265	Kelly	Cliodhna	Orlynn Pk.
Sept	1991	1266	Harford	Miriam	Orlynn Pk.
Sept	1992	1267	Bracken	Caitriona	Orlynn Pk.
Sept	1992	1268	McGrath	Nicola	Minsters Pk.
Sept	1992	1269	Lenehan	Edel	Kelly Pk.
Sept	1992	1270	Murphy	Sabrina	Minsters Pk.
Sept	1992	1271	Murphy	Clare	Ministers Rise
Sept	1992	1272	Brick	Yvonne	Orlynn Pk.
Sept	1992	1273	Mulligan	Stephanie	Minsters Pk.
Sept	1992	1274	Wade	Audrey	Reamount
Sept	1992	1275	Clare	Paula	The Green

Appendices

Month registered in the School	Year	Pupils Register No.	Pupils Surname	First Name	Address
Sept	1992	1276	Kane	Winnie	Orlynn Pk.
Sept	1992	1277	Byrne	Margaret	Orlynn Pk.
Sept	1992	1278	Collins	Edel	Balleally East
Sept	1992	1279	Quinn	Fiona	The Green
Sept	1992	1280	Dunne	Ciara	Minsters Pk.
Sept	1992	1281	McGlew	Clare	Orlynn Pk.
Sept	1992	1282	Doyle	Annine	The Commons
Sept	1992	1283	Hussey	Jeanine	Orlynn Pk.
Sept	1992	1284	Farren	Natasha	Ash Grove
Sept	1992	1285	Grange	Sandra	Orlynn Pk.
Sept	1992	1286	Hickey	Catiriona	Orlynn Pk.
Sept	1992	1287	Lynch	Paula	The Green
Sept	1992	1288	Meagher	Aisling	Orlynn Pk.
Sept	1992	1289	Murphy	Nicola	Ministers Rise
Sept	1992	1290	O'Neill	Mary	Orlynn Pk.
Sept	1992	1291	Skelly	Emma	Skerries Rd.
Sept	1992	1292	Tonge	Ciara	Orlynn Pk.
Sept	1992	1293	Wyse	Lucy	Orlynn Pk.

BIBLIOGRAPHY

Primary Sources:

General:
- Architectural Archives, Irish Builder and Engineer.
- Births, Marriages and Deaths Registers, GRO, Dublin.
- Census Records.
- Church of Ireland Education College, Rathmines, Dublin, Kildare Place Society reading books for primary schools.
- Commissioners of Irish Education Inquiry 1824-25, House of Commons Parliamentary Papers.
- Department of Education and Skills, School Attendance Report, 1929-30.
- Dept. of Education and Skills, Records Management, Schools Roll No's.
- Dublin Catholic Diocesan Archive, Clonliffe, Correspondence re Lusk School.
- Dublin Diocesan Archive, Lusk School/Architects Report, 1965.
- Dublin Diocesan Archives, Clonliffe, Letter from Rev. Fr. Vaughan PP Lusk.
- Genealogy Records.
- Lusk Primary School Registers.
- Mount St. Joseph College, Roscrea, (College Records)
- Primary (Griffiths) Valuations.
- School Inspectors Reports, Lusk Primary School.
- Society of The Sacred Heart, Irish/Scottish Provincial - Archives, Mount Anville, Dublin.
- St. Patricks' Teacher Training College, Drumcondra, Dublin, 1914 – 1960, College Register.
- University College Dublin, Schools Manuscript Collection.
- Valuations Office Dublin, Valuations Records For Lusk.

Bibliography

National Archives of Ireland, Primary Schools Files and Records:

- ED/1/28/No. 32
- ED/1/31/No. 119
- ED/2/15/No. 43/178
- ED/2/15/No. 44
- ED/2/16/No. 21
- ED/2/121/No. 23-24
- ED/2/121/No. 25-26
- ED/4/158-160
- ED/4/161-162
- ED/4/1
- ED/4/2
- ED/4/3
- ED/4/4
- ED/4/5
- ED/4/6
- ED/4/54
- ED/4/56
- ED/4/60
- ED/4/63
- ED/4/66
- ED/4/69
- ED/4/72
- ED/4/155-7
- ED/4/152
- ED/4/152
- ED/4/153
- ED/4/754/78/4/81
- ED/4/788
- ED/4/789
- ED/4/790
- ED/4/791
- ED/4/792
- ED/4/794
- ED/4/795
- ED/4/796
- ED/4/797
- ED/4/798
- ED/4/800
- ED/4/801
- ED/4/802
- ED/4/1372
- ED/4/1503
- ED/4/1505
- ED/4/1506
- ED/4/1507
- ED/4/1508
- ED/4/1509
- ED/4/1512
- ED/4/1515
- ED/4/1516
- ED/4/1518
- ED/4/1521
- ED/4/2121
- ED/4/2125
- ED/4/2125
- ED/4/2131
- ED/4/2132
- ED/4/2213
- ED/4/2136
- ED/4/2137
- ED/4/2141
- ED/4/2142
- ED/4/2146
- ED/4/2151
- ED/4/2156
- ED/4/2162
- ED/4/2168
- ED/4/2174
- ED/4/2180
- ED/4/2198
- ED/4/2199
- ED/4/2205
- ED/4/4522
- ED/9/9001
- ED/9/15495
- ED/9/17749
- ED/9/18306
- ED/9/22631
- ED/9/24870
- ED/9/25914
- ED/11/36/2
- ED/12/8989
- ED/12/8989 Box 143
- ED/12/10833
- ED/12/14826
- ED/12/14826 Box 297
- ED/12/2018

Secondary Sources:

- *Cead Bliain Faoi Rath*, Mount St. Joseph College, Roscrea, Originally From an Article Written By Mr. Liam S. Maher (RIP), English Teacher, Cistercian College (Mount St. Joseph) 1950 to 1987.
- Collins, S. 'Balrothery Poor Law Union', County Dublin, 1839-1851 (Maynooth Studies In Local History), 2005.
- *Dromleigh (Co Cork), Memories of a Country School 1840-1990*
- Education in Ireland, Pre 1900, Irish History Live, School of History and Anthropology, Queens University Belfast.
- Fenton, S. *It All Happened, Reminiscences of Seamus Fenton*, (1948), Publ. Gill and Macmillan.
- Fitzgerald, G. *Irish Primary Education in The Early Nineteenth Century*, Dublin 2013.
- Historical Commentary For 1818, Chief Secretary's Office Registered Papers, (Nigel Johnston, Project Archivist).
- *Irish Times*, Feb. 13th 2010, Article By Garrett Fitzgerald, 'How Religion Made Its Way Into Primary School System'.
- Lewis, S. *A Topographical History of Ireland*, 1837.
- List of School Teachers, Leinster, 1826-1827', (Arranged By Dorothy Rines Dingfelder, Sept. 1982), National Archives of Ireland.
- O'Donovan, B. B.Ed., M.Ed., Doctor of Education, Thesis, DCU, 2013.
- Schooling in The Nineteenth Century, The Kildare Place Society, Exhibition held 2012/13, National Museum of Ireland, Decorative Arts and History, Collins Barracks, Dublin.
- *Land of the horse*, magazine published in association with the RDS, remembering the Irish war horse, p18-19, 2014.

Newspapers:

- *Irish Times*, July 1874
- *Irish Times*, Jan. 24th 1894
- *Irish Independent*, Jan 31st 1956
- *Irish Press*, Jan. 31st 1956
- *Fingal Independent*, July 3rd 1992

Bibliography

Websites:
www.csorp.nationalarchives.ie/context/1818.html
www.nli.ie/en/griffiths-valuation.aspx
www.census/nationalarchives.ie
www.census.ie
www.qub.ac.uk/sites/irishhistorylive
www.dublinnorth.rootsireland.ie
www.geni.com
www.education.ie

Consultations/Interviews

Carroll, Aidan	Dunne Colman	McNally, Seamus
Comiskey, Paul	Gibbons, Barbara	Murtagh, Frances
Cullen, Ann	Johnson, Emer	O'Leary, Des
Devine, Mattie	Kelly, John	Seaver, Patrick
Doherty, Moya	Kelly, Pat	Seaver, Tom
Dunne, David	McNally, Mary	Steale, Deirdre

INDEX

1
1836 OS Map, 11
1870 Parish Map, 12

A
a black eye, 69
Abbeyfeale, 34
Aberystwyth University, 36
adjective, 20
admonished, 16, 17, 27
Alice Reilly, 29
Anne Evlin, 15
Anne Jordan, 16
Anne McCormick, 15
Anne Ryan, 42
Annie (Nan) Dunne, 75
Archbishop, 37, 77
Arithmetic, 19, 50, 71
Arthur Guinness, 3
Ash Grove, 100
Atley, 37, 137
Aungier, 30
Australia, 54

B
BA Degree-Mathematics, 44, 123
Balbriggan, 40, 56, 63, 69, 80, 81
Ballaely Lane, 83
Ballough, 55
Bantry boys N.S., 35
basket-making, 68
Bean an Leasa, 44
benediction, 80
Berry Clare, 81
Betty Murray, 79
big wind, 11
billiard hall, 65
Black Raven, 28,92
blackboard, 18, 19, 22
blacksmith, 69, 96, 104
Board of Public Works, 42
bookkeeper, 96
Boolavouge, 62
Bread soda, 70
brewery, 70, 81
Bridget Connor, 28, 29
Bridget Doyle, 51
Bridget Judge, 36, 39, 45
Bulkey-shans, 70

C
Cabinteely, 45
Cad e sin?, 44
Callisthenic exercises, 51
Captain Bligh, 13
Carnegie Library, 43
carpenters, 104
carpentry, 68
Carrie-May, 80
Carysford, 42
Castlecomer, 57
catechism, 79, 85
Catholic Emancipation, 4
Cead Bliain Faoi Rath, 44
ceilidhe, 80
cess-pit, 35
champion jumper, 69
chilblains, 69
Christopher Gilmore, 15
Christy Rooney, 68
cinema, 73, 92
cleaning of the teeth, 49
Co. Kerry, 35, 39, 40, 41, 42, 45
Co. Tipperary, 18
coach-building, 68
Columbus, 13
Commissioners of Irish Education Inquiry, 4, 6
Communion, 79, 80, 84, 99
confessional, 84
Confirmation, 879, 85, 99
Constable Saul, 40
Coolock, 74
Corduff, 39, 40, 41, 42, 54, 55, 70, 75, 95
Corporal punishment, 93, 94
Corpus Christi, 80
Cow-dung, 69
Craiglockhart, 75
curate, 80, 92
curriculum, 2, 28

D
Daniel Doherty, 97, 98
Daniel Murphy, 35
Darndale, 98
Denmark St., 26, 40
Des O'Leary, 99
diphtheria, 79
dispensary,79
distempered, 48

Donegal, 97
Dr. Cooney, 79
Dr. Fahie, 30
Drogheda Independent, 51
Duffy's Circus, 83
Duncans map, 10
Dungloe, 97
Durkin, 75

E
earache, 70
ecclesiastical superiors, 43
Edinburgh, 75
Edward (Ned) Dunne, 75
Edward Hayden, 69
Edward Monks, 40
Elementary Science, 48
Elizabeth McCaffrey, 45
Ellen Long, 45, 56, 57
Ellen Rooney, 51, 52
Ellie Kavanagh, 66
Emily Leonard, 41
Emyvale, 45
Entertaining Medleys, 13
epidemic, 77
established Church, 2
Eucharist Congress, 79

F
famine, 54, 55, 112
Farm Work, 74
Fear an Leasa, 44
Feis Ceol, 80
Fenton, 35, 38, 41, 42, 45, 47
Fingall Feis, 36, 37, 39
Fingallians, 36
Finglas, 99
first communion, 79, 84, 99
first-aid classes, 52
Folklore Project, 65
forty-hours, 80
four-part choir, 80
Fr. Dan Heffernan, 37
Fr. James McMahon, 77
Fr. Joseph Union, 80
Fr. Mahon, 92
Fr. Vincent Steen, 88
Francis Flanagan, 23
freehand drawing, 50

Index

G
Gaelic classes, 51
gather sticks, 79
geography, 19, 20, 27, 30, 32, 36, 49, 50, 71
Geometrical Drawing, 50,
George Carton, 33, 34
George McNally, 79
Gerry Wynne, 92
goose grease, 69
Gabhlan, Connemara, 57
Grace Dieu, 70
Grammar, 19, 20, 30, 46, 49
groom, 96

H
harness–making, 69
heart-burn, 70
Hedgestown, 57, 58, 74
Henry Howenden, 14
Hethrington, 36

I
immorality, 16
Baggot St. Dublin, 36, 42, 45
Clane, Co.Kildare, 45, 56, 57, 62
inkballs, 84
inoculated, 79
inspectorate, 5, 117
interdenominational, 5, 6
Ionic solfa charts, 46
Irish Training Colleges, 38
It All Happened, 36, 39

J
Jackie Kelly, 66
James Carey, 9, 15
James Carton, 71
James Jordan, 16, 17
James Kelly, 40
James Monks, 45, 57
James Wall, 17
Jane Dillon, 63
Jane Murphy, 16
Jemmy Rogan, 82
Jeremiah Long, 18
John (Pipes) Bentley, 82
John Donnelly, 26, 27
John Dowling, 40
John Kelly, 84
John O'Brien, 17
John Rochford, 14
John Rooney, 69
John Sweeney, 33
Joseph Smyth, 14

K
Kathleen Gough, 81
Katie Hunt, 79, 82
Kelly Park, 100
Kevin Barry, 63
Kilbeggan, 36
Kings Inn St. Convent, 75
Kitty Daly, 79

L
La Touche, 3
Lady of Mercy teacher training college Baggot St, 36, 42, 45, 56, 57, 62, 63
Lambay, 17
Laurence Dunne, 61
Laurence Early, 21
Laurence Philips, 17
lime-washed, 48
Local Crafts, 68
Local Cures, 69
Local Heroes, 69
locum, 40, 41
Londoner, 78
Lord Stanley, 4
Loughbarn, 70

M
Maggie Donnelly, 28
Man O' War, 70
Mansfield, 57
Margaret Coleman, 20
Margaret Owens, 40
Maria Thomson, 16
Mark Taylor, 42, 69
Mary Dillon, 62, 63
Mary Doran, 56
Mary Gaynor, 18, 20, 56
Mary Hogan, 81
Mary Keenan, 41
Mary Kelly, 58
Mary Matthews, 81
Mattie Devine, 89
Maureen McCarthy, 78
Maurice Holly, 38
May Brady, 81
Measles, 77
Michael McCormick, 15
Michael Morgan, 14
Military Farm, 37, 96, 104
Miltown-Malbay, 33
Miss Long, 45
Miss Moloney, 74, 75, 86
Miss Reid, 83
model schools, 3, 5
monitor, 26, 27, 29, 30, 35, 36, 39, 40, 41, 45, 47, 56, 57, 61
Morgans, 81
mortal sin, 85
Mr. Cronin, 38
Mrs. Bentley, 84
Mumps, 77
Munster football championship, 35
Murrays pub, 35

N
nail-making, 68
national education board, 3
Ned Roche, 35
needlework, 19, 22, 46, 49, 71
Nicky Rooney, 65
Nina Rogan, 82
ninepence, 73
North William St. Dublin, 45
Nuns, 77

O
Mount St. Joseph, 44
Oglesby, 66, 82
OLM, 42
organist, 80
Orlynn Park, 100

P
Paddy Donnelly, 71
Palladium, 81
Paraffin oil, 69
parish dues, 82
Patrick J. Dodd, 14
Patrick J. O'Brien, 15
Patrick McDonagh, 15
Patrick O'Shea, 35
Patrick White, 69
Pay Schools, 4
penal laws, 1, 2
penmanship, 19, 47
Peter Leonard, 41
Peter McNally, 92
Peter Seaver, 14
Philanthropists, 2
Phoenix Park, 79
Portaferry, 44
Post Office, 73, 81
postal order, 73
poultice, 69
Powis Commission, 117
Preparatory Colleges, 38
Primary Certificate, 71

Proselytising, 2
Protected Structure', 21

Q
Quebec, 5
Quickpenny, 65, 95

R
Rathenny, 51
Raw beef, 69
Remount, 96, 104
repeal martyrs, 16
reprimanded, 16, 27
results fees, 27, 30
Rev Fr. Doran, 16
Rev. Costigan, 16, 17
Rev. John Fulham CC, 14
Rev. Nicholas Farrell, 23, 28
Rev. Patrick Kelly, 14
Rev. PJ Tyrrell, 15, 16, 37
Rev. Thomas O'Byrne, 37, 42
Richard Hegarty, 35, 46
Richard Peters, 84
Richard Smyth, 14
rifle practice, 52
Ring school, 56
Riverdance, 98
Rocques map, 8
Roddy the Rover, 79
Rogerstown, 14, 69, 95, 96
Rose Kelly, 81
round tower, 8, 11, 83
Royal Irish Constabulary, 40
Royal University of Ireland, 44
rural district councillor, 52
Rush, 40, 41, 42, 43, 45, 61, 62, 63, 64, 65, 81, 95, 96
Rutland St. boys school, 61

S
salaries, 4, 9, 12, 27, 55
sally rods, 70
Samuel Bewley, 3
Sara Mulligan, 45
Sarah Wall, 17
Scarlet Fever, 77
Schools Manuscript Collection, 65
Seaver, 114, 56, 89
Sisters of The Holy Faith, 77
Skerries, 57, 62, 63, 77, 81, 89
skimmed milk, 74
sleuth, 82
Sligo, 45
sodalities, 79
Song books, 47
St Laurence O'Tooles, 57
St. Patricks' teacher training college, 33, 35, 36, 44, 61, 63, 97
Starkie, 27, 36, 37
stone-cutting, 68
strike action, 51
subtraction, 20
Surnames, 96, 105, 106, 107, 108, 109, 111
Susan Philips, 17
Swanlinbar, 45

T
teachers residence, 20, 21, 42, 43
telegrams, 73
thatch, 19, 20, 22, 70
thatching, 68, 70
Ashbourne, 37
The Commission of Irish Education Enquiry, 4
The Kildare Place Society, 3
Theresa Fulham, 80
Thomas Ashe, 37, 40
Thomas Devine, 44
Thomas Evlin, 15
Thomas Keogh, 17
Thomas Knox, 14
Thomas Masterson, 71
Thomas O'Connell, 40, 43
tobacco, 74
Tommy Groves, 66
Tommy Halpin, 69
tooth-ache, 69
travelling show, 80, 83
Trean Hill, 79
tribe of the foreigners, 36
trustees, 12
Tubber Co. Offaly, 56
twelve practical rules, 6

U
University College Dublin, 65

V
vaccination, 79

W
wangle, 70
wart, 70
warts, 70
Wheaten straw, 70
Whitestown cemetery, 64
whitewash, 19, 22
whittle, 70
William Cotter, 33
Willie Bentley, 69
woodwork, 37, 38
Written English, 49